BERNARD SHAW

AND

MRS. PATRICK CAMPBELL
THEIR CORRESPONDENCE

GBS ~~~~~ *BSC*

BERNARD SHAW

AND

MRS. PATRICK CAMPBELL

Their Correspondence

Edited by A L A N   D E N T

NEW YORK · ALFRED A. KNOPF

1952

L. C. catalog card number: 52-6411

THIS IS A BORZOI BOOK,
PUBLISHED BY ALFRED A. KNOPF, INC.

FIRST AMERICAN EDITION

HERE *are the dear letters.*

If I inspired a little of the tenderness of their genius I am proud, not vain. . . .

People talk carelessly, but nobody will think *anything but what lovely letters and what a dear man you are.*

MRS. CAMPBELL TO BERNARD SHAW

FOREWORD
by STELLA M. BEECH

THESE LETTERS *give so intimate and confidential a picture of one aspect of my mother, Mrs. Patrick Campbell, that I would myself have preferred that they were not put before the public during my lifetime. However, my mother expressly stated in her will that she wished the correspondence to be published in full as soon as Mr. Shaw made his letters available. Then Mr. Shaw, when he left me the authority to publish, expressed the desire that "any proceeds arising from the publication should be used for the secondary education" of Mrs. Campbell's great-grandchildren, who are already sixteen and thirteen years old. Therefore a sense of duty to my mother and to Mr. Shaw, and a sense of obligation to my grandchildren, must, to my mind, outweigh any instinctive reluctance I feel about the immediate publication.*

EDITOR'S PREFACE

HERE ARE THE LETTERS interchanged—between 1899 and 1939—by an intellectual giant and a great and beautiful actress, a pair whose brilliance of mind and of personality dominated the English-speaking stage for fifty years.

In preparing for publication a correspondence such as theirs, the editor's function, is, in my opinion, threefold. One, he should cut out all quite irrelevant trivialities and topicalities, and also (so far as is possible) all easily prunable matter that might cause pain or embarrassment to individuals or families still living. Two, he should provide all necessary items of information or explanation in an enclosed paragraph alongside each letter (rather than in the distracting way of footnotes). Three, he should in most other respects keep completely out of the road with his own opinions or commentaries.

The few pages of such a preface may be compared—in my way of thinking—to the few necessary footsteps leading up to the front door of a great house. And in the Shaw-Campbell case it is a complicated much-inhabited hurly-burly of a great house, with laughter ringing through most of its pleasant rooms for most of the time, and hardly a single little chamber locked up or in darkness.

"Hardly a dark room?" echoes the reader, who is but human after all. The answer can only be: read their letters carefully and closely, and find out if you can! Let it be said categorically and at once that nothing that would help to elucidate this pleasing-teasing enigma has been suppressed or excised. This collection is the extant collection excepting only for some passages that have to do with Mrs. Campbell's second husband and have no direct connection whatsoever with the friendship that persisted between Mrs. Campbell and Bernard Shaw. From their own direct and intimate epistolary intercourse nothing has been deleted or omitted but an inconsiderable amount of overembarrassing baby-talk and a certain amount of nonsense verbiage (not at all unlike the "little language" which Dean Swift devised in his correspondence with that other Stella)—gibberish which could have a meaning only for the letter's recipient.

Far more than enough remains to show that these two great ones could be foolish as well as fond, prattlesome as well as witty and wise.

The correspondence begins in the spring of 1899, when Shaw was 42 and Stella Campbell 34. It concludes—rather "fizzling out" as the greatest correspondence will—in the autumn of 1939, when Shaw was 83 and Mrs. Campbell was 74 and within a year of her death. The gaps in the correspondence are curious and not easy to bridge. But it is fairly clear from internal evidence that very few letters, if any at all, were suppressed or destroyed by either sender or recipient. At the date of the very first letter Shaw was known in England only as a trenchant critic, first of music and then of the drama, and as a brilliant pamphleteer on both æsthetic and political subjects. Only one or two of his early plays had so far been acted in England, and then only in experimental conditions. Mrs. Campbell, on the other hand, was in 1899 at the height of her fame and beauty as an actress. She had already created her best and most famous parts—Paula Tanqueray in 1893, Agnes Ebbsmith in 1895, Fedora in the same year, Magda in 1896, and Melisande in 1898.

By the year 1912, when the two began to interchange letters with anything resembling regularity, Shaw had at last become an established dramatist in England, though by no means a popular one as yet. (The historic Vedrenne-Barker seasons at the Court Theatre in London between 1904 and 1907 had done the establishing.) By the same year Mrs. Campbell, on the other hand, had added to her reliable repertoire of successes only the parts of Echegaray's Mariana (1901), Ibsen's Hedda (1907), and Mrs. Chepstow in *Bella Donna* (1911)—the last being a considerable commercial triumph.

So much for England. In the U.S.A. Shaw's fame and success as a dramatist, and as an intellectual force generally, always tended to be in advance of his English reputation. It is significant that no fewer than seven of his best full-length plays had their first world-performance in America. Mrs. Campbell herself conquered New York and Chicago in her first tours there in 1902, 1904, and 1907. She returned yet again in 1910, and later still she was to repeat her London success in Shaw's *Pygmalion* all over the States in 1914 and 1915.

The years after 1912 brought Shaw immortality as well as popularity with his masterpieces, *Heartbreak House* (1921), and *Saint Joan* (1924)—to name nothing else. (Both plays had their first production and first acclaim in America.) For Mrs. Campbell the same years brought only her big Shavian success as Eliza and a belated ovation as Anastasia in G. B. Stern's *The Matriarch* (in 1929). For the rest, she toured and toured with unrewarding parts in unremarkable plays, a respected living legend but none the less an actress-mismanageress. These tours included revisits to the States in 1927, 1931, and 1933, and a long and undisguisedly pathetic sojourn in Hollywood, which found her unemployable because she refused to conform.

By the way of a top step to the outside staircase, one might repeat the American critic Alexander Woollcott's spectacular phrase about Mrs. Campbell in the end being like a sinking ship that fired upon those who tried to rescue it. Or one might quote the English critic James Agate's moving monody on her death, which has things like this: "Her voice was like Casals' cello, and her silences had the emotional significance of Maeterlinck's shadowy speech.

This was an actress who, for twenty years, had the world at her feet. She kicked it away, and the ball rolled out of her reach."

But more apt to these letters, besides being rather less well known and less accessible, is a phrase that has the additional merit of comprehending Mrs. Shaw, a background character who leaps into startling life in the course of this correspondence. It occurs in the course of a letter from Woollcott to Mr. Thornton Wilder in March 1933, and it runs: "Did Ruth [Gordon] ever tell you of that luncheon in our villa when Shaw talked about Stella Campbell for an hour and a half until Mrs. Shaw was driven to beating a tattoo with her salad fork as a way of warning him that she couldn't stand another word on the subject?"

In the course of these few preliminary pages it should have been made clear that, while these two walked hand-in-hand through their quarter-century of close friendship, Shaw's greatness—and with it his popularity—was steadily and triumphantly increasing, while Mrs. Campbell's was more or less steadily on the wane, reaching its ultimate melancholy sundown in California. But throughout that time the strength of her personality, the quickness and sharpness of her wit, were on a par with his own. And it seems to me that this copious sheaf of letters, besides being the hitherto incomplete record of a profound and much-tested friendship, perpetuates the legend of Stella Campbell quite as radiantly as that of Shaw.

ALAN DENT

NOTE ON THE LETTERS

THE HOLOGRAPHS *of the Shaw-Campbell letters have had a complicated history, as may be gathered from the later stages of the correspondence here presented.*

In her will, dated 1934, Mrs. Campbell desired that Shaw's letters should be printed and "published in their proper sequence." She had already cited a number of his letters in her autobiography some twelve years earlier.

In his will, dated 1950, Shaw authorized Mrs. Beech (Mrs. Campbell's daughter) "to print and publish after my death all or any of the letters written to the said eminent actress" (Mrs. Patrick Campbell).

The peculiarities and inconsistencies of Mrs. Campbell's spelling and punctuation have been faithfully reproduced.

CHRONOLOGICAL GUIDE

1856   George Bernard Shaw born, 26 July, in Dublin.

1865   Beatrice Stella Tanner born, 9 February, in London.

1876   G.B.S. moves to London.

1884   Beatrice Stella Tanner marries Patrick Campbell.

1888   G.B.S. becomes musical critic.
         Mrs. Patrick Campbell's first professional appearance
         on the stage, at Liverpool.

1891   G.B.S.'s *The Quintessence of Ibsenism* published.

1892   G.B.S.'s first play, *Widowers' Houses*, performed in
         London.

1893   Mrs. Campbell's first "star" appearance, in *The Second Mrs. Tanqueray*, 27 May.

1895   G.B.S. becomes the dramatic critic of the *Saturday Review*.
         Mrs. Campbell's Agnes Ebbsmith (Pinero), Fedora
         (Sardou), and Juliet (Shakespeare).

1896   Mrs. Campbell plays in Ibsen's *Little Eyolf* with Janet
         Achurch and Elizabeth Robins.

1898   G.B.S. resigns from dramatic criticism (21 May); and
         marries Charlotte Payne-Townshend (1 June).
         Mrs. Campbell plays Melisande to Martin Harvey's
         Pelleas (June), and Lady Macbeth to Forbes Robertson's Macbeth (September).

1899   First note from G.B.S. to Mrs. Campbell, 12 April.

1900   Death of Patrick Campbell in the South African War.

1901   Mrs. Campbell plays in *Mariana* (Echegaray), etc., under her own management.
First note from Mrs. Campbell to G.B.S., 16 September.

1902   First of Mrs. Campbell's many appearances in U.S.A.

1904   Mrs. Campbell plays Melisande to the Pelleas of Sarah Bernhardt, in French.

1904-7   Vedrenne-Barker seasons at Court Theatre, Sloane Square, greatly help to make G.B.S.'s plays known and discussed.

1907   Mrs. Campbell first plays Ibsen's Hedda Gabler.

1910   Mrs. Campbell again tours U.S.A.

1911   Mrs. Campbell in *Bella Donna*.

1912   28 or 29 June. G.B.S. discusses his *Pygmalion* with Mrs. Campbell at her house, and falls "head over ears in love."

1913   Mrs. Campbell in *The Adored One* (Barrie).

1914   Mrs. Campbell marries George Cornwallis-West (6 April) and appears as Eliza in *Pygmalion* (11 April).

1918   Mrs. Campbell's only son killed in the World War.

1920   Mrs. Campbell in *Madame Sand* (Moeller) and with James K. Hackett in *Macbeth*.

xvi

1921   G.B.S.'s *Heartbreak House* first performed in London.

1922–4   Mrs. Campbell tours in Great Britain with her own company.

1922   Publication of Mrs. Campbell's autobiography, *My Life and Some Letters.*

1924   G.B.S.'s *Back to Methuselah* first performed in London.

1928   Mrs. Campbell appears in an Ibsen Centenary production of *Ghosts.*

1929   Mrs. Campbell in *The Matriarch* (G. B. Stern).
G.B.S.'s *The Apple Cart* first performed in London.

1934   Mrs. Campbell begins to appear in minor parts in Hollywood films.

1939   Last letter from Mrs. Campbell to G.B.S., 28 June.
Last letter from G.B.S. to Mrs. Campbell, 21 August.

1940   Mrs. Campbell dies, 9 April, at Pau, in the south of France (aged 75).

1943   Mrs. Shaw dies, 12 September, in London (aged 86).

1950   G.B.S. dies, 2 November, at Ayot St. Lawrence (aged 94).

BERNARD SHAW

AND

MRS. PATRICK CAMPBELL
THEIR CORRESPONDENCE

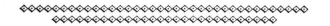

"C & C" is Caesar and Cleopatra, which G.B.S. wrote for Forbes Robertson and Mrs. Patrick Campbell when they were acting together; but the play was not produced until 1906, in New York, when Forbes Robertson played Caesar and the part of Cleopatra was "created" by his wife (Gertrude Elliott).

It was Sir Arthur W. Pinero's play The Second Mrs. Tanqueray *that brought fame overnight to Mrs. Campbell in 1893.*

Shaw had married Charlotte Payne-Townshend on 1 June 1898. When he wrote this letter he had recently had an operation on his foot for necrosis of the bone—hence the reference to the "Xradiograph."

Blen-Cathra, Hindhead.
12th April 1899

Dear Mrs. Patrick Campbell,

We have this house until the 14th May only; so come quickly. Mrs. Shaw will be delighted to see you. But if the words are no plainer than the woman, they will be thrown away on me.

Why not play the first act of "C & C" as a curtain raiser? The public can have the rest of it when I publish it. Or get Pinero to write a sequel. *I* dont mind—and he can have all the fees.

The vegetables have triumphed over their traducers. I was told that my diet was so poor that I could not repair the bones that were broken & operated on. So I have just had an Xradiograph [*sic*] taken; and lo! perfectly mended solid bone so beautifully white that I have left instructions that, if I die, a glove stretcher is to be made out of them and sent to you as a souvenir.

We are having a spell of fine weather here. Why not bring Caesar down to lunch? It would do him good, and dispel all remnants of your influenza.

Yours sincerely,
G. Bernard Shaw.

❖❖❖❖❖❖

"The book" may have been Three Plays for Puritans, *which was published in 1901, and Shaw's "idea" may still be that of* Caesar and Cleopatra. *(See G.B.S.'s letter of 14 August 1937.)*

In the 1912 edition of a volume of these plays, which he gave her in 1914, he has inscribed: "To silly Stella who threw Caesar and Cleopatra *into the waste paper basket from G. Bernard Shaw."*

33 Kensington Square, W.
16th Sept. 1901

My dear Mr. Shaw,

The idea is perfectly delightful. I wish you could see your way to doing it for me.

Please think it out and let me know.

In the meantime accept my warm thanks for your kind thought of me.

I will go through the book carefully—putting myself in entire sympathy with your idea.

Yours sincerely,
Beatrice Stella Campbell.

❖❖❖❖❖❖

The "idea" appears to be Mrs. Campbell's in this letter, just as clearly as it appears to be Mr. Shaw's in the last. Its nature would seem to have vanished into the mists of time. It has been suggested that it concerned a translation of Edmond Rostand's play, La Princesse lointaine, *and the reference to Rostand in this letter strengthens the surmise. Mrs. Campbell is known to have been contemplating a production of that play about this time, but nothing came of it.*

Stephen Phillips was then only known by his Herod, *which had been presented by Beerbohm Tree in 1900. Granville Barker at this time was not known as a playwright but had made his first appearance as a Shavian actor in the Stage Society's production of* Candida *in the previous year.*

Max Beerbohm was well known to Mrs. Campbell and she had staged his play The Happy Hypocrite *in October 1900. Arthur Symons, poet and critic, was later to translate for her the* Electra *of Hugo von Hofmannsthal; and Mrs. Campbell had already produced two plays by Constance Fletcher, whose pen-name was George Fleming:* The Canary *and an adaptation of Rostand's* Les Romanesques.

Gilbert, of course, is W. S. Gilbert, the librettist and playwright, who lived on until 1911, though he had already practically completed his life-work.

10 Adelphi Terrace, W.C.

18th September 1901

Dear Mrs. Patrick Campbell,

I dont think it would do for me to meddle with the fairy scheme: it would give it a flavour of brimstone at once. All the newspaper notices would be sophisticated with usual Shaw nonsense; and the freshness and innocence of the effect would be spoiled.

Besides, one of the great advantages of these entertainments is that nobody cares greatly who the author is. In fact a well known author is a positive disadvantage, since all dramatic authors in England are stale before they reach notoriety. If we had a Rostand, it would be another pair of shoes. As it is, we have only Stephen Phillips; and his reputation would put people on the wrong track even more than mine.

5

Why not try Max Beerbohm? He has just the touch of delicate quaintness you need for the piece. Failing him I can think of nobody but Arthur Symons or Constance Fletcher. Or would you like to heap coals of fire on the head of Granville Barker who has a very fine talent indeed? After all, there must be heaps of young poets who adore you, and could do this piece well enough—if only one knew of them. *Do* give your contemporaries a chance. Turn to the rising suns: I am exhausted, hackneyed, vulgarised, and too old for these games—45 last July as ever was. Try Max. Or, if you like seasoned authors, why not—I am really more than half serious—try GILBERT? *That* would make a real sensation.

Yours sincerely,
G. Bernard Shaw.

❖❖❖❖❖❖

This letter refers to Mrs. Campbell's production of Part I of the famous Norwegian dramatist Björnson's play Over Aevne. *It was translated by Miss Jessie Muir under the title* Beyond Human Power. *As Clara Sang, Mrs. Campbell's performance was the subject of many other congratulatory letters from famous men, including Professor Gilbert Murray, Edmund Gosse, W. B. Yeats, and the Archdeacon of Westminster (these are quoted in her autobiography). George Titheradge was a well-known actor in his day who was at this period Mrs. Campbell's leading man and played Pastor Sang in the play. He died in 1916.*

10 Adelphi Terrace, W.C.
7th November 1901. 5 p.m.

My dear Mrs. Patrick Campbell,

That was a really great managerial achievement. In future, when people ask me whether I go to the theatre I shall say "To the Royalty, not to any other".

6

I think the Hallelujah Chorus might be improved by steeping in boiling water for ten minutes or so before the next matinee. And if Rachael must have a scream at the end, it might be well to give her, at rehearsal, something to scream for. Titheradge was so remarkable a parson that you really ought to play Candida* for his benefit: he would cover himself with glory as Candida's husband; but he is wrong to gurgle like Othello cutting his throat. That scene gets far beyond the screaming & gurgling kind of realism. These physical obstructions and inconveniences have no business among the spiritual agonies. May I suggest, too, that Titheradge's determination to die parrallel [*sic*] to the float with his heels O.P. and his head P, whilst you occupy the corresponding position P & O.P. rather spoils the picture. After all, it is not natural that he should die unassisted, especially after gurgling; and it would be a great improvement if he would breathe his last in the arms of Horatio— say the sceptical parson who wants the miracle. That would compose the picture much better. It is one of the drawbacks to your power of rousing people's sense of beauty, that even trifles jar on it if they are unbecoming.

However, all that is nothing. The impression was overwhelming.

Yours enthusiastically,
G. Bernard Shaw.

P.S. I was greatly touched when Mrs. Theodore Wright, who was a friend of Karl Marx and has been in all sorts of revolutionary circles, got so indignant at the conduct of Pastor Sang, that she clenched her fists and glared at the wickedness of religion instead of giving you your cue—the "My dear" cue. Forgive her: it was a generous slip.

* *Candida* is an old play of my own, with a most parsonic parson in it.

◇◇◇◇◇◇◇

The "beautiful photograph" showed Clara Sang standing with arms outstretched in the doorway ("the miracle"). She is bedridden throughout the play until this moment.

Shaw had to wait for almost twenty-five years before Mrs. Warren's Profession *was publicly licensed. It was acted privately six weeks after this letter was written—by the Stage Society, with Fanny Brough as Mrs. Warren.*

Henry William Massingham, the great editor, was working at this time for the Manchester Guardian. *Later he was editor of the* Nation (*1907–23*). *He died in 1924.*

10 Adelphi Terrace, W.C.

22nd Nov. 1901.

My dear Mrs. Patrick Campbell,

Thank you for your beautiful photograph; but *I* should have photographed you in bed, saying "It's tempting Providence". That was the finest passage in the play. After all, there are lots of beautiful people about; and some of them can perhaps even thread needles with their toes; but they cant take a filament of grey matter from their brains and thread it infallibly through that most elusive of eyelet holes in the top of a dramatist's needle. Besides, that produces a new sort of beauty, compared to which natural beauty is a mere reach-me-down from Nature's patterns. Long ago, when everybody was maudlin about your loveliness, I snapped my fingers—admired nothing but your deft fingers and toes. Now I admire you ENORMOUSLY. You have picked the work of nature to pieces and remade it whole heavens finer. It is the power to do that that is the real gift.

I am in hideous straits about the Stage Society's performance of a play of mine called *Mrs. Warren's Profession*, which Mr. Redford wouldnt license. We had it all arranged beautifully—Fanny Brough for Mrs. Warren—when the

theatre was withdrawn lest the Reader of Plays should revenge himself by suspending its licence.

I wish you had a theatre of your very own; for if the
Lord Chamberlain suspended you, I could make a revolu-
tion within half an hour of the announcement.

The enclosed letter is from one of my reverend Non-
conformist constituents. He wrote to me in great excitement about *Beyond Human Power*. I wrote back urging
him to write to *The Times* and to get a lot of other divines
to sign with him. Unluckily Massingham took the word of
the Lord out of the minister's mouth.

Yours sincerely,

G. Bernard Shaw.

◇◇◇◇◇◇

This note is addressed to Shaw at 10 (*the number underlined*)
Adelphi Terrace, W.C.

*Mrs. Campbell's daughter, Stella, survives as Mrs. Mervyn
Beech. Her son, whose pet name was Beo, became Lieut.-Com-
mander Alan U. Campbell, M.C., and was killed in the First
World War. He died most gallantly.*

Mrs. Campbell was acting at this time in Sir Hall Caine's play
The Bondman *at Drury Lane. In her autobiography she gives
an amusing description of her experiences in this full-blooded
melodrama.*

*In the lapse of nearly five years between this letter and the
previous one Shaw had become an accepted avant-garde playwright, largely through the institution of the Vedrenne-Barker
tenancy at the Court Theatre (1904–7). In the same interval
Mrs. Campbell had toured America three times. Her first appearance there was in New York in January 1902. Between
these American tours she played various parts in London, including Beata in Edith Wharton's translation of Sudermann's*
Es Lebe das Leben (*called* The Joy of Living), *Mélisande, in
French, with Sarah Bernhardt as Pelléas, and she had also pro-*

duced a play called Warp and Woof, *by* "*D.D.*" (*the Hon. Mrs Alfred Lyttelton*). *Mrs. Lyttelton was a great friend of both G.B.S. and Mrs. Campbell, and her name appears frequently in the letters, usually as* "*D.D.*"

33 Kensington Square, W.
8th Oct. '06

Since they were babies my children have come into my bedroom with my letters and sat on my bed and helped me read them. Now the boy is 22 and the girl 20 but they keep up the old habit and this morning there they were and your letter was seized upon and devoured—the girl said "how well he writes music" and the boy said "why does Hall Caine sign himself "G.B.S.".? and then I read it and I said "by jove".

You are right its not a letter to be answered so here are my affectionate greetings.

Beatrice Stella Campbell.

✧✧✧✧✧✧

The Shaw play that Mrs. Campbell saw on "Friday afternoon next" was The Doctor's Dilemma *in the Vedrenne-Barker season at the Court. Granville Barker played Dubedat, and Lillah McCarthy Mrs. Dubedat.*

33 Kensington Square, W.
10th Dec. '06

Your delicious letter has been lost as the enclosed will explain.

I dread seeing my photographs—the days of dewlaps have arrived! God help me and all women! Oh that I had mislaid countless sons and daughters and that they would all turn up today or to-morrow and prevent me accepting an offer to tour in America, that is lying on my table—20 weeks at so many dollars a minute!

I have a book for writing in—"what famous folk revere" —will you answer three questions, and I'll paste them in my pretty book.

I.   What is your belief of the true meaning of the word reverence?

II. What is your attitude towards those things that other people revere?

III. How great a crime do you hold it in art to be brilliant at the expense of filling your audience with pain and wonder by ridiculing those things around which (in other people) the sentiment of sacred reverence has always dwelt?—

I see your play Friday afternoon next.

God bless you for the smiles you make us smile and forgive you for your literary lack-of-taste misdemeanours that make us squirm.

Your Beatrice Stella C.

◆◆◆◆◆◆

Another disconcerting hiatus of silence lasting five years. In this interim both Mrs. Campbell's children had married—her son in 1909 and her daughter in 1911—and Mrs. Campbell appeared, in both England and America, in many since-forgotten plays, though the period begins with her first appearance in Ibsen's Hedda Gabler *(March 1907) and concludes with her success in Sir George Alexander's production of Robert Hichens's play* Bella Donna *(December 1911), adapted from his highly popular novel (written 1909).*

In the same period Shaw gave the world three or four new plays, none of them to be ranked among his major master-

pieces. He was now nevertheless an established playwright. At the end of 1907 the Vedrenne-Barker company moved from the Court Theatre to the Savoy. Of the 988 performances given during their three-year season at the Court, 701 were of Shaw plays, of which eleven were staged in all, several of them for the first time. Within this same interval, too, Shaw enjoyed his first big commercial success with Fanny's First Play, *which was written at the request of Lillah McCarthy and had a first long run of 600 performances.*

In the following letter the "pretty slut" is Eliza Doolittle in Shaw's Pygmalion. *As early as 1897 he had envisaged the possibility of writing such a play, in a letter to Ellen Terry, dated 8 September of that year. He refers to Mrs. Campbell as "that rapscallionly flower girl" and adds: "Caesar and Cleopatra has been driven clean out of my head by a play I want to write for them [Forbes Robertson and Mrs. Campbell] in which he shall be a west end gentleman and she an east end dona in an apron and three orange and red ostrich feathers." The play was written in 1912. For an amusing account of how Shaw read it to Mrs. Campbell see No. CCC1 in the Shaw-Terry Correspondence.*

33 Kensington Square, W.
[postmark: 27 June 1912]

My dear Mr. Shaw,

First of all my thanks for letting me hear the play, and for thinking I can be your pretty slut. I wonder if I could please you.

I want you to tell me what the business proposal is—when, where, and with whom.

Perhaps you will come and see me. We said so little yesterday. I must'nt lose time—my days are numbered surely.

It was a great pleasure to me to see you again.

Yours sincerely,
B. S. Campbell.

❖❖❖❖❖❖

This letter covers both sides of a postcard.

Charles Frohman: the American impresario, who perished in the Lusitania, *May 1915. "Barrie" is J. M. Barrie, the play-wright. About this time he was writing his comedy* The Adored One *with Mrs. Campbell in mind. It was finally produced in September 1913.*

Robert Loraine, the actor-manager, had produced Man and Superman *in America in 1905, with enormous success, he him-self playing the part of Tanner. He died in 1935. "Gerald" is Sir Gerald du Maurier, the distinguished actor-manager, who died in 1934.*

Lillah McCarthy, the first Mrs. Granville Barker, played Ann in Man and Superman, Jennifer *in* The Doctor's Dilemma, *and many other leading characters in G.B.S's plays. He had just finished writing* Androcles and the Lion, *in which the part of Lavinia had been specially written for her.*

Ayot St. Lawrence, Welwyn.
30th June 1912

I have written to Frohman, in the appropriate vein for commercial correspondence, that the Campbell Woman has scooped the entire proposition, and that he is financially outgeneralled and done for. And I have told him to hold Barrie against her if he can. So that communication is finally and delicately settled.

I have written to Loraine that he may sail for America as soon as he likes, but that if he finds Gerald concealed in the same ship, he had better hurry ashore.

To Barker I have broken the shattering news that you have captured me for your own theatre, and that Lillah is a widow in a manner of speaking.

As all these three were waiting for me, I had to let them know at once what to expect. That is the worst of having anything to do with me: you are dragged at once into the brazen atmosphere behind which my poor timid little soul hides and cowers and dreams. But it cant be helped. I tell you only because it is important that you should know that your plans will be known in general to everyone before this reaches you, with a romantic glamor round them and much inaccuracy of detail, but still sufficiently to make it necessary to play with your cards on the table.

Many thanks for Friday and for a Saturday of delightful dreams. I did not believe that I had that left in me. I am all right now, down on earth again with all my cymbals and side drums and blaring vulgarities in full blast; but it would be meanly cowardly to pretend that you are not a very wonderful lady, or that the spell did not work most enchantingly on me for fully 12 hours.

G.B.S.

◇◇◇◇◇◇◇

Georgina was one of Mrs. Campbell's deeply worshipped pet dogs, a tiny Belgian griffon by breed.

The allusion to a solicitor in connection with Granville Barker refers to a quarrel with Mrs. Campbell on a matter of salary in the year 1900. It was taken to court. The affair is amusingly described in the actress's autobiography. Barker won his case. She comments: "Mr. Granville Barker did not look as triumphant as I thought he ought to, and I will go to my grave believing that he owes me £60."

Charlotte—in the last paragraph—is, of course, Mrs. Shaw.

This letter is written on the green paper G.B.S. used when suffering from his headaches—there are several examples of it in the correspondence.

10, Adelphi Terrace, W.C.

3rd July 1912

Beatricissima

I have a frightful headache (dont be alarmed: I am not always ill: only once a month or so); and I am going to be horrid; so pity me. I wonder how your dentist manages. He *must* love you; and yet he cant always help hurting you—deliberately and scientifically hurting you. *I* should plunge a knife into my heart and die at your feet. Yet I am going to pull half your teeth out, without gas. I proceed in my professional literary manner. Hear the essayist. Silence.

The death of J. L. Toole closed a chapter in London theatrical enterprise. He and John Clarke were the last actors who knew what it was to keep a London theatre open on a single star system. Edward Terry, who tried to follow them, failed. Barry Sullivan had already failed. Mrs. Patrick Campbell failed. Ellen Terry failed. Robert Loraine failed. It was always a combination that succeeded: Irving and Ellen Terry, Wyndham and Mary Moore, Julia Neilson & Fred Terry, Bourchier and Violet Vanbrugh, Alexander and Fay Davis, Julia Neilson Irene Vanbrugh, and (oh my heart!) others. Lena Ashwell half-succeeded with McKinnel; then failed. Lewis Waller himself could not hold out single handed. Tree does not try to. In the provinces, yes. In America, certainly. But in London, NO, NO, NO, every time.

Note, oh beautifullest of all the stars, that two of the failures had Shaw parts which were the very Limit of star parts for them. Ellen's skin does not fit her body more closely than Lady Cicely Brassbound fits her; for I am a first class ladies tailor, and I love Ellen and Ellen loves me. Tanner in Man and Superman carried Loraine to the uttermost extremity of what a popular actor can do single handed. His success in America was fabulous; nothing but bitter experience could convince him that it mattered a rap who played Ann or any other part in London. Result: he lost everything he made in America, and more besides; and even in the first fever of the Criterion success, he filled that little house only once. Even in America, with all the prestige of Ellen Terry's enormously boomed farewell tour, Frohman, certain that there would never be less than £300 in the house, found that the figure I had promised him—a little under £200—was the correct one. And in London the piece died out slowly in the suburbs. With Irving as Brassbound it might have saved the Lyceum.

O Stella Stellarum, there is nothing more certain in the process of the suns than that if you attempt management on the single star system, nothing—not even my genius added to your own—can save you from final defeat. Male and female created He them. Your public is more than half feminine: you cannot satisfy their longing for a male to idealize; and how can they idealize a poor salaried employee pushed into a corner and played off the stage? Do you want to be a Duse? A hammer without an anvil! a Sandow playing with paper dumbells! Produce Pygmalion with a twenty pound Higgins, and you will have an uproarious success, just like Loraine. But the house will be under £200. At the end of 15 or 16 weeks, the business will stagger. You will be terrified, and will spend wildly on advertisements. You will drop to £120. Alexander will smile: there will hardly be more than his £116 in it. You will take Pygmalion off and draw away from me. Its successor will fail, because nobody will be able to endure you in anything worse than Eliza; and the very few authors who could give you anything as good will note my fate, and go to Frohman or Alexander instead. You will struggle on until you have lost every farthing; and then it will be America with all its horrors to recoup yourself, and the provinces, or retirement, for the rest of your life, like Mrs. Kendal.

16

Talk of Mrs. Tanqueray looking into her mirror: how do you feel now?

Loraine would not believe this about himself. He does now. He was here yesterday. Your dread of him is as nothing to his dread of you. I explained to him that he is a pig and a Philistine. I reminded him that when Ricketts did that magical production of the hell scene from *Man & Superman*, he (Robert) was simply wretched in his exquisite silver dress, and thought that Ricketts was making him ridiculous instead of immortal. I told him that you were the greatest artist of his time, and that only by a combination with you—to which you would strongly object—could he complete a real London theatre in the full artistic sense. I pointed out to him that if he could join you in a theatre holding £300, it was quite possible that both of you might take as your shares as much as he could get at best with great trouble in America, and more than you could get without him. I told him what you said about him (with exquisite embellishments). I sang "Oh, that breeziness, that BREEziness!" in every key. I rehearsed him making a breezy entry to 33 Kensington Square and knocking Georgina into the area by the mere wind of his impetuousity. I played you shuddering to the inmost fibres of your bludgeoned soul on the sofa. I convinced him at last that he ought to postpone America and stay if only he could persuade you to adopt him and knock some art and some style into his amazing vitality—you talk of leaden feet! he has the feet of Mercury.

Now having told you all this, I grow reckless and will tell you still more terrible things. Du Maurier being lost to us, Loraine is indispensable, I can make the cat play Liza. It wouldnt be *my* Liza because it wouldnt be *your* Liza. But it would be a commercially possible Liza. And I cant make the dog play Higgins. That is a thing that often happens: it is not the best part that is the difficulty. And apart from

17

the part, where am I to find a man to stand up to you on the stage?

You are happy playing with worms. Barker loves worms. Worms never give any trouble; and in plays which can be *produced*, they make the best casts. (Darwin proved that the earth is made of worm casts). But my plays must be acted, and acted hard. They need a sort of bustle and crepitation of life which requires extraordinary energy and vitality, and gives only glimpses and movements of the poetry beneath. The lascivious monotony of beauty which satisfies those who are slaves of art instead of masters of it is hideous in my plays. Well, a man with energy enough to bring up my plays to concert pitch cannot be had and held for a salary. If there is a profit of a thousand a week, he is far more likely to think that he had made it all than to admit that he has made only £500 of it. It must be recognized that he is indispensable to it, just as you are indispensable to it; and indispensables must share.

You dont believe—*yet*. He didnt believe me when I told him that if he wouldnt have Lillah as his Ann Whitefield he should have you, or perish. He perished accordingly; but the play he killed under him was a revival. And now he knows. A new play must not be killed so.

How would you like to write all this with a headache, with even green paper searing your eyes like smoke, and with the far deeper pain of being hateful to one you adore. And all to force you into the arms of Another. But better than the workhouse, which is the end of the Single Star in London.

Who, then, is to be your complement? the John Drew to your Ada Rehan, the Irving to your Ellen Terry? I must have a heroic Higgins, And I must not ruin you. Nor myself. I could not love thee, dear, so much, loved I not money more. *Name your man.*

I have written myself into a condition of complete Sha-

vian fiendishness, I have lived two whole days without seeing you; and now I know that I can go through anything.

Cartloads of chaff are falling on me like snow on Mont
Blanc. Barker spouts Friar Laurence at me untiringly; "Art
thou a man? thy form cries out thou art; thy tears are
womanish: thy wild acts denote the unreasonable fury of
the beast" &c. &c. &c. We were with Barrie on Monday
night: I told him you thought you ought to marry him. He
still longs for you as The Shrew, in spite of Barker, whose
heart you broke by sending a solicitor to tell him that he
had abused your private friendship to take a professional
advantage (what is friendship for, anyhow?). At eleven I
rose and said "I must go". Barrie replied in his slowest
Scotch manner "Shall you be seeing Mrs. Campbell again
tonight?" Such is the ribaldry I have brought on you. I wish
I could fall in love without telling everybody. I shall be 56
on the 26th of this month; and I have not yet grown up.

Edmund Gwenn & Hilda Trevelyan sent today to offer
the Vaudeville on any terms you like under their management.

I know it is all vile, and that I see too far ahead to make
any woman happy. But we great people have no need for
happiness. Nothing like business, is there, after all?

I must now go and read this to Charlotte. My love affairs
are her unfailing amusement: all their tenderness recoils
finally on herself. Besides, I love an audience. Oh, forgive
these blasphemies; but my head is still bad and it makes me
naughty.

at your feet,
G.B.S.

◇◇◇◇◇◇

*This letter is undated, but it is clearly an acknowledgment of
Shaw's missive, dated 3 July 1912.*

Matheson Lang: a popular actor who toured prodigiously, excelled in romantic parts, crowned his career with a memorable Othello, and died in 1948.

33, Kensington Square, W.

I have'nt had a minute to answer your many funny green pages—I wish you were'nt so early Victorian!—I see your point of view clearly.

You must let Loraine have the play if Higgins is more important than Eliza. But he and I cannot be forced into partnership—that would never do.

—one knows, only too well that a 'two star' show is better than a 'one star' and that an 'all star' show is fit only for Kings and Queens! !

The two star affairs you quote were more or less bound by cupid! I suggest Matheson Lang or Aubrey Smith will play with joy the 2nd part and do the easier share of the business.

Before making up your mind you would naturally like to know what theatre and the financial strength of the undertaking: this of course will be put before you, and you will be discreet—I shall know in a few days.

I would be very unhappy if I could'nt feel the very best had been done for your brilliant play—I would far rather lose "Eliza".

My love to you and to your Charlotte too.

Beatrice Stella.

❖❖❖❖❖❖

Lena Ashwell: a distinguished actress who acted with Sir Henry Irving in 1903, created many famous parts, and retired over twenty years ago.

10, Adelphi Terrace, W.C.

5th July 1912

I don't want anything put before me. I am an artist and dont understand finance. I want my Liza and I want my Higgins. If you are unkind about them I shall sit down and cry until I get them. I wont choose between them. I must have my Liza and no other Liza. There is no other Liza and can be no other Liza. I wrote the play to have my Liza. And I must have a proper Higgins for my Liza. I wont listen to reason: I will sit there and howl. I can howl for twenty years, getting louder and louder all the time. I cant have Lang because he is in the east playing *The Devil's Disciple* from Calcutta to Capetown. I wont be offered the Best and then refused poor Bobby, who *is* the best. I will have a better if you can find him, because nobody is good enough for my Liza; but I wont have a worse. I dont want to force anybody into anything: I only want to see my play with my Liza properly supported in it; and until I get that I want to do nothing but yell. If you had a heart you would not be so obstinate and unreasonable. All I ask is to have my own way in everything, and to see my Liza as often as possible. I have gone through my big card index, and could name you twenty far better Higgins than any you have thought of; but they are none of them good enough: I'd rather die than see you dragged down to second class by them: I'd as soon ask you to wear a contract dress at £3 4s. 2d. If you wont have [Loraine] then we must wait until somebody else whom you *will* have comes to the front and proves his mettle. And I shall cry, cry, cry all the time, and there will be a great wave of public feeling against you for your cruelty. And I will write SUCH a play for Lena Ashwell, my dear Lena who really loves me. So there!

G.B.S.

✧✧✧✧✧✧

Cissie Loftus, a clever actress and brilliant mimic, does not seem to have appeared as Eliza after all, in the U.S.A. or anywhere. Nor is there any record of Loraine ever appearing as Higgins.

33, Kensington Square, W.
[undated; approx. July 1912]

Oh darling what a letter!

I call you 'darling' because 'dear Mr. Shaw' means nothing at all—whilst darling means most dear and most dear means a man, and a mind and a speaking—such as you and your mind and your speech! Now please pull yourself together and tell me whether I may get on with business or no. I too have London and provincial rights and I would like permission to play Eliza after Lorrain [*sic*] and Cissy Loftus have finished with it in New York—

If you say 'No', 'No', 'No'—then add 'but you may come and see me whenever you like and Charlotte too'—we are friends.

I long to get on with the whole thing and call rehearsals on Sept 1st or else get off—you know how *much* I want to work with you—and as sure as one can feel—I feel *sure* (Shaw)—There's a nice original joke—

Beatrice Stella.

✧✧✧✧✧✧

Though this letter is undated, it is obvious that "he" refers to Robert Loraine and his projected visit to America.

Georgina's Everilda was apparently another griffon dog.

After September 1912 Mrs. Campbell drops the "Beatrice" from her name and uses the "Stella" only.

33, Kensington Square, W.
[undated; approx. July 1912]

I must hear. Is it with Higgens [*siċ*] he goes? I hope he will clear up his difficulties and come back with money to burn—Anyway he's worth £60— or even £70 a week.

I suppose I must take your note as a serious answer to mine it is *very* sad—and *very* disappointing but better than that you should feel disatisfied [*sic*] or mistrustful—The American offer so far as I know is no longer open—but no doubt somebody will want me—

I send my love to you both and remember when Georgina's Everilda comes I will bring her to your wife.

Beatrice Stella.

◇◇◇◇◇◇

Mrs. Lyttelton: the late Dame Edith Lyttelton—usually referred to as "D.D." (see note to the letter of 8 October, 1906).

"Laurence" is presumed to be Laurence Irving, younger son of Sir Henry.

The taxicab accident occurred during the long run of Bella Donna. *Mrs. Campbell was away from the theatre for a fortnight and was then sent by her doctor to Aix for treatment. But she was very ill for a long time (see note to undated letter on page 25. In her autobiography she quotes several letters of sympathy, and then concludes the account: "There was one who, perhaps through the intelligent grasp of his genius, understood a little the nerve rack of my illness. Himself living in dreams, he made a dream-world for me. Only those who can understand this can understand the friendship Bernard Shaw gave to me by my sick-bed—the foolish, ridiculous letters he wrote me, and his pretence of being in love with me. He revelled in the mischievous fun and in the smiles he brought to my face. He did not care a snap of the fingers at the moment what anybody else might say or think."*

33, Kensington Square, W.

[22 July 1912]

Do you know you are very foolish, and not a little mischievous—I am rather ashamed of you.

Mrs. Lyttelton told me some of the contents of your letter—she had taken your nonsense seriously and wondered why *she* had never heard I had got poor Laurence sent away. What an absurd thing for you to fool inaccurately about! !—and why didn't you tell her I would have been *delighted* to act with Loraine—but not to have gone into partnership with him—

Can it be that Dr. Almoth [Almroth] Wright's letter to *The Times* applies to men as well as to women—and your sense of proportion has wobbled? ! !—

I am delighted Loraine takes your play with Cissy Loftus to America. She ought to play Liza BEAUTIFULLY and it would be wicked not to have it with *her* here when they come back—

I hope you will have a nice holiday.

My black eyes and bruises and swellings Fripp expects to have gone down by Thursday and I will play again then.—

Yours,
Beatrice Stella.

They tell me I missed the end by a hairs breadth, it was an astonishing experience—

33, Kensington Square, W.

[postmark: 24 July 1912]

Oh my dear don't trouble to justify yourself. We understand—But I do wish you would'nt send me your photographs—I dislike photographs, I have given all yours away at the theatre—My dresser particularly liked the one of you as Jesus Christ playing the piano. I hope to be out of bed and playing again on Thursday, which will mean only laid

up a week—after missing haemorhage of the brain by a
hair's breadth according to Sir Alfred Fripp—I can paint
out my black eyes and swollen face—if only the queer pains
in my head go.

Yours,
Beatrice Stella.

I am *quite* sure if Cissy Loftus will work hard she will
play "Liza" *splendidly*—and suit Loraine's style far better
than I—and suit your style too—far better—remember—the
Morbideza [*sic*] that will creep out in my work—so bad for
yours!

◇◇◇◇◇◇

"The enclosed" is a press-cutting:
*"Mrs. Patrick Campbell has had a severe shaking through her
taxicab colliding with another near the Albert Hall. Her head
smashed through one of the windows, but she was not badly
cut. She will probably resume her part in* Bella Donna *at the
St. James's Theatre to-morrow."*
The wedding was that of the Marquis of Anglesey.
*Florence Farr was an actress and a musician of great talent.
She was a close friend of Shaw's and appeared as Louka in the
first public run of* Arms and the Man *in 1894. She was also a
pioneer of Ibsen. She entered a Vedantist seminary in Ceylon
in 1912 and died there in 1917.*

33, Kensington Square, W.
[postmark: 25 July 1912]
The enclosed will explain my mishap—it was a blind-
ing bang—my head rose 6 inches and then the haemorhage
came down my face under the skin, and I have been a sight
of sights with aches and pains in every inch of me and
bruises as large as saucers—stooping to pick up Georgina

who had fallen from the seat saved my face—I am afraid I cant play again—the play is off on August 1st.

—I go on Tuesday with Sir Edward and Lady Stracey in their Rolls Royce to Aix—we take it easy 5 days and stay there 3 weeks he does the cure, we enjoy ourselves we take a chauffeur—I shall miss Marjorie Manners wedding and I am sorry—but I couldn't have gone with two black eyes and a swollen jaw—

You know it is a serious thing to carry the mischief and the sorrows of our unborn children within us—your 5 sons and your 4 daughters—haunt your aura—and three unborn daughters haunt mine I am sure—

—Indeed I wont even bother myself for one instant again about 'Liza'. I so absolutely *believe* in Cissy Loftus and Loraine for the parts.—

All success to your rehearsals and your holiday and my love to both you and Charlotte.

Stella C.

Florence Farr is so full of joy at her Ceylon enterprise it is nice to feel as she does and I am glad she has such an outlook.

33, Kensington Square, W.
[postmark: 29 July 1912]

Both Sir Edward and Lady Stracey were very amused and delighted with your letter and book—May Stracey begged me to write and say it would be grand, and that you rather owe it to me, and that chivalrous spirit that dwells somewhere within you—to let us have "Liza" to take with us for me to read to her—so that she will hear what the world will never hear now—we would treasure the M.S. and let you have it back faithfully—and we would let no other soul see it—

—My Stella used to sing a song which I told her was silly,

and she declared was funny—your last letter reminds me
more of it than your others—

> He's mad, mad, mad,
> He's clean gone off his nut
> He cleans his boots with strawberry jam
> He eats his hat whenever he can
> He's mad, mad, mad—

—I hope you too will have a lovely holiday and not need
your 'cap and bells' all the time—and that bladder-whacking
of yours, that makes my dear friend D.D. jump, and imagine its really a bump!
My address will be

> Hotel Mirabeau
> Aix-les-Bains
> Savoie
> France—

I start to-morrow after 8 days in bed—with two black
eyes—and some screw-like pains in my shoulder.

Yours affectionately,
Beatrice Stella.

Hotel de Russie, Bad Kissingen.
9th August 1912

Stella, Stella: all the winds of the north are musical
with the thousand letters I have written to you on this journey. But at last the car's gears got jammed at the fall of
evening; and as I live (by vegetables)! I *stood*—stood on
my straining legs on that hillside for ten hours, keeping up
the spirits of my chauffeur and warding off ghosts and foreign devils from him whilst he took the whole transmission
to pieces and put it together again. I found a village and a
clean double-bedded room in a *Gasthaus* for Charlotte and

her sister; and they slept happily. I and the chauffeur kept up magnificently, and greeted the dawn with the exultation of men who had not turned a hair. And that day we did not turn many hairs. But the next (which was yesterday)— my word! I tell you, my good woman, that if you expect to find any romantic nonsense about me, you are greatly mistaken. My knees are out of order: my calves are like a shop assistant's where there are no seats behind the counter. I shall not feel romantic about you again for at least ten minutes.

But this is not what you want to know. The original manuscript of *Pygmalion* you cannot read: it is in short-hand. The typed copy with my corrections which I read from at DD's has been through the hands of the compositors in Edinburgh, and would not be fit for your lily-white hands even if it were within my reach instead of—I presume —in London. And the first proof, which I brought with me, has gone back to Edinburgh, scrawled with corrections and cuts and interpolations. I posted it only a day or two ago, and cannot reasonably expect the corrected proof by Mon-day, when I start for an excursion down the Tyrol. I want to pass the Stelvis Pass, where the car can get up 9000 feet into the snows of the Ortler, and I can hear a few words of Italian on the other side before turning back. It will be hard to turn back, knowing that I have only to push on to Tresenda, turn to the right, skirt Lake Como, hurry through Milan, dash through the Little St. Bernard (being myself the Great St. Bernard), make through Albertville to Chambery, and then be in your arms in an hour. But back I must turn for all that, leaving your arms empty and, let me hope, aching.

Now from Kissingen to Bornio, which is the Italian foot of the Stelvis, is about 400 miles, all of which has to be retraced; and when a journey of 800 miles includes crawls

up endless hairpin zigzags to 9000 feet, it is likely to be a
matter of ten days. That means that I shall not be back here
until the last half of the week ending 24th August, when,
if you are still at Aix, I will send you a rough proof of
Pygmalion. I warn you beforehand, however, that if you
once read it you are lost: you will be at my feet at once
with your dark hair looking dyed because of the gleaming
of my brown shoes through the roots.

If you by any chance leave Aix before the end of the
month, let me have a line to this hotel. Charlotte will be
here all the time. She gasps in rarified air whilst her sister
wallows in mud at five marks per gasp and per wallow; and
the Stelvis cannot tempt them to intermit these voluptuous
cures for overeating. Neither of them, by the way, is in
the least ill; but Charlotte wants to get thin, and her sister
wants to get plump; so they have both agreed to be asth-
matic and have treatments. I have taken the waters myself—one mouthful, which will suffice for the rest of my life.

Is it Lady Strachey you are with? Your letter reads like
Strachey which suggests nothing to me but a Colonel in the
Guards of whom I knew something (in connexion with a
famous opera singer) thirty years ago. If it is Lady Strachey, what will she think of me when you trail your victim
before her? I solemnly protest that when I went into that
room in Kensington Square I was a man of iron, insolently
confident in my impenetrability. Had I not seen you dozens
of times, and dissected you professionally as if you were a
microscopic specimen? What danger could there possibly
be for me? And in thirty seconds—oh Stella, if you had a
rag of decency it *couldnt* have happened. I always thought
that if I met you I should ask you to play. I looked at the
piano; and I said "Good God! fancy listening to *that* when
I can listen to her". Is this dignified? Is it sensible? At my
age—a driveller—a dotard! I will conquer this weakness, or

trade in it and write plays about it. Oh Lord! I hope it isn't
Lady Strachey: she is such a nice woman; and I had to dis-
gust her before with certain savageries in a little piece called
Press Cuttings. *She* cannot be made the dupe of my ridicu-
lous illusions about you. I am like the brigand in *Man and
Superman* with his Louisa (who was our cook, by the way).
Still, O Stella, I kiss your hands and magnify the Life
Force for creating you; for you are a very wonderful
person.

That doggerel of Stella's—Stellinetta's—nearly cost the
life of myself and the three people I was driving; for instead
of minding my work I kept composing millions of additional verses, in proof whereof I send you three or four
of the least poetic and most intelligible. The one profane
rhyme is not my fault: jam inevitably suggests dam. Stellinetta is rather a wooden little devil, by the way; but perhaps the baby will wake her up—not that I want her to be
wakened up; for she is rather exquisite as she is. I once
puzzled her frightfully by a piece of Irish folly. We were
sitting in the front of a box at the Savoy at some idiotic
performance of *Arms and the Man;* and the audience gave
me a sort of ovation at the end. My impulse was to rise and
bless them (I often feel like a Pope—should have been one),
but Stellinetta was talking to me; and to appear conscious of
anything but her would have been a breach of gallantry.
So I betrayed not the faintest consciousness of the applaud-
ing house, and hung on Stellinetta's words. She didnt see
it a bit, and thought I was cracked, poor infant! And Charlotte was furious, and said. I had been guilty of a gross breach
of public manners. But it was pleasanter to be gallant to
Stellinetta than to smile at a mob of gushing Shavians. I am
the servant of the public, but not its adorer. And I will not
begin another sheet or I shall never get to bed. And so
buona sera, Beatrice.

G.B.S.

Stellinetta sings to her Banjo.

1.   He's mad! mad! mad!
        He's gone right off his chump
He cleans his boots with strawberry jam;
He thinks the world of my silly old mam
Who doesn't value his plays a dam
        For they give her the blooming hump, dear girls;
        They give her the blooming hump.

2.   Yes, he's mad! mad! mad!
        He's regularly deranged,
He began by falling in love with me;
And when I got married he loved D.D.;
But now he prefers my Mammy; and we
        Say a sane man couldn't have changed like that
        A sane man wouldn't have changed.

3.   Oh, he's mad! mad! mad!
        But not so mad—ha ha!
As he'll be, having chucked Alexander up
When he brings his mischievous candour up
And succeeds in getting the dander up
        Of my southern blooded Mamma, dear girls;
        Of my lovilly dark Mamma.

4.   Then hurrah! rah! rah!
        He'll never be my Papa;
For however he loves and however he longs,
My Mammy and I wouldn't touch with the tongs
Such a silly old man with such silly old songs:
        No, we'd rather marry the Shah, dear girls;
        We'd rather marry the Shah.

        (Banjo *ad lib*—Plunk a tunk a bunk chunk etc. etc)
Kissingen
August 1912.

Hotel Mirabeau, Aix-les-Bains.
Tuesday, 13th Aug. 1912

I am sending your poem to Stella and if she doesn't
bring a laughing babe into the world it won't be your fault
—or mine—

You seem to be having a merry time.

I am looking at a glorious world, when I look up—and
out—but the scullery maids in their pearls and fashions with
their bloody nails and sealing-wax lips make my hair stand
on end—I have never been to a fashionable cure place before—I am a little astounded. I didn't realise quite—"laugh
and the world laughs with you, snore and you sleep alone".
Send 'Liza' quickly I leave on the 25th. I must hurry back
and see about a job—I would like to travel for a year—with
a letter a week from you—

Lady Stracey is the great great grandchild of *the* Sheri-
dan and her mother was Motley the historians daughter and
her Aunt Lady Harcourt, her sister is Mrs. Hall Walker
whose horse won the Derby for King Edward the VII.

By the way do you know the story of the tipsy gentleman who had to propose the health of the King and the
Queen and he didn't know which came first—he waited a
moment and then said "Gentlemen the Quink"—

I think the enclosed is a good idea we might sell the seats
and give Loraine the money to pay his debts and then he
would be able to accept the salary he is worth.

—Yes General Stracey sung duets with Trebelli before I
was born—

Beatrice Stella.

Perhaps someday, if you are very good and behave properly at rehearsal I will write you a love letter.

◇◇◇◇◇◇◇

Max Linder was a French film-comedian of great charm and inventiveness, and Chaplin has somewhere acknowledged indebtedness to his methods. He died at forty-one in 1925, after having been reported missing in the war and mourned all over France and Britain.

"Fanny" is Fanny's First Play, and "Voysey" is Granville Barker's fine play The Voysey Inheritance.

A note in Mrs. Campbell's handwriting is attached to the copy of this letter stating that the original was sold. [See her letter of 5 April 1938, from New York, in which she informs G.B.S. she intends to sell some of the letters "singly."]

Hotel Excelsior, Nancy.

19th August 1912

I have just opened up communications with Charlotte after harrowing misadventures which have landed me here instead of nearer, my Star, to thee, at Bormio. She says that Clark (the printer) has sent revises of *Pygmalion*, and that she is checking the corrections. I am writing to her to send you one of the revises. If my letter reaches her the day after tomorrow, and she acts on it promptly, you may get it in time for a reading on Saturday night. On second thoughts, I'd better wire to her.

My misfortunes are too prosaic to be narrated. Briefly, on my way south, in a townlet some 20 miles north of Ulm, the car ruptured a vital organ. Then came all the bothers that follow such accidents—refuge in an impossible inn with no bedclothes and primitive sanitation, taking the car to pieces in a shed to find what was wrong, putting her together again, getting horses to drag her to the nearest railway station, negotiating for transport with a country station master, persuading her into a truck after baffling the plans of the shunters for smashing her by impossible methods. following her to the frontier, getting her across it through a French station and a German station (not on speaking terms) with two customs houses to negotiate, speaking German fluently to the Frenchmen and French fluently to the Germans and understanding neither of them (I am the most deplorable of linguists); all this is simply tragic for me, who am so shy that I would rather write three plays than ask my way anywhere; and yet I have to do it with an air of energy and resource and get it through somehow. On such occasions I miss Charlotte, who, when in the smallest difficulty, demands information and assistance from every bystander (giving them copious and detailed information as to every relevant or irrelevant event of the last three months) and generally gets them too. The things of this world bruise my soul. A trumpery bother like this is more fearful to me than one of the campaigns of Cæsar. Stella, do not ever bully me: you don't know how easily frightened I am. Women never do realise what timid weak creatures men are.

However, here I am, with the car safe in its native dock at the Lorraine-Dietrich ateliers, and every air of having got out of the emergency in a masterly manner; and here I shall be for a week and perhaps a fortnight. And here, too, is your letter, which I wanted to think about, or rather to let provoke me to tell myself stories about you. (If you knew all the adventures we have had already in that imaginary world which is my real world, you would blush to the remotest contours of your enchanting person—*that's* a nice thing to say, isn't it? (Good God! will I never be a grown up sensible man?) So to get some quiet and avoid being run over in absence of mind I went into a hairdresser's, forgetting that I had had my hair cut only the other day, with the result that I am mown all but bald. I did not wake up to what was happening until the man started on my eyebrow, probably mistaking it for a supplementary moustache because it turns up at the end in the Mephistophelean manner. As it is, I am cropped to the white, like a fox terrier.

If the sun is shining in Savoy, and you are motoring much, make them put the hood up from twelve to four, and ask the chauffeur to give you some lubricating oil to rub on your countenance. If you don't, it will peel. *I* use a skin food; but engine oil is cheaper and equally effective. And wear a silk mask with goggles in it (they are the only really bearable goggles); so that if the heat is quite infernal, the screen can be put down and the wind of the car's movement let play on you.

There is a peculiar charm about Savoy. Rousseau was quite right; it is the only possible scene for a sentimental romance. You don't feel hard and heroic there; you don't suffer the indescribable heartbreak of Ireland; you don't loathe the scenery for being prosy and mediocre in spite of its blatant picturesqueness as you do in Switzerland; you feel human and affectionate, and you are conscious of an infinite charm of happy sunny French elegance, and an absence of care and grind which exists nowhere else. It is really Arcadian; and now that I think of it I am not sure that you ought to be allowed there; you are too disturbing in your wicked and splendid attitudes, though I suppose all this Brinvilliers-Borgia is as complete an imposture as the G.B.S. of the popular journalistic imagination. Anyhow, in Savoy one becomes as a little child again. It has the XVIII century charm, the charm that made people play at being ideal shepherds and shepherdesses instead of swaggering in the modern manner as some thing powerful and destructive. Aix is an outrage on it. All 'cures' are horrible, except that the hotels don't overfeed you as they do in places where people are presumed to be in sound health. And I doubt if Aix is capable of the amazing fabric of fraud, quackery, imposture and humbug which the Germans organize at places like Kissingen, with their artificial

Sea Breeze, and mud baths, and rarified atmospheres, and whey, and grapes, and devil knows what not.

Fortunately they hurt nothing but one's pocket. This gabble that I am writing is to fill up the time until I recollect—oh yes: I have it now.

Do you ever study the cinema? I, who go to an ordinary theatre with effort and reluctance, cannot keep away from the cinema. The actor I know best is Max Linder, though I never heard his voice or saw his actual body in my life. But the difficulty is that though good looks and grace are supremely important in the cinema, most of the films are still made from pictures of second, third and fourth rate actresses, whose delighted willingness and energy, far from making up for their commonness, make it harder to bear. There is one woman whom I should shoot if her photograph were vulnerable. At Strassburg however, I saw a drama which had evidently been played by a first rate Danish (or otherwise Scandinavian) company, with a really attractive leading lady, very sympathetic and expressive, without classical features but with sympathetic good looks, like Kate Rorke in the best days of her youth. Here I saw a *Femme Fatale* who was a fine figure of a woman, but so hard that she wouldn't have been fatal to anything in my house except a black beetle if her foot happened on it. Also a *Belle Mère* who was a little more fascinating—so much so, indeed, that the audience applauded loudly when her husband, on looking out of the window and seeing her squeezing lemon juice into the medicine of her step-daughter (to whom acid was fatal) seized a gun and shot her *sans phrase*. It is something to have people care whether you are shot or not. But she was only £15 a week at the very outside. Now all these Dramas are dramas of *Bella Donna* in one version or another. Twice I have seen a version called *The Judgment of Solomon*, which would have pleased me better if the bad mother hadn't been absurdly like Florence in her most maddening good natured aspect. Besides, the baby, in spite of all the efforts of the performers to stifle it half the time and hide its cavernous mouth the other half, was evidently howling all through; so that Solomon would have been justified in having it cut in two merely to stop its noise.

Now I ask myself why should these mediocre ladies be preserved to all posterity whilst nothing remains of you but a few portraits which cannot reproduce your living charm. Nobody who has not seen you move—seen you "live and move and have your being"—has the faintest idea of your fascination. I could make prettier photographs of women who, in action, are grimacing kangaroos. It would be well worth Pathé's while to pay you £5,000 for a film, even if you make it a condition (which I should by no means advise you to do) that it was not to be exhibited in London. Think of that immortality—of beauty imperishable! Suppose you learnt that Mrs. Siddons had had the opportunity of doing this, and hadn't done it through some snobbish scruple or other, wouldn't you swear at such little-minded folly? Think of being a beautiful old lady with white hair, able at last to enter a room full of men without seeing them all coming on guard at once with the Almroth Wright terror of sex slavery in their souls, and yet able too to see yourself at the height of your vigor and militant beauty! You say you want a job; why not this job, since Lubin is away and THE job must wait for him or some other Adonis capable of standing beside you without being ridiculous.

Which reminds me that Barker writes that he is glad that I am "taking no risks" with *Pygmalion. Voila ce que l'on dit de moi! Voila ce que l'on dit de moi! Voila que l'on dit de moi! Voila ce que l'on dit de moi—oi—oi—oi—oi. Dans les gazettes de l'Holla* ♪♪♪ *nde!* (But what do you know of Offenbach? you're too young). Barker is a brute. It is

not my risks (and I am risking my heart's blood) but yours
that I should be thinking of, if I were moralizing or com-
mercializing the situation. As it is I am a simple egotist,
wanting nothing more than my own way. The wretched
Fanny is still running and shows no sign of any greater ex-
haustion than has been chronic with her from the first. But
he has to produce *Voysey* presently or pay off his company, which he can't afford. So I have advised him to bring
Fanny to a violent end, and apologise to the public, plead-
ing that he can stand her no longer. The relevance of this
to our affairs is that it will stop my income, and that I am as
anxious as anyone can be to have a lucrative success with
Pygmalion. As the gentleman in *Bleak House* says, il fo
manger.

Love letters! *Sancta simplicitas!* When did you ever
write me anything else? As if the magic were not strong
enough without that! No: let me write; and do you pray
for us both; for there is always danger when that devilment
is at work. Let us take life as it comes, and love and hate
and work without dramatising it more than we can help.
Once, in my calfish teens, I fell wildly in love with a lady
of your complexion; and she, good woman, having a sister
to provide for, set to work to marry me to the sister. Whereupon I shot back into the skies from which I had descended,
and never saw her again. Nor have I, until this day, ever
mentioned that adventure to any mortal; for though dark
ladies still fascinated me they half laughed at me, half didn't
understand me, and wholly thought me cracked.

So your host *is* that gallant guardsman. *She* was a dark
lady too, with laughing childish teeth, and a voice like ripe
plums. Oh Maffio Orsini and bella Venezia—"*Men di sue
notte limpido*"—I can't make grammar of this; but that is,
right or wrong, the echo I hear in my memory—but you
are too young to know anything about Donizetti. Those
old Italian operas are still full of beauty and romance to me,

except when they do them at Covent Garden, when I simply can't keep my mind fixed on them. Lord Esher made me try Tetrazzini and *La Sonnambula* (which I knew by heart when I was 12) one night but it was no use. Oh, that inane cantilena! I wonder could *you* make it interesting to me. Tett could sing anybody's head off; but she was a Musical Tub.

Your G.B.S.

33, Kensington Square, W.
[Envelope postmarked 31 Aug. 1912]

It's a real delight to read this nonsensical play of yours. But I *do* wonder what you'll do without me for Eliza!

The play came too late to Aix.

You don't deserve to be clever as you are and it's not that you are *so* clever—it's just your exhuberant [*sic*] and mischievous mind.

I hope you are quite safe after your motor mishaps. I got sick of Aix and went on to Chamonix and without a guide and in Louis XV heels lace stockings long skirts and a floating veil I climbed down the mountain unaided and tripped upon the *mer de glace*—

Why I would be only too glad to do your 'Kine' work if you'll get it for me—I don't know where to apply.

Yours
Beatrice.

◇◇◇◇◇◇◇

"Beo," Mrs. Campbell's son, had written a farcical play called The Dust of Egypt, *which was produced at Wyndham's Theatre by Sir Gerald du Maurier and then sent on tour by him.*

33, Kensington Square, W.

[postmark: 2 Sept. 1912]

I hear people have read your play. The first one said, "Did his mother suckle him"?

the 2nd. "No chance anywhere for your beauty and nobility"

the 3rd. "By jove there's a fortune in it! the brilliancy of the man! and the joke—the enormous joke of your acting a girl! ! !

Directly Sir Edward and Lady Stracey return I will read it to them—but I tell you I cannot keep up the exhuberance [*sic*] as you did—and the beloved Irish accent! which I believe the serpent had or Eve would never have noticed the apple far less eaten it—

—I wish you would get me a cine engagement—why not write me a dumb crambo play—

Do something quickly or I shall have vanished to America. I am not going to live much longer and I must tidy up!

Beatrice Stella.

Beo's play is going like wild fire in the provinces and has been bought for America—

I hope its not raining all the time, and that you are still enjoying your holiday—

❖❖❖❖❖❖

"Helen" is Mrs. Alan Campbell, Beo's American wife. "Florence" is Florence Farr, who had just left for Ceylon, never to return.

The postcript about "Jim"—J. M. Barrie—is of particular interest since there is in his collected and published letters a characteristic specimen, dated 7 September 1912, to Mrs. Campbell herself. It is in all probability an answer to her "insulting" letter, and it begins:

40

*"I thought when I saw your nice little monogram that it
meant you no longer adored G.B.S., and that you had crossed
the street again to me. [Shaw lived opposite Barrie in Adelphi
Terrace.] You see, I had watched you (a bitter smile on my
face) popping in at his door instead of at mine. For the moment
I am elated though well I know that you will soon be off with
me again and on with him. He and I live in the weather house
with two doors, and you are the figure that smiles on us or
turns up its nose at us alternately. However, I would rather see
you going in at his door than not see you at all, and as you are
on elastic, I know that the farther you go with him the farther
you will have to bound back."*

A cable from America offering a fine tour of a one-act play
by Sir James Barrie brought Mrs. Campbell hurriedly back
from Aix, but the course of baths she had been taking appears
to have had an adverse effect on her health. She was ordered to
bed by the doctors and kept there for six months. It was a
further three months before she was able to act again.

33, Kensington Square, W.
[undated; *c*. Sept. 1912]

Are you safely home again? I think it is a pity you
sent me "Liza" for now I am ready with her tomorrow! !
When I found you really *did'nt* want me I cabled to
America accepting their terms—alas! (thank God)—too late!

Some afternoon when you are not tired out by rehearsals
please come and eat some grapes and nuts—my son and his
wife are here and they are both quite "off their heads" to
meet you. As for Helen she bursts into shrieks and shrieks
over Liza and whenever I look a little pale and tragic she
says "say Aaaaaaah ow ooh, Aaeeeeeeeeeeh ow-ooh" and
then she laughs and laughs until her hair comes down—you
wont be able to withstand Helen—

I miss your eight sheets of green paper—you easily tire!—

I thought Loraine had gone to America, what a pity we

can't meet and let him see what a really charming harmless person I am—I'd have a nice grousy or pheasanty supper with bananas and apples and nuts, any time you say—and Charlotte too if she will cease to regard me as a middleaged minx—

It is sad to think Florence has gone—and so happy she was saying Goodbye to the lot of us!—

Yours
Beatrice Stella.

I wrote dear Jim an insulting letter meant for the two of you.

◇◇◇◇◇◇

This letter was written to Shaw by Mrs. Campbell's daughter-in-law, and by "Stella" she means, of course, Mrs. Campbell herself.

33, Kensington Square, W.
13th September 1912

Dear Mr. Shaw,

Stella has asked me to write you a *"funny letter"* (!) —as she has not sufficiently rallied from the upsetting effects of your play-reading to write one herself. (I never realized before what was meant by the expression "Laughing yourself to death.")

If I had seven right hands I might be able to take down some of the many witticisms that she will soon send you herself, but, as it is, perhaps I had better not dull their effect by any (vastly better!) ones of my own.

This letter would be almost a series of dictated messages, were Stella not fast asleep at this moment with Georgina wound tightly around her neck.

Being her trusted secretary I ought to tell you only the

glorious fun *she* had over your play, and how *she* appreciated (*really*) your coming—head-aches and all—to read it to her.

But please, may I say in a very low voice, which couldn't possibly wake her up, that Beo and I are *much* too proud to speak to any of our old friends since you let *us* hear it, too, —and that never in your life have you given two people more real enjoyment and red-letter-day satisfaction.

The doctor says she will soon be well as ever if only she will "rest" now,—so you will doubtless receive shortly an even more illegible letter than mine.

Until then I am supposed to send you all her *bon mots* and thanks (which you can imagine more easily than I can write them!)

I've put all of ours in, too, though perhaps they should be sent "under separate cover" as this letter is intended to be sacred to Stella.

very gratefully,
Helen Campbell.

⟡⟡⟡⟡⟡⟡⟡

The "Christian Martyr play" is Androcles and the Lion, *which was first produced in September 1913.*

Shaw had sent Ellen Terry a description of how he had read Pygmalion *to Mrs. Campbell in the presence of "D.D." "And then—and then—Oh Ellen; and then? Why, then I went calmly to her house to discuss business with her, as hard as nails, and, as I am a living man, fell head over ears in love with her in thirty seconds."*

Ellen Terry answered three days later with a note that said:
"It was a joy to get your letter. I'm in love with Mrs. Campbell too, or rather I'd like to be, but something tugs me back. She is amusing and was nice to me in America. The flower-girl idea is thrilling."

Ayot St. Lawrence, Welwyn.
28th Sept. 1912

How are you?

This is a business inquiry: you are now an important part of my property; and I cannot have you running down. It is useless to appeal to me for sympathy. My wife is ill; my mother is ill; I am rehearsing two plays simultaneously; and if an earthquake swallowed half the habitable globe I should only laugh. Up to a point I can sympathize: a slight cold or a moment of unhappiness would not try me too far; but if I let myself get tender over serious misfortunes I should die. Just now my heart is like the nether millstone: I could drive a steamroller over the shrieking Georgina without a ray of pity.

If I had another play ready I should read it to you just to find out whether you are really ill or not; but I have nothing but the Christian Martyr play, a bellowing roaring business, which would unroof your house and leave you naked beneath the worshipping stars.

And, anyhow, I never encourage illness. When I saw you last you were in bed; but you had the energy of 10 tigresses; and your remarkably fine neck would have carried the pediment of the Parthenon like a feather if you had been snatched from between the sheets and set up as a caryatid.

It is I who need sympathy. I have just had a letter from a Suffragette, beginning "Poor ill-used darling."

Dont tell Helen to write to me: she must be perfectly sick of the subject of your ridiculous and probably imaginary illness. Get up; and console ME.

Ever,
G.B.S.

33, Kensington Square, W.

8th October 1912

Dear Mr. Shaw:

There is something rather uninspiring about your strict injunction in your last letter to Stella: "Please don't let Helen write to me",—and I long for a typewriter to do away with the unwelcome personal element of this letter,—which she *makes* me write, really!

She's so worried about your "anxious boots",—and is longing to see you and really laugh again, though she has barely begun to recover from the destructive effects of your last visit. I think I can safely say that she is better today, and much more cheerful. The doctors are greatly encouraged about her, and we all hope that in a week or two she will be able to sit up.

The last few days of gradual improvement have been rather antidoted by the arrival of Madame Bernhardt (*en masse!*) at eleven o'clock this morning,—the doctor having issued instructions half an hour before that "Mrs. Campbell is to see *no one on any account*"—(except Mr. Shaw, if he calls.) The time between 11 and 11.27 this morning is a confused nightmare of much mole-skin and sable being helped up six flights of stairs,—and exhausted cries of "*Oh! Mon Dieu! Ces escaliers! Vertige! Vertige!*"—to a running accompaniment of *Oui-oui's*, from Beo. Then an aftermath of brandy and vinegar salts, and a promise to *revenir bientot.*

If Stella survives, perhaps you will come too, before long, and tell her all about your first night! It is cruel that she can't be there to see it. She sends you all possible good-luck messages instead.

Yours very truly,

Helen Campbell.

P.S. My motto has always been "*A bas* self-sacrifice!"

45

The play in which Aubrey Smith appeared at Liverpool was called Instinct, *produced originally in Paris in 1905—a translation of the best play of Henry Kistemaekers, the Belgian dramatist. It eventually came to the Duke of York's Theatre in London. The one-act plays by Pinero and Shaw which had failed there were respectively* The Widow of Wasdale Head *and* Overruled (*on this occasion apparently called* Trespassers).

"Caesar" is Forbes Robertson, who received his knighthood in June of the following year.

Midland Adelphi Hotel, Liverpool.
23rd Oct. 1912

Stella,

You must be either better or dead. Say, oh fairest, is your excellent white bosom still straitened, or are you up and about? If you are, it is your duty to write to me. I hope you have lost your good looks; for whilst they last any fool can adore you; and the adoration of fools is bad for the soul. No: give me a ruined complexion and a lost figure and sixteen chins and a farmyard of crows' feet and an obvious wig. Then you shall see me come out strong.

Everybody is down here—Ellen Terry (God knows why!), Forbes Robertson, acting stupendously well, Martin Harvey, and Aubrey Smith & Lilian Braithwaite. Aubrey has got hold of a good play by Kistemaekers, and gives a fine performance in it. I am trying to persuade Boucicault to put it up at the Duke of Yorks with Barrie's Rosalind, Pinero's play having failed flatly and mine aggressively. They simply hated it. They couldnt help laughing once or twice; but such angry screams of reluctant mirth were never before heard out of hell.

And this was the play *you* put into my head. I had been with D.D. with her board up

46

```
┌─────────────────────────┐
│                         │
│      TRESPASSERS        │
│       WILL BE           │
│      PROSECUTED         │
│       Alf. Lytt.        │
│                         │
└─────────────────────────┘
```

and then I was sitting with you, with no board up, and the idea suddenly flashed into my imagination, and led to this ruinous failure on the part of the silly public.

I shall never quite get over it—I don't mean the failure; I mean the falling in love. I havnt been quite the same man since. Have you been quite the same devil? for I suppose you *are* a devil: they all tell me so when I go on raving about you. Well, I dont care. I have always said that it is the devil that makes the hell; but here is a devil who makes heaven. Wherefore I kiss your hands and praise Creation for you, and hope you are well as this leaves me at present thank God for it. This is the Irish formula, which by the way I should have adopted earlier in this letter, as every sentence would then have begun with Dear Stella. I used to write letters for Irish servants when I was a child. "Dear mother I hope you are well as this leaves me at present thank God for it dear mother I saw Bridget on Friday and she desires to be remembered to you dear mother I hope you got the flannel petticoat safely dear mother &c &c &c &c &c &c &c &c &c &c"

I shall be here until Sunday morning, I expect. Caesar on Friday. I confessed my infatuation to Caesar. He was very nice, but seemed to think I wouldnt be able to stand it.

I have just recovered from one of the famous headaches, and am not quite sane yet.

G.B.S.

◇◇◇◇◇◇

"The great genius" is J. M. Barrie. He became Sir James Barrie, Bart., a year after this.
Lady Savile was a friend who had just died. An affectionate note from her is printed in Mrs. Campbell's autobiography.

33, Kensington Square, W.

26 Oct. 1912

Well darling I am not in heaven, neither have I sixteen chins and what bosom is left me is still straightened. In a week they say I shall be able to sit up—The great genius who lives opposite you, and whose one act plays *are* a success came to see me yesterday and didn't look at me with horror—

Will you come Monday or Tuesday at 4 o'c and make me laugh and convince me it's worth while getting well?

I want you to bring me that play of yours that I hear is "religious, noble and poetic" but you insist on a revolving stage. When you think what you *can* do, you know the public are right not to accept your play at the Duke of York's—though had the actors played with an Irish accent it would have gone like wildfire!

For the life of me I could'nt recognize any resemblance to D.D. or myself—you *blind blind* man—

Poor Violet Savile—I loved her very much—she was arranging to come here and to be carried up to my room by "two able bodied men" and every day she had roses sent to me from Rufford—and now he has sent me a little diamond

48

and emerald brooch she always wore as a keepsake! The sorrow of it all catches me at the throat.

I send you my love—mind you come Monday or Tuesday.

Stella.

◇◇◇◇◇◇

Forbes Robertson had appeared in the first English production of Caesar and Cleopatra *in 1907. This revival at Liverpool appears to have been in the nature of a try-out for the production of the play in his farewell season at Drury Lane the following spring.*

Miriam Lewes was a brilliant actress of rich experience. She played many Shavian parts, and appeared memorably with Robert Loraine in Strindberg's The Dance of Death *in 1928. In corroboration of Shaw's story, one can vividly recall her turning a few sensational cartwheels as Mrs. Vincent Crummles in a Nigel Playfair production at Hammersmith in 1927.*

Edlaston, Shropshire.
27th Oct. 1912

Alas! I shall not be within reach of you on Monday or Tuesday, unless an uncontrollable transport of longing to see you tears me away from my clear duty to return to Liverpool and see them through another rehearsal of Caesar. The performance on Friday was a specially disastrous dress rehearsal. The intervals totalled up to 1 hour 16 minutes. Oddly enough, all the great passages went splendidly; but the details and the small change of the play went to—well, to blazes. Such dryings-up and wrong cues and the like were never heard. To my taste the climax was reached when the end of the fourth act was approaching and the stage was darkened for the discovery of the murdered Ftatateeta. Cleopatra said "It is dark and I am lonely" with

49

such convincing naturalness that the sympathetic electrician on the prompt perch consoled her instantly with a flood lime which deluged the stage with light and sent me into a hysterical convulsion of laughter.

I didnt mean that the people in *Overruled* (alias *Trespassers*) were like you and DD, but that the idea of the play came into my head that day when we were sitting together on the sofa, just 24 hours after DD and I had careered all round Chelsea in a taxi. It gave me the situation—*my* situation. But when I put *you* on the stage, Strauss and Hofmannsthal and an Orchestra of 100 volcanoes will be nowhere, though I will do it with my little finger all the same.

I should love to read you *Androcles and the Lion*—has earth or heaven anything better to offer me than reading my plays to you (except perhaps living them with you?); but I am a little afraid too, because it is a bawling, shouting, roaring, bustling, brutal affair, and an hour and a quarter long. It might worry you and tire you. However, it's in three acts; so you can take it an act at a time if you like—an excuse for coming three times. Then there's *Misalliance*, a masterpiece which I suppose you never saw, in one act three hours long. The heroine is an acrobat, a beautiful Polish acrobat; you shall play her when you have learnt how to dance on a high wire.

That reminds me of a recent conversation with Miriam Lewes:

G.B.S.—Miss Lewes: did you ever really want to be an actress? Didn't you want to be an acrobat?

MIRIAM (gravely) Mr. Shaw: I *was* an acrobat. (Curtain).

Revolving stages present no difficulty. You can buy one like a fender or a hearthrug, and put it down on your own stage. They are made in Germany.

I am staying here with Charlotte's sister, Mrs. Cholmondely. I may get conscientious and go back to Liverpool for

Tuesday; but here I must *rest* until Tuesday morning anyhow; and the journey up, even if I dont go back to Liverpool, will take a whole day. So I shall not be in London
until Thursday at the very very earliest. It is appalling to
think that I have written nothing these three months—no
new plays to read to you. What could I not have written
in that time?

The new prologue to *Caesar*, a twenty minutes sermon, a
masterpiece of Shavian rhetoric, was received with stupefaction. Then a man in the gallery said "It's all true, though",
and it was applauded reverently. But I am in a cold fit on
the part of the public; *Pygmalion* will be a failure. What
matter, since you will share it with

G.B.S.

33, Kensington Square, W.
[postmark: 30 Oct. 1912]
Then to-morrow Thursday at 4 o'c and you'll bring
Androcles and the Lion even if I would rather you talked
than read—

Stella.

Ayot St. Lawrence, Welwyn.
30th Oct. 1912
O beautiful illustrious, I have mountains of work
upon me here, and cannot return to town until Friday
morning as ever will be . . . I cannot find *Androcles* here,
and am not quite sure that Gilbert Murray returned it to
me when I sent it to him to Cromer; but if it be within my
reach in London I will come on Friday at 4 and—unless you
write forbidding me—bellow it in your coral ears until
Kensington Square shakes down its railings. O brave high-
souled lady and cleanser and inspirer of my trampled spirit,

I would the post were in hell, since it will not wait another moment.—

G.B.S.

33, Kensington Square, W.

1st Nov. 1912

Oh darling! I think D D and I behaved like ungrateful savages, and you so good, and so gentle with us—and so kind to come and see me at all and honour me by reading your *brilliant* play—

—Oh dear me—its too late to do anything but *accept* you and *love* you—but when you were quite a little boy somebody ought to have said "hush" just once!

Grateful
Beatrice.

◇◇◇◇◇◇◇

This letter in Shaw's handwriting was written from Granville Barker's house in Kent.

It is on a single sheet of notepaper and ends abruptly with the one word "belief" at the top of the back of the sheet. There is no punctuation after the word and the rest of the page is blank, giving the impression that the writer was interrupted in the middle of it. The letter was never finished or signed.

Stansted, Wrotham, Kent.

3rd Nov. 1912

O glorious white marble lady,

What was done to me in my childhood was nothing at all of an intentional kind. I wasnt spoiled; and I wasnt helped. No direct ill treatment was added by anybody to the horrors of the world. Nobody forbade me to discover what I could of its wonders. I was taken—and took myself—

52

for what I was: a disagreeable little beast. Nobody concerned himself or herself as to what I was capable or becoming, nor did I. I did not know I was different from
other people (except for the worse); far from being con-
ceited, I hadnt even common self-respect. I have discovered
all my powers from the outside, with incredulous astonish-
ment, or rather I have discovered that everybody else hasnt
got them. My shyness and cowardice have been beyond all
belief

◇◇◇◇◇◇◇

*It is fairly clear that this letter crossed Shaw's of 3 November
in the post.*

33, Kensington Square, W.
4th Nov. 1912

I am very unhappy because I hoped you would send
me a word saying I hadn't behaved abominably—

I feel now you didn't *want* D D to hear that play at all—
and that it was only the horror of my thin green face that
made you say "as you like"—my temperature is going up to
105 point 6—telephone something that will make me feel
less a culprit—I have lost your telephone number—

—Remember how you snatched away Eliza—sending the
news by Loraine, and I only turned the other cheek.

Be patient with me. I have been a widow for 12 years and
a grandmother for four days and within the last few weeks
I nearly gave life the slip.

I send you my love and I am sorry I was a churl and you
had no tea and your hands were cold.

Stella.

◇◇◇◇◇◇◇

This is obviously a reply to G.B.S.'s unfinished letter of 3 November.

33, Kensington Square, W.
7th November 1912

Three times yesterday I tried to write, and my temperature went up to the moon!

I love the "dirty scrap of paper", but whats that about "shy" and a "coward"—

I see you—as sensitive as Keats—as timid as a lamb—and that "want of taste" we grumbled at, is a sort of Swank—thats not a pretty word, but it will do. . . . These letters of yours are traps—traps like your Irish accent—

There is a tract called "Led on step by step" that's whats happening to me!

—And wasn't it a pure blue heaven to me too?

The goodness of you to come and forgive—

—I'll whisper something—"I'm afraid of the Keats, and the lamb"—

Bring yourself and the Rodin article and the penny tract soon—

I hope all the sick people are feeling better and you not looking and feeling fifty-eight notes to the Octave!

—dearest—Stella.

10, Adelphi Terrace, W.C.
8th November 1912

Stella, Stella

Shut your ears tight against this blarneying Irish liar and actor. Read no more of his letters. He will fill his fountain pen with your heart's blood, and sell your most sacred emotions on the stage. He is a mass of imagination with no heart. He is a writing and talking machine that has worked for nearly forty years until its skill is devilish. I should have warned you before; but I thought his white hairs and 56 years had made his philanderings ridiculous, and that you would beat him at his own game and revenge his earlier victims. I pray still that you, great actress as you are, are playing with him as he is playing with you. He cares for nothing really but his mission, as he calls it, and his work. He is treacherous as only an Irishman can be: he adores you with one eye and sees you with the other as a calculated utility. He has been recklessly trying to please you, to delight you, to persuade you to carry him up to heaven for a moment (he is trying to do it *now*); and when you have done it, he will run away and give it all to the mob. All his goods are in the shop window; and he'll steal *your* goods and put them there too.

But don't cut him off utterly. He is really worth something, even to *you*, if you harden your heart against him. He will tell you that you are too great a woman to belong to any man, meaning, I suppose that he is too great a man to belong to any woman. He will warn you against himself with passionate regard for you—sincerely too, and yet knowing it to be one of his most dangerous tricks. He will warn you against his warning you, not meaning you to take any warning; and he will say later on "I told you so". His notion of a woman in love with him is one who turns white and miserable when he comes into the room, and is all one wretched jealous reproach. Oh dont, dont, DONT fall in love with him; but dont grudge him the joy he finds in being in love with you, and writing all sorts of wild but heartfelt exquisite lies—lies, lies, lies, lies to you, his adoredest.

G.B.S.

◇◇◇◇◇◇

This is a good example of Mrs. Campbell's epistolary style which does not always translate easily to the printed page. The word "really" in the first line is underlined five times in strokes of gradually diminishing length, the word "me" in the second line seven times. And the whole letter is dashed off with an impetuosity that has no time for a full stop or even, sometimes, conventional capital letters.

33, Kensington Square, W.
14th Nov. 1912

You didn't *really* think that I believed you came to see me because you were interested in *me*. I knew it was Liza and I was delighted that you should be so businesslike in such a bewilderingly charming way—

I see how things are going—and you musn't think of me anywhere but still in bed gazing at the cracked Kensington Square ceiling—and a calm and safe peace too!—

No indeed—not for one minute did I flatter myself!— Cissy Loftus—Lillah—Dolly Minto—Gertrude Kingston—or Lady Bancroft (she would be the best). I can see them all in "Liza".

My love to you,

Stella.

I hope all is going well tonight and our dear friends not killing themselves.

33, Kensington Square, W.
18th Nov. 1912

No more shams—a real love letter this time—then I can breathe freely, and perhaps who knows begin to sit up and get well—

I haven't said "kiss me" because life is too short for the kiss my heart calls for. . . . All your words are as idle wind—Look into my eyes for two minutes without speaking if you dare! Where would be your 54 years? and my grandmothers heart? and how many hours would you be late for dinner?

—If you give me one kiss and you can only kiss me if I say "kiss me" and I will never say "kiss me" because I am a respectable widow and I wouldn't let any man kiss me unless I was sure of the wedding ring—

Stella (Liza, I mean)

Ayot St. Lawrence, Welwyn.
18th Nov. 1912

. . . If I looked into your eyes without speaking for two minutes (Silent for two minutes with an audience even of one! Impossible, cried the fiend; but I don't care) I might see heaven. And then I should just trot off and do ten years hard work and think it only a moment, leaving you staring.

Do you know, I dont hate you one little bit. I am clearly in my second childhood (56, not 54); for you might be the Virgin Mary and I an Irish peasant, and my feeling for you could not be more innocent; and yet there is no relation into which we could enter which would not be entirely natural and happy for me.

Such concord will make me silly. Let us work together and quarrel and come upon all sorts of incompatibilities. Our music must have discords in it or you will tire of it.

I think you are getting well. I hear a ring, I see a flash in your letter. The able courageous Stella is stirring. And perhaps she will put me away with the arrowroot. No matter: I shall rejoice and glory in her. If I could bring her a thou-

sand of the most wonderful lovers, she should have them;
and I would polish their boots—and perhaps occasionally
their brains—for her with entire contentment.

Goodnightest G.B.S.

33, Kensington Square, W.

[postmark: 26 Nov. 1912]

That was a most nice letter—of course you have
guessed I have had a 'set back' and I have been very ill—or
I would have written. Please when you have time come and
see me, and tell me what to do to be hale and hearty again.

Stella.

❖❖❖❖❖❖

The "volume of plays" may have been Vol. II of the Plays
Pleasant and Unpleasant—*an edition of this appeared in 1913.*
Vol. I appeared in 1912. Both volumes of this edition were
given by G.B.S. to Mrs. Campbell in May 1914.

Belloc is Hilaire Belloc, the essayist, critic, poet, and contro
versialist, whose eightieth birthday has recently been celebrated.

William Poel was a distinguished and influential man of the
theatre who founded the Elizabethan Stage Society in 1894.
His work was enthusiastically praised by Shaw the critic.

Ayot St. Lawrence, Welwyn.

27th Nov. 1912

Oh, all they say is true. I have no heart. Here I am,
with my brains grinding like millstones, writing a preface
for my long belated volume of plays, and stopping only to
bring my quick firers into action by hurling a devastating
letter into some public controversy. Grind, grind; bang,

bang; broken heads and broken wings everywhere within
range; "and this word Love which greybeard calls Divine,
be resident in men like one another and not in me: *I* am myself alone". (Applause, started by the tragedian himself
with his boot heels).

Stella! Who is Stella? Did I ever know anybody named
Stella? Cant remember: what does it matter? I have articles
to write and the preface to finish. I have to debate with
Hilaire Belloc in the Queen's Hall on the 28th January.
Not an advertisement has appeared, and the hall is nearly
sold out already. (And actresses talk to me of their popularity!). Belloc shall perish. I try to get back to Elysium and
Stella; but a tempest of blighting, blasting withering argu-
ments bursts out of me and scorches all the trees of Paradise.
I want no Stella: I want my brains, my pen, my platform,
my audience, my adversary, my mission. I read Belloc's
book (*The Servile State*, ha! ha!) the other day. I will tear
it to rags. Collapse of Socialism, says Chesterton in *Everyman*. I have already scattered his collapse to the four thousand winds of hell. Parents and Children: that is the theme
of my preface. The tears of countless children have fallen
unrevenged. I will turn them into boiling vitriol and force
it into the souls of their screaming oppressors.

Stella! Who is Stella? A woman, Well, can she love a
human dredger? does she want to clasp brass to her bosom—
oh, her bosom! I remember now—the jade!—when she first
took my hand she shook it so that it touched her bosom,
an infamous abandoned trick: it thrilled through me,
through all my brass for hours. That must have been cen-
turies ago: I was young and foolish then and could be
thrilled. What did she care for me then? What was my
knuckle to her—it caught me just on the knuckle—more
than a mutton bone or a door knocker? Bear witness, all ye
clouds of Kensington Square, that I did not move a muscle.
Had she felt what I felt she would have risen up into the

skies and set me there at her right hand. Am I the man to
whom that happened? No; the grindstones are at work; it
is to their sparks and their whirring that I thrill. Press the
levers of Babbage's Calculating Machine to your bosom
Stella; and—oh, I am lying: this unlucky recollection has
knocked Belloc out of my head and almost made the grindstones stop. It is well that you are ill; if you were to appear
in the front row of the balcony of Queen's Hall on 28th
January, I might betray my cause; for women always pity
the vanquished and hate the insolent conqueror. Think of
me always as the hero of a thousand defeats; it is only on
paper and in imagination that I do anything brave.

All the same, it is certain that I am a callous creature; for
I have let you write to me twice—no; that cant be. I *did*
answer. But would not a man with a grain of heart have
written ten times? Oh I have been as hard as nails for a fortnight past. I was when I began this letter.—I shall be so again
when I post it. But now—just for a moment—only a moment—before the grindstones begin again. Perhaps I shall
sleep well tonight; it is hard to put a man of brass to sleep.

And now I must stop myself resolutely for a moment,
and think of somebody besides myself. I am being kept
down here for the good of my health and to save the grindstones from interruption. On Sunday I must go up to town;
for I have to address a meeting in the East End in the afternoon and speak at the William Poel dinner in the evening.
And I shall spend next week in London. On Monday I have
to lecture for Lena Ashwell at her Three Arts Club—something about whether professional artists can have any self
respect—or is it Tuesday? Anyhow, Monday and Tuesday
are crammed. Later, I may have an afternoon. Your set-
back makes me desperate: I had set my heart on your getting well with a rush this time. Oh you must, you must,
you shall be torn out of bed and shaken into rude health.
Or else I will get into the bed myself and we shall perish to-

gether scandalously. Oh, why cant I do anything? What
use are grindstones after all? Goodnight, and forgive my
follies.

G.B.S.

❖❖❖❖❖❖

*Shaw had spent a month in Paris in 1906 being modelled by
Rodin. There are two busts and a bronze mask of him in the
Rodin Museum in Paris, besides the bust that was in Shaw's
house at Ayot St. Lawrence. The article on Rodin referred to
here is to be found in the volume called* Pen Portraits and Re-
views *in the collected edition of Shaw's works.*

33, Kensington Square, W.

2nd Dec. 1912

Most dear man of brass, full of grindstones and
things!—its a sad woman thats writing to you—for the doctors tell me that in 6 weeks I have made no improvement
and they cannot let me lie here much longer—and—Oh, but
I am not going to tell you—I was such a green sick skeleton
those days I didn't write and I am so glad you didn't see
me—You are raging against the world—I see bits about it in
the paper—a letter in the Westminster. I should like to hear
you on January 28th.

—I must see that Rodin article. I hear about someone calling it "subtle humour"—and another raging in anger against
it, and I want to know what its all about—

—I think if you don't come and see me rather soon there
won't be me to see—I forgive you your follies sure enough—
think of mine!

Stella.

◇◇◇◇◇◇

An envelope has been pinned to this letter with the postmark
8 November 1912, but a copy made by Mrs. Campbell when
she was writing her autobiography bears the date 8 December
1912, and the reference to the "bad week" shows that it was
written when she was expecting to undergo a dangerous opera-
tion.

33, Kensington Square, W.

8th Dec. 1912

It was beloved Blake who wrote "Bend not a joy
towards yourself and spoil the winged world"—
—You know where you left my friend?—well the top-
most bough and the highest tree, with wings strong enough
to fly up to the sun—is where indeed is a "joy fit for Paradise"—

Write something beautiful about Blake for me—and when
I am well talk to me about him—he wrote too "Damn braces
bless releases"—

Did I once call you a clown? I expect it was when you
said "I am God"—

This week is going to be a bad week—I won't be able to
write for a few days—my friends must fold their hands for
me—

My eyelids are heavier than I tonight—I am glad we met.

Goodnight

Stella.

There are parts of your letters I cannot reply to, except
by golden silence.

◇◇◇◇◇◇

The Hazlitt reference is to the great essayist's Liber Amoris,
which records his miserable love affair with Sarah Walker, the
maidservant in a house where he lodged.

10, Adelphi Terrace, W.C.
8th December 1912

My dear Mrs. Patrick Campbell

It is so many years since I have heard from you that I have lost all hope of your retaining any kindly feeling for me. I am like a dentist: there is so much that is wounding about my work that I am continually afraid of your going back to hard thoughts of me in my most detestable moments. *Misalliance* may have revived all your dislikes. The truth is, I need a letter every ten minutes to encourage me and silence my guilty conscience. I dont like myself well enough—though I admire myself enormously—to expect anyone else to like me.

And then I seem to remember adown the long years that my last letter was maudlin and depressing. It was written in a moment of deep feeling; and it is unprofessional to write under the influence of deep feeling: that is, it isnt useful or helpful, and it is selfish (I actually wrote "isnt"). I can only plead that I was most frightfully in love with you.

Today I am self-controlled, as you may gather from this merry note. I am holding myself in with a grip of steel. My mouth is like Ibsen's. My heart and soul are like water within me; but the ice crust is unbroken. I now have a mystic theory of your illness; it is a trap of the Life Force—the *Élan Vital.* I once fell into that trap. I will explain viva voce. I recovered. You will recover. But the traps of the Life Force sometimes set up a morbid routine out of which the victim has to be shaken. Do you know that I staggered about on crutches for 18 months, during which a sinus (a hole) going down through my foot to the bone kept filling up and breaking down, filling up and breaking down, just like your temperature. Eighteen months: think of that! One day I got a bicycle and tried to ride it with one foot. I presently had an upset, and came down on the ruined foot that had not borne my weight for all that time. It curled up under my own weight like a shaving. It swelled to the size of your house; and you could have walked into the sinus; an amazing spectacle. Then, when it regained its normal size, I had it X-rayed, to see what was happening to the bone. Also I stopped dressing it. It got well in a fortnight—shaken out of its morbid routine.

Now I wonder what would happen if you told the doctors that you distinctly recollect that you swallowed a brooch at rehearsal in a transport of fury and that you can feel it in your appendix. Insist on being X-rayed to detect and locate the foreign body and see what will happen. Those rays are rum things; they will upset the routine that the illness has started; and they wont hurt or harm you (I speak from experience: I have had my inside X-rayed as well as my foot). I am overwhelmingly convinced that you want a change of some sort or a shake. Once, in Bayonne, I snatched Charlotte from the tomb by suddenly, in desperation, rolling her about and pummelling her from head to foot, whereupon, amazed into a protest of all her vital forces she got up *well*, to the stupefaction of her sister, who had despaired of her life. I dare not pummel you because you are sore and I would die rather than extort the tiniest squeak from you; so it must be done by rays—light rays, life rays. Remember, they will really go through you and disentangle things and clean up morbidities and kill things and do all manner of things. So make them begin with that exploring operation.

I should like to see you if I may some day next week (*this* week it will be when you get this). I have a very indelicate question to put to you on a matter of business which I have put off and put off; but I have been a little uneasy about it all along; and now I think I had better ask it and have done with it. Could you spare me a moment on Tuesday afternoon? I had intended to chain myself to the gate here and have a week in the country, as my speech at the Irish meeting on Friday—violently overacted—finished me almost; but now I am forced to produce a hasty revival of *John Bull's Other Island* for Boxing Day, and this means rehearsing every day from tomorrow on.

I am assailed by demons who ask me whether I have read Hazlitt's account of his infatuation with the slavey, and lead me to open books with reproductions of Isabey's miniatures of Napoleon and Josephine. I reply that Hazlitt and Napoleon are all right, but that if all the saints, and all the angels, and the Blessed Virgin were all rolled into one beautiful woman; and all the prayers and adorations and loves and worships they draw to themselves were concentrated into one holy passion, it would all be as—no room to finish. Guess the rest.

G.B.S.

◇◇◇◇◇◇

This letter is undated, but was in all probability written in answer to the preceding.

Trench was Herbert Trench, a poet of distinction and also a theatre-manager. He produced The Blue Bird *and* King Lear *at the Haymarket. Tree and Alexander are, of course, Sir Herbert and Sir George, both famous actor-managers.*

> 33, Kensington Square, W.
> [undated]

What a dear funny letter.

I dont think you may come tomorrow. I may already be in the tureen—or the greater part of me! ! ! !

Is it my salary you want to know. I played for the Irish people for nothing—for Trench for what he could afford—for Tree for all I could get, for Alexander what he offered—for you—for love—

How foolish to talk this way with the tureen staring me in the face—

I told your brooch story to the doctors who were here
this morning. One lost his temper and let out like this—"Are
people fools? Can't they see the great physical suffering in
your face—don't they know it is only your extraordinary
temperament that has enabled you to stand a fever and suffering and confinement to your bed for nearly four months
without flinching? Don't they know we have watched you
carefully and have waited as long as we dare!—You *act*
and they don't see the poor sick woman whose pulse and
heart tell us the truth". I nearly wept but I gave a valiant
shrug and pooh!

Its a pity the operation has to be—but as someone said
"you cannot expect the Almighty to cut your toe-nails"—
Poor Hazlitt's Slavey—poor, poor Josephine—poor Stella.

◇◇◇◇◇◇

*"That question" was undoubtedly a question of how Mrs.
Campbell stood financially.*

*Lena Ashwell, Gertrude Kingston, and Elizabeth Robins (an
Ibsen pioneer)—all notable actresses.*

33, Kensington Square, W.
9th December 1912

It seems absurd to let tonight pass without writing a
word of thanks—I can't think why I was horrified—there's
no doubt about it I was—for a moment—I knew what you
meant, and felt, but somehow it seemed to me so odd—even
darling D D after all these years has not asked *that* question
she knows poor me and my vile pride—she has looked mysteriously at me lately as though she meant to ask someone
something—Bless you—you were brave—and now I'll tell
you a great secret—I know as much about Blake as would

fill a thimble—and I know six little pieces by heart for the piano and if you heard me play one of them you'd box my ears—and when I come out of that "home" its to be Mrs. P.C. and Mr. Bernard Shaw, and even if Charlotte does think I am a lunatic she might have let you bring a card for her!—oh of course you dont' leave cards—oh dear oh dear— Lena Ashwell—Gertie Kingston—E. Robins—how can I compete with these women? Your wife will never like me— I think she is *wonderful* to have left you *21*. Thursday coming perhaps you might telephone up and ask how I am— I think I leave here Wednesday—I wish I was dining with you at the Ritz tonight both of us 21!—and you in evening dress and I looking lovely too! Oh no, I mean I wish it was a wet night in the park and you were speaking and I was giving away pamphlets and leading the applause . . . I wish I had all your words and your beloved Irish accent to dress my dreams and then someone would listen to me—and I *did* have something to say its too late now—If you can read this scribble you can read me.

Goodnight

Stella.

If they get me well I'll tell you why.

9th Dec. 1912

Why yes of course I have just written to you—Don't tell any one you have seen me today. I promised the doctors.

Stella.

◇◇◇◇◇◇

Lucy was Bernard Shaw's sister. She had been a professional singer.

Mrs. Campbell declares in her book that when she told G.B.S. she wanted to visit his sister Lucy, who was an invalid, he replied: "Go; she will tell you lies about my childhood; the rela-

67

tives of great men always do." Lucy, older than G.B.S., toured
the provincial stage with her husband, who was a singer also.
G.B.S. and William Archer went to Greenwich one evening
in 1889 to hear them both in Dorothy. Hesketh Pearson tran-
scribes Shaw's account of Lucy's death in 1920, and tells us:
"The brother and sister had lived for many years in different
circles and had seldom met."

10, Adelphi Terrace, W.C.
10th Dec. 1912

Silly silly Stella
The male resumes his predominance. So you think
that *that* required courage? Shall I tell you the calculations
I have been going over in my head ever since you became
ill? Listen.

Money. She must have money to go on with. Has she
any? Let me see. £116 a week all through the run of *Bella
Donna*. Half to the bankers to pay off debts. That leaves
£58 a week going to her credit. But it also proves that the
bankers must have allowed her to overdraw recklessly. For
that the bank manager ought to be sacked; for there are no
securities: she told me she had saved nothing. Unless the
bank has insured her life, the manager's conduct in permitting the overdraft is unbusinesslike to the verge of malver-
sation. Therefore either the manager or the firm (or more
probably all of them) is in love with her. That being so,
they may say "Perish the bank: let her have the last sover-
eign in the safe rather than she should have a moment's
anxiety". In their place I should have that impulse.

But business is business: in practice there is a limit to all
overdrafts. That limit may be approaching—may be already
reached—must be near enough to cause some anxiety. Are
there friends—for pride is no use: when you *must* have
money you must take it or raise it—must, must, must, must,

MUST. DD—Savile—who *is* there? But if they didnt offer and insist she might go to a money lender. She would. Delicacy: thats the difficulty: a woman is visibly spending money like water and earning nothing; and people talk of delicacy! Thank God *I* have no delicacy—no good taste—she said so—oh sweet revenge, to turn myself, like Jupiter with Danae, into a shower of gold! Only, I havent gold enough: I'm not rich; and there's Mamma and Lucy and others; and I am a member of a firm; Charlotte & Co. No; it doesnt run to a shower.

How much will she need? No: I must be prudent: how little can she scrape through with? There's the rent, the Xmas quarter. Then Xmas boxes, bills, nurses, doctors. Of course she is saving a lot by being in bed: no dressing, no taxis. The thought that there might be a bill of sale on that piano is like a dagger. Insistent problem: how much will make her quite free from anxiety until she is up again? And how much can I afford? No use pretending to be opulent: I'm not. The Xmas fortnight: would £250 get her over it?

Oh God! to offer Stella a filthy little £250! I spit on myself. But she says she cant keep money—gives it to whoever asks her—despicable weakness! Better perhaps dole out a little at a time: other fortnights will follow Xmas. How much can I afford? Ass! why ask that question over and over again? You know perfectly well that you want to give her a thousand pounds. Very well: put your cheque book in your pocket and go to her and ask her. If she does not want it there is no harm done: you are no use: that is all. If she does want it, and will not take it: there are ways—artful ways—guileful ways—but the simple way is sincere, and will do. True she will suddenly realize that I am, after all, a stranger to her; but what of that! she is not a stranger to me; and she has forfeited the right to refuse, because she has given money, and would give it to me if I wanted it. Can I seriously believe that she will say "Insolent stranger;

you have violated my pride, my privacy, my feeling that I must be a star and not a candle lighted by a man with a match. Ring the bell; and have yourself turned out".

I wasnt a bit afraid of that. And that is the whole argument that ended yesterday.

My grandfather used to say that no living man, prince or pauper, could refuse a five pound note if you crackled it under his nose. Why did I not get a thousand pound note and crackle it under your nose? Say what you will, there's something dignified about a thousand pound note. Wouldnt you like to take it and burn it before my face? *Quel geste!* I could take the number, swear to the burning, get another one, and crackle that too.

Stella, if those bankers—no: dont be angry: I only say IF, I F, I F, I F. And so enough of that. Only, dearest, if you ever want anything ever so little, remember, crackle, crackle, crackle, crackle.

If it pleased you to give that to the Ragbag, think of what it would be to me—but no no no: it would not be the same: it would be like nothing on earth. Oh, to call it an obligation! to thank one, in that high heroic way, for N O T H— I N G! to deny me—oh, yes, yes, yes: I am making a lot of it; I have, as you say, no taste. But if I *had* any taste, I should have risked making it impossible ever to ask you anything. Was not that a sacrifice? No: for I have had everything— the sun and moon and all the stars of heaven.

I have just seen *Troilus and Cressida*. Oh Stella—

"with such a strained purity"

Believe it, oh believe it. Troilus was about twentyone.

Come! I swore I would not go on like this. I remember how women used to appal one when they fell head over ears in love. No mortal woman shall enslave me, though a divine woman may free me. To business again. As to cards Charlotte is a perfect dragon for cards; and you may depend on it there would be some terrible breach of etiquette some unwipable-out insult, if she gave me a card for you. Besides, she does not know. You have never revealed yourself to *her;* and do you think I am going to tell her that my supposed anxiety about *John Bull's Other Island,* which I have to produce single handed in Barker's absence for Boxing Day, is quite another anxiety, and that in spite of the most desperate pressure of time, I simply could not attend to my business to-day, and amazed the company by my absence of mind? How could she feel sure that it made no difference to her, with her sensitiveness and susceptibility to worry? She has heard no news of you for six weeks at least, and would not presume on an acquaintance which was only an accident of your acquaintance with me. She also is proud: she makes you her best bow, saying, "I am quite aware that it is my celebrated man you are interested in, great artist, and not in me". And perhaps also "I am not included in your conquests?" Though, as to that, she has a calm way of taking it for granted that no woman can resist me; and when her affections and interest are not engaged her feeling seems to me an odd mixture of shrugging her shoulders at them because they cant; and being indignant or contemptuous if they can. She doesnt care much for women; and she hasnt found you out yet, though you may have remarked that when you accidentally called on her she said the right thing with a touch of high courtesy just as you said it to me that day when I read you the play at D.D's. But your relations together must make themselves: I must not meddle. *She* was very ill lately: I had an anxious moment.

But this is not the moment to think about cards. This is the day of battle; and when the trumpet sounds, goodbye to dreads and terrors: they are for cowards like me (I am your knight of the white feather, brave Stella): you must march with the colours flying and the music in D Major. And you shall leave for me the address of that home which will be the home of my heart while you are there. And you shall play those six tunes to me (that is all Paderewski and Hofmann have): but I will show you a way to have more; for I can play Chopin's Sonatas and Ballades and feel your fingers guiding mine as I play, though I only make a little lever tremble. And I love you for ever and ever and ever, Stella. And I agree that when you are well we shall be Mr. Bernard Shaw and Mrs. Patrick Campbell; for Stella means only Stella; but Mrs. Patrick Campbell will mean my treasure, my darling, my beloved, adored, ensainted friend of my very soul.

Oh, before you go, my Stella, I clasp you to my heart "with such a strained purity". A thousand successes, a thousand healings, a thousand braveries, a thousand prayers, a thousand beauties, a thousand hopes and faiths and loves and adorations watch over you and rain upon you. Goodnight, goodnight, goodnight, goodnight, my dearest dearest.

G.B.S.

33 Kensington Square, W.

[postmark: 11 Dec. 1912]

Well not the tureen to-morrow—after all—Your letter! well I never! I never did!!—Sherlock Holmes! he's nowhere—only you did *not* get the name of the Jew. . . . P. S.— – 50%

Stella.

◇◇◇◇◇◇

"Lillah and Granville" are Mr. and Mrs. Granville Barker.

33, Kensington Square, W.

12th Dec 1912

It was rather mean of me not to tell you that I laughed until I cried over your letter, and then I cried until I laughed at myself for being such a booby—and I remembered how you had maligned me for years and years and now you are bent on breaking my heart,—You don't read my letters to Lillah and Granville do you? remembering always that no gentleman ever compromises a lady!!

Would you mind *lending* me some bacteria? the doctors cant find any in my blood and they want some to cook and replace—they say now a horse's, but I would much rather have yours. I promise to return whatever is left over—

I longed for you to be here and throw all three doctors out of the window.

Stella (la dangereuse)—

Its a dreadful thought but I believe I shall suddenly jump out of bed and take a taxi to—

◇◇◇◇◇◇

Of her declining to play in Michael and His Lost Angel *by Henry Arthur Jones, Mrs. Campbell says in her autobiography: "I did not like forsaking my manager, or offending Mr. Jones, or foregoing my salary; but there was something in that play I could not stomach."*

Agnes Ebbsmith was her leading role in Pinero's The Notorious Mrs. Ebbsmith *(1895). For the Crown was an adaptation by John Davidson from a French play by François Coppée (presented under Forbes Robertson's management at the Lyceum in 1896).*

Eleonora Duse, the great Italian actress, had been seen by Mrs. Campbell, but only in modern plays like Magda. *In her book she says: "To me she was too sad, and too slow. But in her work there is great dignity, sincerity, and a fine introspection—and a tremendous appreciation of the nobility of suffering."*

Ayot St. Lawrence, Welwyn.

4th Jan. 1913

Dearest liar:

I have found you out. You have been tormenting me for weeks because I wrote odious things about you in the past and because I did not come to you sooner; and I, poor timid soul, always ready to believe that I was callous and brutal in those days, have squirmed with remorse. Well, yesterday Calvert wanted a copy of that American reprint of my *Saturday Review* articles which I so dread; and I got it for him. And before I sent it away I screwed my courage up and forced myself to read the articles about you. And what a revelation! what a relief! what a triumph! Never did a man paint his infatuation across the heavens as I painted mine for you, rapturously and shamelessly. Not a line would have jarred with my wildest letters to you. Firstly, *Tanqueray*. Sweep this silly piece away and let us hear this glorious woman play: it is only an unbearable interruption to her. Then *Ebbsmith* smashed, pulverized, flung into the dustbin: it proves nothing but that Mrs. Campbell is a wonderful woman. Then *Romeo and Juliet*: "Mrs. Campbell danced like the daughter of Herodias": away with the play away with Shakespear, away with Juliet: nothing of it remains except her dance and that shall endure for ever. Then I came to *Michael and his Lost Angel*; and I trembled; for I well remembered how Jones read that play to me, and what he had done for you (by this I mean how much pains he had taken to write the part for you), and what he hoped from you, and how he was at the height of his achievement then, and how heartlessly you flung him aside and trampled on him. And he had been entirely kind and helpful to me. I said to myself: "I cannot have forgiven her for this; I dare not read the next notice." But I nerved myself, and did—the notice of *For the Crown*. Criticism? Just Gods! A mad rapture of adoration. Not even silence about Jones, but an open declaration that sacrifice was worth it if only it pleased you. Ten thousand Jones and Pineros and Shakespears were nothing in comparison. I would not hear even of your acting. "On the highest plane one does not act, one *is*". I would not have even Juliet: Stella, Stella, nothing but Stella. Nothing that you could do was wrong: everything was a glory. And you, wretch, dare reproach me for this because I did not say "Mrs. Campbell's rendition of the potion scene was sound and scholarly; and her readings of the text were original and profound." That was what you wanted, Mrs. Crummles. And I rolled Pinero in the dust beneath your feet (the feet I kissed with my pen since I could not reach them with my lips) and I told Jones publicly that he was fortunate to be insulted by you; and these two men are my friends and never breathed a reproach, whilst you say that I treated you shamelessly and did not appreciate you. Are you not afraid of drawing down lightning on yourself? I! I, who burnt up Shakespear so that his sparks might whirl about you in a halo of glory. Did I not come to you? Did I not march in your train with all my trumpets in D major and my trombones in D flat major? And you would not come to my squalid second floor in Fitzroy Square and give me the nail of your little toe to kiss! Even Duse threw me a haughty word; but you resented my inadequacy when I, the greatest critic in the world, had proclaimed you the most wonderful woman. You even persuaded me that I had been cold and mistrustful—that my love for you is a new thing. It shines in every line I wrote about you. It goes back for years and years and years. And yet it was nothing to what I feel now. It's quite true that I did not know you deeply and nearly then, but I did adore you and sing dithyrambs to you as to a goddess. I challenge you passionately to produce one word that has ever been written of you by anybody that is more abandoned in its confession, that shouts more recklessly to all the world that the writer is your utter captive.

Now let me be sure a moment. I am in custody down here; but tomorrow I come up for the committee of the Society of Authors; and when that is over I dine with the Barkers (at six); and I must catch the 10 o'clock train from Kings Cross. I have things to discuss with Barker; but they need not keep me later with him than half past seven. It is ever so long since we last met; and I have a million things to say. For instance, that you are my most tranquillizing friend and my most agitating heart's darling, and that I will delight in you, whether you are kind or unkind, long after all the seas gang dry, my love. And so good night, with unfathomable blessings.

G.B.S.

12, Hinde St. [Nursing Home]
16th Jan. 1913

I'm getting on splendidly and but for a cough that wrenches and weakness for want of food I should feel quite well—

—Don't you love this picture? I lend it to you for a few hours then you must send it to me back again. I expect you'll see me before I'm dressed up in the drawing room—

Stella.

◇◇◇◇◇◇◇

Lady Horner is "another friend who never flattered me, and often delighted in teasing me."

12, Hinde St.

18th Jan. 1913

Sleeves indeed—a spun steel veil from head to foot.

Its nice to lie here and remember your coquetries, and my iron will—and its nice too to remind myself that you have Charlotte and Barker, and Barrie and Belloc to take care of you—

That coast walk seems to have been an hysterical affair, rather like my Helen preparing my bedroom at 11.30 p.m. for the sweep, when there were four maids to do it for her in the morning! bless her—This happened the night she left me here and saw my empty room.

I banged your windows open.

Beo and Helen played golf with Savile yesterday and had a jolly day. Today she is here for the first time—I didn't want her to see me with my eyes starting out of my head—

Darling D D came yesterday and proposed her house at Wittersham for me to get well in—but "not for a honeymoon" she added! Lady Hamilton is pressing Malta—Lady Charles Beresford, Brighton. but I expect I shall convalesce twice daily at the Hippodrome.

—3 weeks here first. When you have finished walking and finished with Belloc come and see me. I have had quite a lot of visitors today—I am sorry you've been too busy to write.

Stella.

Sunday. 19 Jan. 1913

Only Helen and D D and Lady Horner today, I am as well as I have ever been. next week I shall hold receptions.

✧✧✧✧✧✧

Willie Clarkson was the most celebrated wigmaker of his day. He died in 1934.

Cashel Byron's Profession was one of Shaw's novels (written 1886). The Admirable Bashville is a dramatic adaptation from it in blank verse.

"Bowlby" (Sir Anthony Bowlby?) was one of Mrs. Campbell's doctors.

12 Hinde St.

24th Jan. 1913

I wonder how the twins are—I wish they were my twins—I think its dreadful—your headaches and stomach-aches. I don't feel inclined to write to you, I think all this walking and talking such a bore—I wish you two . . . oh well its none of my business and perhaps I'm jealous!

I am rushing bounding and leaping into health—*now* I am dangerous indeed! Everyone spoils me. Clarkson the wigmaker sent me some white hyacinths.

What a vile habit to read my letters 'aloud. How I detest letters written for an audience—in hopes of publication after death—Lord Chesterfield Madame de Sevigne Bernard Shaw —give me the impulsive, undated, unpunctuated, unreadable letters of a Campbell—

—A "treacherous liar" indeed and who can sing again the song another had drawn from one's being?—or mark the pause—the pulsation—the anguish?—silence is the only way, and then the truth creeps in.

I read *Cashel Byron*—what adorable nonsense—and Lydias manners! ! ! !—I wish I had married a pugilist—could he whistle in tune? I once knew a man a little like him but he whistled out of tune—and was only at his ease with servants and shopgirls—

—I tell you again and again you can find heaps and heaps of Elizas—but you will only find one who will put the touch of song into her—the touch of the universal rythym [*sic*] . . .

. . . I know why you get a stomach-ache after eating jam, and you're sick after porridge—and you get head-aches—from talking too much! . . . but that too is not my business. . . .

—The two Knights and the Baronet who toyed with my entrails found me perfectly healthy, and dear Bowlby said I could have 6 more children. D.D. said "nonsense at our age" which is *absurd* for I am two years younger than she is in spite of that clicking machine at the back of your head —If you read a single word of this letter aloud,—May you lose the power of speech just when you are about to crumple Belloc up.—I hope I shall see you on Monday, its too paltry to wait until after the 28th—

Stella.

◇◇◇◇◇◇

"Gabiest" is represented by G.B.S.'s signature, which is re-peated fourteen times, at every possible angle—sideways and upside-down—careering madly over the remainder of the page.

10, Adelphi Terrace, W.C.
29th January 1913

It has come back to me that my mother used to say "prise to your queen" when she wanted to warn me that my queen was in danger. I suppose it was prise; but it may have been preeze, or preys (on the analogy of keys) or anything. I cant imagine that I have been playing chess; or that I remembered so much about it.

I am not a bit in love now. I enjoyed myself enormously. You are such a jolly playfellow. And such a child! an old fashioned child! I should like to spend an hour every day

79

with you, in the nursery. I no longer want you to act for me. I cant bear the idea of your having to work: you are not grown-up enough. And you dont want me to be busy, but to come and play. I am so tempted that I must set up a barrier of engagements between us. Tomorrow is full, Saturday is full, Sunday is full. On Monday, I come from Ayot for the Committee of the Society of Authors, and return by the 10 o'clock train from Kings Cross. Are visitors permited in the nursing home from half past—no: from 7.45 to 9 in the evening?

I am trying hard not to act. There are such wonderful sorts of relations, such quaint comforts and happiness, and close-together-nesses; and babes-in-the-woodinesses, besides being in love, which, as you point out, my diet and feeble nature forbid. I may have moments of being in love; but you must overlook them.

And now, having expressed myself with carefully punctuated moderation, I shall go to bed quite calmly, and sign myself, oh loveliest doveliest babiest

Your gabiest
G.B.S.

◇◇◇◇◇◇

Gaby Deslys was a celebrated French vaudeville artiste of the period, for whom Sir James Barrie once wrote an entertainment entitled Rosy Rapture.

"Sir Anthony" is one of the doctors (Bowlby?).

In the last paragraph Mrs. Campbell quotes from G.B.S.'s letter of 4 January.

12 Hinde St.
31st Jan. 1913
Hours for visitors from
12 AM to 11.30 PM.

Sweet Gaby Deslys—I mean Gabiest—

Yes a child—"I was a child and she was a child that" etc. Its good for you to be with children—to play in the nursery of my heart.

Chess—a game for Kings and Queens—Mary and George —Deidre and Naisi—I didn't tell you the splendid thing I heard about Tuesday; though I suppose nothing really pleased me quite so much as "When he spoke of religion there was a tone of reverence and sincerity that made me feel the man has grown more real more sincere"—

Calvert has got to be thanked for that and other effects—

So you are too busy—too many appointments—the nonsense of it—too busy too many appointments—well you are too busy—

A Prince of Lovers! theres something to be proud of indeed,—And to write such poems as the one I read you last night—you promised me one—you slept with the promise unfulfilled—not 21—56 *that*.

I will come and work for you soon—but I must be idle a little longer or I will never get back my "Bring forth men children only" blood and iron constitution!

Sir Anthony told me this morning I have another fortnight in bed and that months of fever leave their mark upon ones strength not to be gotten over quickly—

So dont sneer so heavily at me because my spirit inclines a little longer towards idleness.

I know as well as any man that life is a mangle and we've just got to turn and turn—and turn. . . .

This is a fool letter—so is yours—*please* send me some more of your books—and your plays to read. I didn't sleep

81

a wink last night—and now its 11 a.m. and I am going to shut my eyes

Good night
Annabel Lee

contd.

So you're no longer in love that means I may someday become a respected friend of the family, and who knows have cards left upon me!—

—No-one can go to sleep at 11 AM its ridiculous

What letters you would get if you didn't read "bits aloud" and they were quickly put into the waste basket—

The British Museum indeed! how this trick of yours annoys me thinking everything appertaining to yourself will eventually find its way to the British Museum—

I adore and at the same time detest your fears and tremblings and bewitching timidities—'late for dinner' 'not fit to work' unmanned "if within a fortnight of a public appearance you shake the hand of a sick widow you professed to love!"—if only you'd eat red steaks and drink beer your spirit would be meat, I mean meet to mate—no I dont mean that—

What was that you said? "Stella are you not afraid of sudden lightning"—and then you said something else—theres a deal to remember and cope with.

Stella.

10, Adelphi Terrace, W.C.
31st January 1913

O tormenting letter, I am troubled again. I did not think I should relapse so soon. I have slipped out of the real world.

Do something for me. Read the enclosed proofs for me of

82

my new edition of *The Quintessence of Ibsenism*. The preface is new. The chapters on the last four plays—after *Hedda Gabler*—are new. The chapter (p. 171) on what is the New Element in the Norwegian School? is new; so if you have read all the rest before, you can turn at once to these, though there are new scraps in the rest. If you find anything wrong, mark it (they are first proofs, uncorrected); and say any silly thing that comes into your head about it, no matter how crudely: I will do the polishing and extract the quintessence. Oh! Oh! If it bores you, but it oughnt [*sic*] to. Some of the new stuff—*Little Eyolf*, for instance—is terrible and wonderful. Read between the lines.

Barrie has finished the great new play for you which is to extinguish Eliza. He may not have told you, as he may feel some delicacy about interfering with me. So *I* tell you. Make Frohman pay you a colossal salary; but dont be too unkind to Boucicault. And when you have spoiled the Egyptians, spend it all on Eliza and me.

I scribble in great haste—going out with Charlotte to try a car, and darent be an instant late.

Oh why, why, why did I fill up this afternoon? If only I could steal a minute before dinner; but I darent, darent, darent: youd make me late and then—

G.B.S.

12, Hinde Street.
3rd Feb. 1913

No I am too feeble witted to entertain you and Jim at the same time, besides as he would explain to you it would break the Weather House—

At *6 o'c* someone who is troubled, and who troubles me deeply will be here—so it must be 7.45. rearrange your life for today—perhaps you cant—I hope you can—

Isnt it wretched about D.D.—how could you refuse?—

Your letter written under "domestic and intellectual pressure" is abominable.

Beatrice.

Ayot St. Lawrence, Welwyn.
4th Feb. 1913

Yes: I suppose it was abominable; but my life consists of miles and years of that sort of abomination; and for just a moment of something else I have to run to you. Work, work, worry, worry, brains clattering, dating, punctuating, committees, speeches, snatching three lines to you and talking Insurance Act and the newspaper over my shoulder all the time, and then slipping the letter into my pocket lest anybody should see the address and be heartbroken: that is the sort of thing that you vaguely lump into a cloud of abomination as Suffragettism; but it is 99-100ths of my life.

It has been a lovely spring day; and I am alone here; and I have walked seven miles, and put in a "brilliant" morning's work. (Call me brilliant once—only once; and farewell for ever). Yesterday was a devil of a day. A day of sentimental self-sacrifice: the thing I have always disdained immeasurably as something that could never touch *me*. Yet what happened was this. On Thursday we lunched with S.B. In the middle of the meal she very devilishly asked me point blank how you were, and watched to see how much damage that shell would do when it exploded. And indeed the damage was not cleared away until Sunday—or, to be precise until midnight on Saturday, the interval being extremely miserable. Now if I had done what I wanted to do last night after dinner I should have started all that misery again; and when it came to the point I had not the heart to do it. When there are two people of whom one can stand almost anything in the way of privation, and the other is so sensitive that it is horrible cruelty to children to look

84

coldly at that person (or warmly at anyone else), why, the hardy person must suffer and the sensitive person be spared. And yet there is a deep down violence to one's innermost nature in such sacrifices which gives me bad moments. However, it cannot be helped; thus it has always been; and thus, I suppose it always will be.

Anyhow, I had not the power to write anything in *The Philanderer*.

They are coming for the letters. Send me a word or two: I shall be alone here until Friday evening—perhaps until Saturday afternoon. Meanwhile I shall have the happiness of having nothing to make me anxious, and lots of work. I should live in a lighthouse and work, work, work; for I am a slave by nature.

All of which is not very amusing, is it?

G.B.S.

◇◇◇◇◇◇

The fact that G.B.S. did not destroy Mrs. Campbell's letter in spite of her request, seems to indicate that he had regard for her criticism, and in a later letter (20 March 1913, from Leamington Spa) he writes that he has "altered the bit about Hedda, since you insist. . . ."

"I am God": see Mrs. Campbell, 21 May 1932.

To be torn up and thrown into the waste basket *please*.

12, Hinde St.,
5th Feb. 1913

re proofs.

I couldn't do what you asked. I should write myself an ass on every page—

But your "Hedda" makes me very sad—not one little bit do you understand Hedda—your interpretation of "do it beautifully" positively made me scream—her love—her shame—her physical condition—her agonizing jealousy—even the case of pistols—you're wrong at all points—did you think about it at all—or is it just your adoration for bl——y plain facts that makes you so indifferent to all the poetry, the universal truths and beauty that lie behind and beyond?—

—You miss it all dolefully in *Little Eyolf*—the fact is you write carelessly sometimes—And with whom are you quarrelling? Be calm dearest, be gentle with fools—And why take it for granted that your reader doesn't know what you know, and isn't agreeing with you?

You seem to have a simpleton always in your minds eye. . . . The fact is you have too much brain—you tumble up against it—I admit my heart thrills as you bravely 'get there' —but oh my, you do turn such inadvised St. Catherine Wheels?

Chesterton chastises you—*I* know whom it is you serve— Long ago you wouldn't have made me angry if instead of saying "I am God" you had said "I am *my* God", or if you had said—all the women who have loved me said "I was their God"—because . . . If one wasn't afraid of your turning Catherine wheels in ones heart, how one would adore you. . . .

I knew by instinct what Ibsen and the rest of them *taught* you—But then I had a father who only read and talked Darwin, and a mother who loved only Dante—and whose soul was steeped in beauty.

re The Philanderer

Well I have read it, and I am ashamed to say I didn't laugh—it offends me. I find it ugly—some mischeivious [*sic*] personal experience.

If I don't see you before the 9th write to me for that day is my birthday—

Jim came. I hope to God he doesn't feel as sad as his face

Dear,

This is the only book I could find. It has the chronological guide in front of the book. Evidently this lady Mrs. Patrick was a big thing in #1 his life. Sorry if it's not what you wanted but I tried.

Love,
Jane

STUDENT PERSONNEL SERVICES

DORMITORY INSPECTION SLIP

Dormitory_____ Room_____

Occupant_____

Charges or Demerits:

Total demerits_____

Total charges_____

White — Occupant
Yellow — Business Office (charges)
         V-P, House Council (demerits)
Pink — Head Resident

Inspected by_____

Date _____

looks when he isn't smiling! he told me about the play—
delicious fun—

I was alone all the evening because you are the slave of
your appointments with the exception of those you make
with me—

Stella.

Feb 5th.

Your letter this morning upsets me because it isn't
fair—not a bit. It reads sincerely too—and makes me want to
say many things.

I should like to play a game of chess for a birthday treat,
unless you are engaged up to Christmas.

If a woman whose name I know had the pluck of a mouse
she would treat with charm and sympathy the woman, or
women, Mr. Mouse took an interest in. When Mrs. Mouse
would find that most women could play 'cricket'

Oh dear dear most dear Mr. Mouse—

Dead as Caesar for four months I lay until Mr. Mouse
nibbled—

No not "brilliant" but oh Mr. Mouse can run so swiftly
in and out of traps its wonderful—but when Tabby mews—
he trembles!

—x x x x x x x x x x x x x x x x x x x x x x—and so on—and
so on—and so on—

Ayot St. Lawrence, Welwyn.

6th Feb. 1913

Stella, Stella Stella Stella Stella Stella Stella Stella
Stella Stella Stella Stella Stella Stella Stella Stella Stella
Stella Stella Stella Stella Stella Stella Stella Stella Stella
Stella Stella Stella what is there left to say?

I have just played all sorts of things, almost accurately, I
dont believe I could get a headache if I tried. I drove from
Hatfield faster than a man should drive in the dark.

What an enormous meal of happiness! They will wish you many happy returns of Sunday. Sunday! I laugh hollowly. When I am dead let them put an inscription on 12 Hinde St HERE A GREAT MAN FOUND HAPPINESS. Wagner wrote up on his house Hier wo mein Wahnen Frieden fand (Wahnfried sei dieses Haus genannt) (if I recollect it aright). Nobody can translate it; but I understand it. I will write on the sky someday.

I was only twenty minutes late for my appointment; and if I had been wise enough to miss it altogether I should have saved £300; for that is just what keeping it cost me in money. What it cost me in absence three hundred millions could not pay for.

Her last words as we parted (very affectionately on my part) were "I never know where you spend your afternoons. Once I never thought about it—never doubted. Now —I always imagine—" I see you, like the Flying Dutchman, once in seven years; and I am supposed to see you every seven minutes. It is amazing to myself that I dont. How is it that I will get up and trudge through the mud to any sort of miserable work, but that I must always let heaven come to me? I should not have come up today but for that silly committee and two other utterly frivolous businesses. It is incredible. How did I get it ground into me that happiness is always picked up on the way and must not be sought? Yet there is something in it: it came nobly off today. Stella: I *WAS* happy. Was! I *am*. I shall never be unhappy again.

You cannot have this in the morning because the evening post, at six, had gone before I returned; so this must wait until morning (12) and will reach you in the afternoon—oh Stella Stella Stella Stella Stella Stella

G.B.S.

◇◇◇◇◇◇

There is much about Shaw's regard for William Morris in the letters to Ellen Terry.

John Palmer: distinguished critic, scholar, and playwright, who has long been resident in Switzerland.

Ayot St. Lawrence, Welwyn.

7th Feb. 1913

Now a last line; for this is my last night alone. I wish I could write verses. Why do not rhymes come tumbling into my head naturally, as they did into Morris's? I have to play things, sing things, repeat things that you set jingling in my head. It seems to me that all the poets have been in love with you; for they seem to have said everything; and my words that would praise thee are impotent things, and I was a child and she (you) was (were) a child in a kingdom by the sea; and it is undeniable that the moon never beams without bringing me dreams and the stars never rise but I see the bright eyes, and so on and so forth; but if I try to make verses for myself I can think of no rhyme to Stella but umbrella, and only too damn' well I love Mrs. Campbell and horrors of that sort. The thing should rush into my head or come to my hand as prose does, ready made. I never have to think of how to say anything in prose; the words come with the thought: I often have to argue a thing carefully to get it right; but when I have found the right thing to say it says itself instantly; and matters of feeling dont even have to be argued. Yet when I want frightfully to ringle-jingle with words they wont come that way. I suppose its want of practice: If I had always written in verse I probably couldnt write in anything else, which would be a nuisance. When Morris talked prose in criticism of things he didnt much like, he was often at a loss for a word, and used me as a dictionary. I used to hand him the word he was looking for; and he would snatch it up with relief, though he could sling rhymes without having to think about them, and used to look at me with incredulous disgust when I told him that when I wanted a rhyme I had to try down the alphabet: Stella, bella, sella, della, fellah, hell a, quell a, sell a, tell a, well a, yell a, Campbell, bramble, gamble, ramble, etc. etc. He did not consider poetry worth all that trouble; and I agree: I always tell people that if they cant do three quarters of any art by nature theyd better sweep a crossing.

Besides, Masefield has written the poem for me. What I want to do is to play my harp. It has so exquisite a touch that I can play it with my lips. So far I can play only harmonies at the treble end; but some day I shall sweep all over it in great chords; and the heavens will ring; and I will put in a great bass.

My mother cut a wisdom tooth when she was 80. I ask myself sometimes am I cutting a folly tooth at 56? Still, one has to become as a little child again—in that kingdom by the sea.

I have been reading John Palmer's book on the censorship (he is my successor on the *Saturday Review* now, and much the cleverest of the lot); and he says "Mr. Shaw is a militant Puritan, to whom the west end theatre is definitely the gate of hell. He hates the aphrodisiac play etc etc". O Stella Aphrodite, am I really a Puritan? "The beautiful Puritan pansies"—yes, I think I am. Goodnight. The birds will cover us up with leaves.

G.B.S.

10, Adelphi Terrace, W.C.
14th Feb. 1913
Stella: I must break myself of this: there is some natural magic in it, some predestined adorability for me in

you, that makes me quite reckless when I am within reach of you. It is the dark lady the child dreamt of.

Tomorrow is cram-full—full I tell you: I have not a moment between lunch and my train. And yet I know that I *can* break through and snatch a moment between 4.30 and 5.45, which is the very last second.

Oh what a will-less creature I am! I have taken my farewell, gone back for my last appearance, returned for my positively last appearance, and am madly going again tomorrow for my last appearance but 500,000,000,000,000,-000,000,000,000,000,000

Something was worrying you—but what is that to me? Once I was capable of being helpful—even wanted to be helpful. Now I am a mere predatory creature seeking my prey, my mysteriously natural prey. A parasite. I! *I*! ! ! It is worse than the tide that I turned to swim against and after five strokes found myself ten yards farther out. Only then I tried but couldnt. Now I could but wont try. That is the dangerous symptom. For I tell you I could. I feel in me the strength to do things a hundred times harder. And I *wont*—yet. Not until the very last moment.

I have never missed the train yet—nor saved it by more than a few seconds. If I ever lose it I shall never come again; for then I shall know that I am not strong enough to save either you or myself, and must fly. So oh Stella, dont ever let me lose it. Dont let me hurt anyone to whom I am bound by all the bonds except the bond of the child to the dark lady. For then I should know myself to be an utter brute and my halo would go out like an extinguished candle. Oh this loathsome but necessary conscience! And oh! this wild happiness that frees me from it!

I saw you first in a dream 43 years ago. I have only just remembered it.

G.B.S.

◇◇◇◇◇◇

Hayden Coffin was a comedian and light-opera singer who died in 1935. Mona Limerick: an actress who distinguished herself in Miss Horniman's repertory company at Manchester. She was the first Nan in John Masefield's play of that name.

The Mitre, Oxford.

22nd February 1913

What a day! I must write to you about it, because there is no one else who didnt hate her mother, and even who doesnt hate her children. Whether you are an Italian peasant or a Superwoman I cannot yet find out; but anyhow your mother was not the Enemy.

Why does a funeral always sharpen one's sense of humor and rouse one's spirits? This one was a complete success. No burial horrors. No mourners in black, snivelling and wallowing in induced grief. Nobody knew except myself, Barker and the undertaker. Since I could not have a splendid procession with lovely colors and flashing life and triumphant music, it was best with us three. I particularly mention the undertaker because the humor of the occasion began with him. I went down in the tube to Golders Green with Barker, and walked to the Crematorium; and there came also the undertaker presently with his hearse, which had walked (the horse did) conscientiously at a funeral pace through the cold; though my mother would have preferred an invigorating trot. The undertaker approached me in the character of a man shattered with grief; and I, hard as nails and in loyally high spirits (rejoicing irrepressibly in my mother's memory), tried to convey to him that this professional chicanery, as I took it to be, was quite unnecessary. And lo! it wasn't professional chicanery at all. He had done all sorts of work for her for years, and was actually and really in a state about losing her, not merely as a customer, but as a person he liked and was accustomed to. And the coffin was covered with violet cloth—not black.

I must rewrite that burial service; for there are things in it that are deader than anyone it has ever been read over; but I had it read not only because the parson must live by his fees, but because with all its drawbacks it is the most beautiful thing than can be read as yet. And the parson did not gabble and hurry in the horrible manner common on such occasions. With Barker and myself for his congregation (and Mamma) he did it with his utmost feeling and sincerity. We could have made him perfect technically in two rehearsals; but he was excellent as it was; and I shook his hand with unaffected gratitude in my best manner.

At the passage "earth to earth, ashes to ashes, dust to dust" there was a little alteration of the words to suit the process. A door opened in the wall; and the violet coffin mysteriously passed out through it and vanished as it closed. People think that door the door of the furnace; but it isnt. I went behind the scenes at the end of the service and saw the real thing. People are afraid to see it; but it is wonderful. I found there the violet coffin opposite another door, a real unmistakable furnace door. When it lifted there was a plain little chamber of cement and firebrick. No heat. No noise. No roaring draught. No flame. No fuel. It looked cool, clean, sunny, though no sun could get there. You would have walked in or put your hand in without misgiving. Then the violet coffin moved again and went in, feet first. And behold! The feet burst miraculously into streaming ribbons of garnet coloured lovely flame, smokeless and eager, like pentecostal tongues, and as the whole coffin passed in it sprang into flame all over; and my mother became that beautiful fire.

The door fell; and they said that if we wanted to see it all through, we should come back in an hour and a half. I remembered the wasted little figure with the wonderful face, and said "Too long" to myself; but we went off and looked at the Hampstead Garden Suburb (in which I have shares), and telephoned messages to the theatre, and bought books, and enjoyed ourselves generally.

By the way I forgot one incident. Hayden Coffin suddenly appeared in the chapel. *His* mother also. The end was wildly funny, she would have enjoyed it enormously. When we returned we looked down through an opening in the floor to a lower floor close below. There we saw a roomy kitchen, with a big cement table and two cooks busy at it. They had little tongs in their hands, and they were deftly and busily picking nails and scraps of coffin handles out of Mamma's dainty little heap of ashes and samples of bone. Mamma herself being at that moment leaning over beside me, shaking with laughter. Then they swept her up into a sieve, and shook her out; so that there was a heap of dust and a heap of calcined bone scraps. And Mamma said in my ear, "Which of the two heaps is me, I wonder!"

And that merry episode was the end, except for making dust of the bone scraps and scattering them on a flower bed.

O grave, where is thy victory?

In the afternoon I drove down to Oxford, where I write this. The car was in a merry mood, and in Notting Hill Gate accomplished a most amazing skid, swivelling right round across the road one way and then back the other, but fortunately not hitting anything.

The Philanderer, which I came down to see (Mona Limerick as Julia) went with a roar from beginning to end. Tomorrow I drive to Reading and thence across Surrey into Kent to the Barkers. The deferred lunch at the German Embassy will take place on Monday. Unless I find at Adelphi Terrace before 1.15 a telegram forbidding me ever to see you again, I *know* I shall go straight from the Embassy to your bedside. I must see you again after all these years.

Barrie is in bed ill (caught cold in Oxford a week ago) and ought to be petted by somebody.

I have many other things of extreme importance to say, but must leave them until Monday. By the way you first said you were leaving Hinde St on the 23rd; but you said last time to Lady Jekyll "Another ten days". If you are gone when I call I shall hurl myself into the area and perish.

And so goodnight, friend who understands about one's mother, and other things.

G.B.S.

10, Adelphi Terrace, W.C.
26th Feb. 1913

Quite nice simple people, the B's. It was the quietest and unaffectedest of dinners.

Next week will be a week of oratory—two orations—Monday and Thursday.

On Friday and Saturday the afternoons are filled to the last moment. On Sunday I shall be at Ayot. On Monday committees and oratory as aforesaid will occupy me wholly. On Tuesday you may have fled to Brighton. This seems to justify me in coming tomorrow if I may. As you must take a drive if you can, I will not come until 5. If that is too early, or if you are tired of my importunities, send me a wire before 2.

Remember that I am always your saint and that my ectasy will survive disembodiment. My deepest and lastingest happiness beggars all desire. You must always sit enthroned in heaven for me for at least a little while. If you stop doing that, my unbreakable (or perhaps broken) heart would harden. Everything else I can do without, though not, as you must know, through indifference.

It is an enormously unreasonable demand to make on a mortal woman; but I make it, manlike, because I do not believe in mortality.

G.B.S.

95

12, Hinde St.
27 Feb. 1913

"Jack" is the *deaf* Colonel who called when you were here—and who is married to Mrs. Cornwallis West's—Sister—Col. John Leslie—Lord Ribblesdale arranged four days ago to come at 5 o'c today. I wanted to hear all about his girls engagement—and that would have bored you.

—I drove to the Zoo at 2.30 with the poor man who has had a haemorrhage and whose wife is related to Hanney. I patted and *kissed* a cheetah—and made roaring noises at a lion and stroked a Penguin.

How calm a day when you don't see that popular actress!

I have been thinking a great deal and "setting myself before myself" and lo! I find I adore sentiment—the sentiment of love—of youth, of religion, of babies, of nursery fires, and a thousand things—and I adore too acrobats—on wires or mental—Oh dear—oh dear—dear dear—dear—all roads lead to the hole in the ground or the door in the oven.

I'm stumped

10, Adelphi Terrace, W.C.
27th Feb. 1913

Cruel stony hearted wretch, snatcher of bread from a starving child, how had you the heart? how could you? do you know what it means to me? I want my plaything that I am to throw away. I want my Virgin Mother enthroned in heaven. I want my Italian peasant woman. I want my rapscallionly fellow vagabond. I want my dark lady. I want my angel—I want my tempter. I want my Freia with her apples. I want the lighter of my seven lamps of beauty, honor, laughter, music, love, life and immortality. I want my inspiration, my folly, my happiness, my divinity, my madness, my selfishness, my final sanity and sanctification, my transfiguration, my purification, my light across the sea,

96

my palm across the desert, my garden of lovely flowers, my million nameless joys, my day's wage, my night's dream, my darling and my star.

And you deny them all to me with six conventional words that do not even scorch the paper they are written on.

Very well; I will stay away, I will forget, I will drudge, I will do without, I will grind out articles and speeches amid the ruins of my temples and the fallen leaves of my trees. I will do my duty and relieve it with hideous laughter, joyless, hard, dead.

Friday, Saturday, Sunday, Monday, not a moment, not a chance, not a possibility, four eternities:

O cruel, cruel, cruel, cruel, have you no heart at all?

G.B.S.

◇◇◇◇◇◇◇

"Hawk" was Bouchier F. Hawksley, Mrs. Campbell's lawyer and business adviser for many years.

"The baby David" was the grandson of Mary Lady Elcho, a close friend of Mrs. Campbell's.

12, Hinde St.
[undated; between Jan. and Feb. 1913]
Hawk can be terrible—so non-understanding—he ended by saying "Well do as you like. I don't agree with you—you are taking the line of least resistance. You are wrong—what I suspect I knew to be the better way, but it is difficult for you and unpleasant" and then he added—as kind as kind could be—"don't tire yourself my dear—dont let all these people tire you".

Dear old Hawk, the kindest and best friend on earth, if only he would understand that I *cannot* be guided in matters of *taste* in business—and that's where he's at sea—

Oh you Sherlock Holmes! How horrid he was to you. I don't think he sees you as a real person—

What a day it has been, a little of Hauptman's book—most wonderful—then lovely ladies full of foolishness and prettiness, and then the baby David—I must'nt forget a telegram —and a letter—I learning to walk—and then a great man playing at ball!—

And then bitter business—

But three words singing with sweetness to take to bed. "Mother of Angels"—I know nothing about to-morrow.

Stella.

10, Adelphi Terrace, W.C.

28th Feb. 1913

Who mashed Stella?	Who made her smile?
I, that rejoice	Dis very chile
In a nice Irish voice	With my wink and my wile.
I mashed Stella	*I* made her smile
Who'll be her man?	Who is a fool?
Why, he that can,	I, as a rule,
Apollo or Pan,	(The happiest fool)
I'll be her man.	*I* am a fool.
Who kissed her toes?	Who clasped her tight?
Who d'you s'pose?	That wasn't right.
And also her nose?	Oh, the delight!
I kissed her toes	*I* clasped her tight.

Who is her friend?

Stella's true friend?

World without end

I am her friend.

G.B.S.

Stansted, Wrotham, Kent.

2nd March 1913

Words cannot describe the matter-of-factness of this morning in the country after a drive of an hour and a half in the small hours last night. I feel like a solicitor; and instead of paying you ridiculous compliments and pretending to be sentimental I ask you why you do not take your solicitor more into your confidence. Your calm instinctive attempt to deceive me about your house—the certainty that you will hire a flat at about three times the rent you will get for 33 (that is what always comes of attempts to economize)—your hints about Australia (where, as Lillah says, having been there, they want "beef" rather than brains & beauty)—the knowledge that you *must* be hideously in debt after this ruinous illness—your entourage of society people who are always offering their friends everything and giving them nothing except motor rides that cost more in tips than taxis, and meals and hospitality—that can be had at half the price at a hotel—your notion that because I am selfish in the afternoons I cannot be businesslike in the morning—your ridiculous idea that you can always be a goddess to me (or that you could ever be anything else) and must therefore never exhibit yourself as a mortal with cares and anxieties and worries—that likeness between us that makes you believe that Beo's arrangements are all wrong and makes me believe that *your* arrangements are all wrong (unless I revise them)—all these things stimulate my meddlesomeness to the highest degree. Of course if you bother me with your wretched affairs they will worry me; but suppose my fears and suspicions as to your being in serious difficulties worried me more! Two heads are better than one when a situation has to be considered. Always hear what a committee has to say, even if you dont accept the conclusions.

Or, if youd rather not, dont. But if you suppose that you

are heroically keeping my mind quite easy about you, you
are mistaken. And the mind is master in the morning. You
think, because you see me only when my mind has had
enough of work for the day that I care for nothing but
roses and rapture. But between breakfast and lunch I scorn
them. Wait until you see me at rehearsal! You think that I
wont never—that my prey will escape me. You err. I shall
cable Shubert tomorrow that he can have *The Philanderer*
if he will engage you for Julia and produce me first or
rather take a theatre for *me* to produce, you and Loraine,
et quelques poupées.[1] And then, *then* we shall see.

Here is Lillah—I must break off and prepare for the car.

G.B.S.

◇◇◇◇◇◇

*Beatrice and Sidney Webb, Socialists and reformers, were
Shaw's oldest and staunchest friends and associates.*

10, Adelphi Terrace, W.C.
4th March 1913

I have to spend the next weekend on Beachy Head
with the Sidney Webbs and the editorial staff of our new
paper, to plan our campaign. The occasion is one of tremendous importance, and admits of no distractions or levi-
ties of any sort. From Saturday to Monday I shall be deeply
serious and very busy.

Still Beachy Head is not so far from Brighton as London
is. Suppose I take the car (I may have to leave it if my beloved invalid is convalescent enough to use it), then I should
leave London early on Saturday. I might lunch at Brighton

---

[1] Valabrègue, the soldier-diplomat husband of the prima donna An-
gelica Catalani, was said to have believed that all the essentials for a good
performance of opera were "my wife and a few dolls," by which last he
meant supers.

if I made good time in spite of police traps. I might call on my friends there—even take them for a spin in the car—after lunch, and yet reach Eastbourne in time for dinner. I might even steal a visit to Brighton after lunch on Sunday. What do my friends in Brighton think of it? Are they full of engagements? Have they forgotten me? Are they fed up with ducal motor cars?

I asked Lillah what Australia was like. She said it was immense for a first visit, except that you had to spend your entire salary on clothes, as large crowds followed you in the streets and you were entertained daily at Government House and the like. She thinks you would have an enormous vogue. And that is all the comfort I got by asking. What I wanted to be told was that the notion is ridiculous and ruinous.

I scribble late. I will say nothing deeper. Goodnight
G.B.S.

◇◇◇◇◇◇◇

Laurence Tadema was the daughter of Sir Lawrence Alma-Tadema, the painter, who died in 1912.

Caxton House, 31 Oriental Place, Brighton.
6th March 1913

Had you better come? I have been talking to Laurence Tadema about you—My goodness! "Part of the scourge that is in the air"

"On his death bed I pity him"

"He walks into your heart with his muddy goloshes and then walks out leaving his muddy goloshes behind him"

"His love is epistolary"—"He has no respect for the feelings of those who love him"—

"Don't give him affection he will surely hurt you".

101

You had better not come. I cannot be so brave.–Helen
wants a menu for your luncheon Saturday and Sunday.
No. Dukes have not offered me motor drives–
I have bumped no-one with my bath chair.
I hope your beloved head is better.–
Stay and write your articles and talk away on Beachy
Head, but if you do come wire a menu to Helen–

Stella.

◇◇◇◇◇◇◇

*Arthur Bourchier was a popular actor-manager who died in
1927.*

10, Adelphi Terrace W.

12th March 1913

I'll write no more: you can read me in the *Morning
Post*, stamping, ramping, goring, bellowing, and being pif-
fled at by Harold Cox. I am clean out of heaven and in the
mud of the streets again. I am correcting proofs, speaking at
meetings, writing articles, and wallowing in what you call
bad taste. Being busy, I have no time to bother about being
happy, no time to bother about other people being happy.
The vibrato vibrates: I radiate the breeziness of Loraine, the
bonhomie of Bourchier, the brilliancy of G.B.S. The headache has taken the poison out of me. I let my life escape me
before the poison went; and now I am an empty digestive
apparatus, with a brain clacking at the top. Well, let it
clack. If my soul is dead, I can go on clacking until my
brain dies too. If not, it will wake in due time, and I shall
be in the magic gardens again with everything veiled in
dreams and a voice whispering two words that touch me
even now.

Meanwhile, you have nothing to do; and Brighton is a
bright dull place–the worst sort of dull place. You had bet-

ter learn Barrie's play: mine you can learn when the time comes: I cannot tolerate people who come perfect to the first rehearsal: I like an empty head for my ideas. I long for —no I dont: I am curiously indifferent about that play. You do not write to me, but so long as you are not lonely or bored, why should you? You can always whistle for me when you want me.

G.B.S.

Brighton.
13th March 1913

I tried to read *The Case for Socialism* but I heard a thrush singing all the while—

I have just read Harold Cox—but I still hear my thrush— Sometimes the note sounds like a cry—and the cry like a call, and the call—"Stella"! "Stella"! "Stella"!

Your letters—a carnival of words—how can I answer with my poor whining beggars?

Its warm and wonderful here. Helen went up to London yesterday and so I am alone—she will come back to-night— and the thrush sings and sings away!—

◇◇◇◇◇◇

"Beatrice" is Mrs. Sidney Webb.

10, Adelphi Terrace, W.C.
13th March 1913

Now you have upset everything again with your thrushes and nonsense; and I am whistled back as infatuated as ever. This thing is getting ridiculous. Yesterday I was al- most free: now a scrap of paper brings everything to me

103

again and makes a baby of me. Free, I could have been of
some use to you, like old Hawk. Unfree, I am a mass of
childish wants and dreams, no use to anybody. I think I will
write down the character sketch I gave Beatrice, and read it
carefully through when my infatuation has utterly transfig-
ured you. Oh, if only you were alarmed, and could struggle, then I could struggle too. But to be gathered like a
flower and stuck in your bosom frankly! to have no provo-
cation to pursue, and no terror to fly! to have no margin of
temptation to philander in! to have a woman's love on the
same terms as a child's, to having nothing to seize, nothing
to refuse, nothing to resist, everything for nothing, the gate
of heaven wide open as in my story, to have striven fiercely
all my life for trifles and have treasures at last offered for
nothing, to miss the resistance that has become to me what
water is to a fish, to hear tones in a human voice that I have
never heard before, to have it taken for granted that I am
a child and want to be happy, to draw the sword for the
duel of sex with cunning confidence in practised skill and
a brass breastplate, and suddenly find myself in the arms of
a mother—a young mother, and with a child in my own
arms who is yet a woman; all this plunges me into the wildest terror as if I were suddenly in the air thousands of feet
above the rocks or sea. The measure of that terror is the
relief with which I felt the earth yesterday—as I felt the
stone when I was swimming my last stroke. Yet here I am
caught up again, breathless, with no foothold, at a dizzy
height, in an ecstasy which must be delirious and presently
end in my falling headlong to destruction. And yet I am
happy, as madmen are. What does this sound like from me,
the supersane man? I am not otherwise mad; yet I am stark
raving mad in this matter unless you are indeed and in truth
an extraordinary person, a genius, a half goddess, wonderfully lovely, wonderfully tender, and simply sincere and
pitiful and—oh for the word: I am at last at a loss for one—

when you take me up and say . . . I cant write those two words: they can exist only in my holiest memory now.

And this—*this* you have done by a couple of day's silence, a couple of days hunger, a couple of days brazen descent into an accustomed despair, and at the end, a scrawl —a little whisper of poetry and petting and thrushes and the like. Oh Stella, Stella, Stella, I no longer regret anything; so take care, take care: next time it may flash out at a look, a word, a rustle of your dress, a nothing. I must stop, or I shall begin to write utter nonsense. Goodnight.

G.B.S.

31, Oriental Place, Brighton.
20th March 1913

I couldn't answer your 'Policeman' letter—The earlier one—well you know what *that* was to me—almost fit for the British Museum—to line a wild birds Nest!—but the 'policeman' hurt dolefully—Did you send it to sport your "style"? bless my soul—Or your principles?—My dear—

Well the wind blows here—the air is wonderful—and it snows—and it hails, and then again out comes the sun and its quite hot.

—I want some tea, and chocolate—and cake and jam, and thin bread and butter—and sweet nonsense—and the best man in the world by my side—I hope all is well with you—there was something of backyard repartee about that 2nd M.Post article of yours—"style" again?

The flat project seems impossible—and so is Kensington Square—I go up to-morrow for a few hours and see what I can do—and touch my piano perhaps—

"I heard the thrush sing and knew the child a child of God—and I held out my heart to him in my two hands, but he tossed it into the air like an orange peel—and turned on his heel, but my thoughts followed him like birds, and whirled about him, and the smallest settled on his lips and when he would whistle his gay tune, he found he could not —for every time he drew his lips together lo! the little bird kissed him." From the Hindu.

Stella.

Regent Hotel, Leamington.

20th March 1913

Barbarous wretch: do you think I can live by imagination alone? Have you nothing to say to me? I badly need some sort of humanizing; for all this talking has put me on stilts. On Tuesday Winifred Holiday called on me on business of the last importance, which turned out to be that I should make a great religious peroration that night. Which I did, shamelessly, and not only brought down the house, but quite touched the bishop in the chair. Forbes Robertson also had an oratoreal success. You dont appreciate Forbes: you have no taste for the classical. Last night at Blackburn I gassed—its the only fitting expression—for an hour and a half, and did another religious peroration. After that I scintillated in the Mayor's parlor, being screwed up rhetorically to such a pressure that I sparked at every touch and terrified and disconcerted the chambermaids and waiters at the Old Bull by my intensity. Mrs. Siddons saying "Will it wash?" was nothing to me. Today, after missing connections all over the L. & N.W. system I got to Coventry and had the motor bike explained to me far too late to start on it for Ayot (80 miles); so I resolved to spend the night here. And here I am. I seem to be always spending nights in hotels now, alone; and I ask myself every time—but no matter.

I do not seem to be recovering in the least. And yet it seems to me that you must be returning like a stretched and let-go elastic to your old aloofness and hostility to my school. Then I remember something and see that that is impossible. Still, I should be much happier if I could receive some assurance—not unreasonably often: say every ten minutes or so—that—that—that—that—

I dont know why: I cant write. Writing is no use. I have written everything, said everything. And I am saying it still. Only, I want to say it so that you can really feel it.

I am still quite mad and quite sane and quite fifty different things all at once; but I dont want to write it now: I want to live it. I cant do anything with this pen and paper. I shall go to bed and think about it.

In the morning I brave the bike at last and shall ride up to Ayot on it or perish.

Lots of things have happened about you: I'll tell you if we ever meet again, which I tell myself in desperation seems never going to happen.

Wont you say something to me?

No: its ridiculous to be importunate: its infernal to be expected to write. You shant be bothered.

Still, just—

Oh, Stella!

I should like to see you most frightfully.

If only——

Stella, Stella, Stella.

Da capo.

And Stella, Stella, Stella, Stella, Stella, Stella.

And so on for a thousand bars ·/. ·/. ·/. but perhaps you never copied orchestral parts and dont know that that means the same thing over and over and over again.

Foolish. So great a rhetorician ought to be able to end with a fine peroration. But I cant.

I ought to tear up this resourceless letter. Better send it, though, to show you how much I need to have my inspiration renewed.

The velvet dress, the velvet dress, the velvet dress.

Do *you* get distracted in that way? But you cant: you

have lots of people to make an atmosphere for you. I am alone in a hotel after two days wandering like a lost dog.

I have altered the bit about Hedda Gabler, since you insist. I knew there must be something wrong, though you couldnt tell me what; for out of the mouths of babes & sucklings cometh wisdom. It was Ibsen's fault partly: his insistance on Lovborg being shot in the abdomen, thereby bringing out Hedda's "do it beautifully" as meaning "Dont spoil yourself" led me to emphasize that point with a slash; but of course that was not what Hedda thought she thought, which was that the memory of it should always be a treasure to her. Shall I put a footnote to say that the original version was quite right, but that Mrs. P.C. insists on my altering it, and that as I am violently in love with her I cant help myself?

G.B.S.

Ayot St. Lawrence, Welwyn.
21st March 1913
GOOD FRIDAY.

Good Friday? No, the day is ill
That severs me from what I like
And gives me but a graceless spill
When riding on a motor bike.

This letter should be written by Beo at the age of 16. This morning I went to Coventry, got the wretched thing started in pouring rain after many unsuccessful kicks; and rode 77 miles to Ayot in 3¼ hours. As I had never touched a motor bicycle in my life this might have ended in slaughter. Once coming suddenly on a vehicle round a corner, and meaning to stop, I did the wrong thing and launched the machine forward like a thunderbolt. But there was a passage the size of a needle's eye, and I shot through. It looked like a superb stroke of motorbiking: it was really a murder-

ous blunder. A few yards from our gate there is a bad corner. Elated by my 77 miles and my 57 years I took that
corner too fast. Result; I went into the bank and fell one
way whilst the machine happily fell the other. It only broke
its lamp, and I broke nothing. The vibration of 40 miles an
hour on bad bits of road, and the excitement and confusion
of a roaring wind in one's eyes (I didnt goggle) mingled
with the terrors of the novice as to what to do if anything
in the nature of an emergency came up, made a sort of boy-
ish adventure of the thing. Decidedly I am a fool to torment myself with such games. However, the thing is done.
I *can* ride a motor bicycle; and now I would sell the machine
for twopence. Men *are* fools, especially timid ones like me,
always defying straws because the straws frighten them.

And that is all the news, except domestic news, which
need not be told because all its incidents are the effect of
illness, which makes mountains out of molehills, and doesnt
understand the real mountains.

Barrie's play is announced to follow the next Peter Pan
revival, which means early in 1914. Is that *your* play? Have
you settled anything with Frohman?

Saturday
A letter! Who will take the silly bicycle for half a farthing? I dont remember the policeman letter. I never wrote
it. And anyhow, one needs a policeman sometimes. I knew
the flat would be impossible. 33 is characteristic, historic,
sacred (to me), and you cant do better without becoming
a slave of an establishment, like me. Some day there will be
a tablet on that house and generations of Romeos and Juliets
will visit it and pray there on the anniversary of my first
visit and my first falling in love.

The post is going. Oh, I must work, and slang Harold
Cox, and be a policeman. If I stop to think about myself and
you, the situation becomes desperate. With you I forget
everything. Away from you I remember everything when I

have time; so I must leave myself no time and be a machine
—all I am good for. I MUSTNT be in love; but I *am*.
You have beaten me—my first defeat, and my first success.

G.B.S.

❖❖❖❖❖❖

Leonora was Barrie's alternative title for The Adored One.
*"Viola" and "Felicity" are Sir Herbert Tree's daughters, the
elder of whom, Viola, was to produce a revival of* Pygmalion
*in 1920 at the Aldwych Theatre. She figures in the correspond-
ence at that period.*
*"The Rutlands" are the Duke and Duchess of Rutland. The
Marchioness of Anglesey was the eldest daughter of the Duke
of Rutland.*

Brighton.
25th March 1913
I wont be alive in 1914—starved to death long before
that!—It would have been joy to get the simplicity and
fun and beauty of *Leonora*—just as it would have delighted
me—and almost killed me to try and get your dear slut
Eliza—and I would have gotten her to your liking somehow!—but I cannot come and beg and weep to you people—
You seem to have enjoyed risking your life on that vile
machine. I wish you had come this way.
I haven't a purple or a velvet dress. . . .
I have always been an odious letter writer—you have
made me worse—grumbling that I can neither punctuate nor
spell, and like Irving am ungrammatical—you literary trades-
man you!
Foolish things have been happening here—I chaperoning
a party including the three Tree girls and a lot of young
men to a dinner in a private room on a Sunday night at the
Metropole The manager opened the Ballroom at 12 o'c.
Musicians came down in overcoats over pyjamas. Russian

dancers were imitated—shoes kicked off—hair came down. Viola was wonderful, and Helen and Beo and Felicity deliriously happy and the other young men pleased to have me there to take care of them all.

Then there have been two dinners and a luncheon at Lady Charlie Beresfords—and scandal talk galore!—And many a rendez-vous at Cheesemans oyster shop—The Rutlands—Angleseys—Helen and I in a room 6 ft. square—outside it at the bar niggers from the Pier eating their oysters and drinking stout and cracking jokes—on a little brown bench —others sitting patiently waiting until there was room at the bar—or the little room empty—the Duke wild with joy— Helen laughing herself silly over the childishnesses of Dukes and Lords and Ladies. Georgina sulking because she doesnt like oysters, and loathes the smell of lemons, vinegar, and red pepper—Anglesey declared the only time he ever ate an oyster he was sick *at once* thereby arousing our curiosity. . . .

In the afternoon we go to Rottingdean—there are a lot more people there—To-day we both motor with Savile to Worthing—and have tea somewhere.

At night I read *The Fool in Christ*—there are bits of you in that book its strange—and I have waded about in the Balfour Snippets—heavens how dull!—and so I live and I waste—and I grieve.

Domestic peace be with you.

Stella.

The Old Sugar Loaf, Dunstable.

26th March 1913

Stella, what luck! What a day! We started from Ayot for Holyhead just after midday with everything smiling on our journey, lovely weather, roads in first rate condition, car going superbly, Charlotte almost happy. An

hour later a new car with two ladies and two gentlemen
shot out of a watersplash on a by-road right across me and
across the whole road. I was coming down hill. The road
was as smooth as steel and as hard. To put on the brakes
hard meant a skid, an upset, and a wild stramash into the
other car. To go ahead meant to smash those two ladies into
splinters and probably kill the the men too, not to mention
what might happen to our own iron nose. To swerve meant
to charge a miniature mountain range of hummocks crossed
by a drain and crowned by a terrible telegraph pole. So I
charged them. The miraculous result was that not a soul
was hurt or even physically shaken; but the car! I spare
you the technical specification of her ruin. When we dug
her out of the hummocks she looked as if a colossal Georgina had worried her for an hour. Back she goes tomorrow
morning by train for a new front axle and springs and a
dozen other comparative trifles. It was a first class accident,
and the fact that we did not even get a shock (we should
have been hurled through the windscreen) remains unex-
plained.

I thought Fate was exhausted after that. But Fate wasnt.
I phoned for a car to take us on. It left London at 3.20; but
at 7 there was no sign of it; and we had to resign ourselves
to a night here. A little after 7 it arrived. And the driver
was drunk. He made desperate efforts to conceal his condition from me; but when we were at dinner he broke out,
smote the waiter on the nose, and was hurled into outer
darkness by the landlord. Where he is now heaven knows!
I have phoned to Daimlers for another car. If it comes, and
the new driver is sober, we shall leave at 9.30 or 10.

We cross from Holyhead to Kingstown on Saturday;
and my address thereafter will be c/o The Right Hon. Sir
Horace Plunkett, Kilteragh, Foxrock, County Dublin. And
I beg and pray for a line to meet me there from the woman
whom I still love beyond all reason.

Loraine cables that he wants to produce *Pygmalion* in London in April, and "is Campbell available?" I have replied "Campbell supreme April impossible".

I read *Pygmalion* (very badly) to the Scott Gattys yesterday. It's amusing and effective; but oh how utterly inadequate! It was good enough for that strange woman; but now, now, now, now, NOW!

I must stop, though I have a million things to say, as the accident involves correspondence and business before bed.

For nights past I have sat down to write to you, and thought of you instead until I had to lay down the pen without a word written. It is past letter writing with me. There are things one cannot put on paper. I have written everything that is writeable: The rest must be *viva voce*.

Goodnight, oh beautifullest and adoredest.

G.B.S.

Kilteragh, Co. Dublin.
2nd April 1913

This place will kill me presently. The air is like ether: it goes through my bones; and I work, work, work, hurling off articles and despatching arrears of business, and writing volleys of letters—all but the letter I want to write; and when it comes to that I can do nothing but dream and say long strings of darlings and silly things and do nothing. This house is just like a picture by Picasso; and it is right in the focus of the circle of hills from Killinay, where I dreamt my boyhood away on the east, to the Three Rock Mountain on the west. And oh! the shapes of those hills! no Englishman knows what an outline is: in all my long career in England I remember only one thing that fits those lines and belongs to their beauty, and that is a white throat on a bed near High st. station.

Who is Leonora? Is she the heroine of Barrie's play? I

113

dont know: I havent read it. I have written to ask Barker whether Barrie is still faithful or whether he has given it to Irene. But Barker has not answered; so perhaps he has gone to Algeciras after his Lillah; or possibly he is waiting to find out from Barrie the answer to my question.

I note, as per your esteemed letter, that you cannot beg. I can, and do, at your feet, imploring, adoring and trembling, and having no proper pride at all. So be at peace, proudy-dowdy-dearest, and know that your telegram conjured up floods of affection from the four corners of the earth and drowned me for hours and hours and hours.

Charlotte has suddenly got well, and changed from a fiend into a green eyed mermaid, smiling and fascinating and dressing in diamonds and generally dispensing charm and childish happiness. What is more amazing, she actually refers to you without fury, even with raillery. "Did you go to Brighton that day at Beachy Head?" Boundless contempt for both of us, but no more hatred, almost a joyous contempt. She realizes her superiority now. Quite right too; for you and I see two barefooted playmates on the hills; and she is what you, like a dear ignorant colleen-*contadina* as you are, sum up as a Suffragette. Dont grudge her her contempt; for the difference between that and the sick hatred and fury her illness produced is for me the difference between heaven and hell. She cannot, like you, laugh through her last gasp.

Do not suppose, however, that I do not know that you are a great and wonderful woman, and so beautiful that all the stars are not too fine to make a necklace for you, and that there are secret places in the world where there is nobody else but you.

Oh if it were not for this new paper, and Horace Plunkett's agricultural co-operation, and these serious political schemes in which so much of my work lies—if only I were a gay creature like Viola and Felicity and the rest—I would

fly with you and play Higgins to your Liza in little fit-ups
in obscure places as Mr. and Mrs. Vincent Crummles, and
stay with you at public houses, and raise up a family of Infant Phenomena. But our destiny is higher.

It is post hour; and I have already delayed this letter
many days.

Yes, coming, coming,—I must go.

Oh the two beauties I was born to love! Ireland's and
Italy's, how they scorch my veins.

G.B.S.

◇◇◇◇◇◇◇

*Twenty-five years later, when Mrs. Campbell sent a copy of
the following letter to G.B.S. to remind him of what he had
written, he returned it with the following words on it:*
"Wicked wicked letters.
*"How often I warned you never to give money to a beggar
who begs well! He is a professional. I am amazed at this proof
of the unscrupulousness with which I practised my professional
tricks on you. Still, it was very delightful.*
(signed G.B.S. 18.3.39)."

Kilteragh, Co. Dublin.
3rd April 1913

This is only a supplementary letter to send you a
scrap of a communication just received from Barker—in
reply to my enquiry about Barrie. I enclose also an article
which may amuse you as a specimen of the way the young
lions now roar—at the old pioneer. I get a certain pleasure
from this sort of rebellion: when things are alive young men
go on like this. And I have, still, only to raise my paw—!

I drove into Dublin today and cursed every separate
house as I passed. All the old longing for beauty and blessing gets stirred up in me; and as I come back into the country

you are no longer that popular actress Mrs. Bella Donna, but my girl, my beauty, my darling, barefooted, dusty petticoated, or my mother of angels, or a dozen lovely wild things that would greatly astonish the young lions of the St. James's stalls.

They have sent me a dummy copy of the new paper; and it's SO ugly. Quite damnable. Unless one does everything onseself—but bless you, I don't care. [*Here a line and a piece have been cut away*] nor ever dissever my soul from the soul of the beautiful Cammabelle Lee.

So if you are idly curious as to whether I am still in love with Stella, the answer is yes yes yes yes yes yes yes yes yes yes yes yes yes yes yes yes yes yes yes yes yes yes yes yes yes yes yes yes yes and a million times yes. Cannot help it. Am quite sensible, quite able, quite myself, and yet a lad playing with you on the mountains and unable to feel where you begin and I leave off. And if you tell me that *you* feel like that the sky will not be high enough for me (isnt that a nice Irish phrase?) Heavens! how delicious it is to make love to you ! ! ! ! !

G.B.S.

33, Kensington Square, W.
8th April, 1913

I really wrote you a delicious letter 3 days ago but when I came to look it over barely one word was legible. I thought only the greatest love in the world could make excuses for such unseemly unsightly ~~penmanship~~ scrawlsmanship—as a matter of fact one tiny word in your supplementary letter sent me astray. . . .

Here am I writing in my bed in Kensington Square once more!

If those young lions could hear what I have heard their heads would be bowed in worship, their hands raised in

prayer—the angels sing at sweet visionings the song my singing bird sang to me.

I send you one of your letters to read that somehow has
missed the waste paper basket. . . .

Yes I think Barrie will be faithful if I can *wait*. What will
you be I wonder—

My love to you
Stella

Kilteragh, Co. Dublin.
9th April 1913

Stella, Stella: N E V E R do that. Innocent that you
are, you are full of the most dangerous indelicacies. Have
you ever dodged elusively round a room, with a weeping,
howling, red faced, swollen, aged, distorted-featured man
pursuing you with a letter in his hand, pressing on you the
documentary evidence in your own writing that you once
loved him or pretended to? If you had, you would die
rather than serve a love letter up cold to the writer. True
this letter isnt cold in that sense, and perhaps never will be;
but it's so inadequate, so thin, so artificial compared to my
memory of that blessed time! above all, the sight of my own
writing brings back other letters to other people that also
were sent back; and I cant endure it when you are concerned. I nearly hurled it into the fire with a scream: for
nobody but you would I have forced myself to read it. The
warning in it was honest: I was bound to give it; but dont
take it. Still, it is yours; and I send it back to you to destroy
if you like. Do anything with it except show it to me. All
that paper love is nothing: the real thing is in the marrow
of my bones and the roots of my nerves.

So the queen of heaven is back in her shrine. When you
said you were writing in bed, and for a moment I thought
you might be ill again, I asked myself was it a wild hope or

a wild fear. Oh the Life Force never laid a deeper trap than that illness that gained for me the entry to the sanctuary. I shant know what to do now that you are up. My perfect bedside manner is no use in a drawingroom. There is the piano, of course; and you will play it to me; but I want my harp.

For three days I have been thwarted at every attempt to write to you. I am stealing this letter from my bedtime. On Friday night we cross to Holyhead; sleep there; start in the morning by car for Shrewsbury, where we shall probably sleep on Saturday night: and on Sunday come on to Ayot St. Lawrence. On Monday I must come up to Adelphi, as I have to lecture in the evening in Gravesend. On Monday afternoon perhaps—perhaps—I could starve until half past three—a line to Adelphi on Monday morning, or to Ayot on Saturday night or Sunday would stop me—let it not be written—oh, the flood is rising again—goodnight beyond words.

G.B.S.

◇◇◇◇◇◇

A motor-car in which Isadora Duncan's two small children were sitting ran backwards into a river, and both were drowned. Gordon Craig, Ellen Terry's distinguished son, was their father.

"D.D." and Lord Savile are friends who have already been mentioned. "Oscar" is presumably Oscar Wilde. Mrs. Campbell prints a note from him in her book.

The Crock of Gold is the fantasy by James Stephens, and The Great Adventure a highly successful play by Arnold Bennett which had begun its long run three weeks earlier.

33, Kensington Square, W.

15th April 1913

I am a little ashamed of you where do you find it in your heart to blame me? Its a mean trick—and Adam's! Such a day one would have loved only to have thought of life and happiness. I open the paper to read of Isadora Duncan's heart rending sorrow—poor Singer—poor Ellen Terry, poor Gordon Craig—poor all of us that have hearts to ache. It is as though one must go to her these first awful days and try to keep her from going mad—She can never dance again— love to her will mean death—and the sight of little children will always break her heart—she loved them and defied the world with their loveliness—it's pitiable—

I threw your letter into the fire quickly—I remember nothing in it but the general unfairness and some low joke I couldn't follow.

D.D. is back—happy to be home again. Alfred is in bed with influenza—he shot a young lioness, they all shot her together I think—I feel rather dull about it. D.D. asked me whether you made "love" to me I said you made "advances". Yesterday afternoon a friend lent me her motor and I drove into the country alone. In the evening Helen and I—in dia- monds and dignity—dined with Lord Savile. He insisted on my reading Oscar's letter—people ought never *knowingly* to write for publication they lie, and lie, and lie—and the better they write—the better they lie—the tragic waste of it. . . .

—It must be beautiful at Ayot today . . . that poor girls misery weighs upon me. . . .

. . . At a meeting of the Kensington Square Garden Committee two old ladies asked whether anything could be done to stop the birds singing. "It disturbs us at half past four in the morning and makes a great deal of noise in the late afternoon"—So one can grow old enough to mind a thrushes song!

Barrie has my copy of *The Crock of Gold*—if Charlotte hasn't read it get it from him she will love it—Couldn't you take D.D. and Charlotte and perhaps me too—to *The Great Adventure we*, D.D. and I, would love it.

I forgive you and I will help you to live a little nearer to that superiority you assume—you have treated me meanly —I will treat you generously—I will accept the blame you put upon me— . . . Grief must be turned into *beauty* if only Isadora is able to *feel* that—if only I could do—or say something to help her—

Stella.

33, Kensington Square, W.
21st April 1913

I dont understand why you didn't encourage me to come to Gravesend or why you persist in making me think myself "Oh you beautiful doll",——a silly goose grandmother—one who can play two or three little pieces of music quite nicely when she's alone but before company misses her notes and gets the giggles—

Whats the difference between being addicted to drink and overlaying your baby—and being addicted to work and neglecting your hearts love?

There's that thrush singing in the Square, that bird has *time* to sing! And I believe he is singing "Oh for a thousand hands to hold my beloved. She is a thousand virgins and my song ravishes them all!"

—Somebody said the other day it was a blackbird and not a thrush—I wonder—and I wonder whether you will keep your appointments, and remind yourself of them by looking in your book.

Stella.

SHAKESPEAR SONNET

Oh wherefore in my heart that was so hard
Hast thou these tender places made to come?
Dost thou not know how I must stand on guard?
How I must keep that voice of nature dumb

That bids me to a tranquil fireside turn
And thou there with our child upon thy knees,
And makes this springtime hurt me like a burn
Because we cannot play beneath the trees?
If I give way to thee, am I not lost,
Divided, doubled, thrown quite off my track?
If I forego thee, can I bear the cost
Of craving every hour to have thee back?
  Oh dearest Danger, I must love thee less
  Or plunge into a devil of a mess.

Ayot St. Lawrence
22nd April 1913

                    Ayot St. Lawrence, Welwyn.
                        22nd April 1913
    You see what comes of being good. Sonnets and ten-
dernesses that make the heart sore.
    I come up tomorrow afternoon: I have to dine with Lena
Ashwell Thursday afternoon, two committees. Friday evening, *Caesar and Cleopatra*. Saturday, back here.
    Oh these fine spring days!

        But what are vernal joys to me?
        Where thou are not, no spring can be.

My mother used to sing in what used to be called an
Orpheus quartet.
    My sister found among my mother's belongings the cap I
used to wear as a baby. Had anyone suggested such a possibility I should have laughed him (or her) to scorn. We
never know anything about our parents. See *Misalliance*,
passim.
    I was suddenly asked today whether you were at Adelphi
Terrace yesterday. I said no, and confessed to a conversation through the telephone—truth so far as it went. I men-

tioned that you wanted to make a party for *The Great Adventure*. I said "She cannot understand why you dont love her". "That shows some good in her" said Dear Mrs. Dignity.

I felt positively domestic on Monday night—as if I had been married to you a thousand years and had never got the least bit tired of you. It was divine of you to come to Kgs. X with me. I hope you got back without any shocks. I told him to drive quietly and bribed him sufficiently to pay for the few minutes difference it made to him.

Perhaps I am dull when I feel domestic. But you wouldnt think so if you could see into me. Perhaps you can.

G.B.S.

◇◇◇◇◇◇

The Barrie playlet is possibly Half an Hour, *in which Irene Vanbrugh appeared at the Hippodrome five months later.* Rosalind *was another Barrie playlet.*

10, Adelphi Terrace, W.C.
26th April 1913

BUSINESS.

It is not certain that Barrie's sketch is gone irretrievably to Miss Vanbrugh. She is engaged for so long ahead with *Rosalind* and other matters, that it may be possible for you to get it back again. In that case the difficulty (I suppose) will be with the Hippodrome, which is doing well enough with *Ragtime* (as I guess) to dispense with a new and expensive attraction. At all events I advise you to ascertain at once from Barrie whether he can enable you to fill up the summer with a variety engagement if you consent to sign on at once for *Leonora* in September at the Duke of

Yorks. Better tell him that you will not insist on £300 a week at the halls. It is too much.

I further advise you to regard the Duke of Yorks offer as of very great importance, and to make Barrie feel that nothing but the urgent need of feeding your starving infants prevents you from engaging yourself for it. If you secure it, the contract will be something to overdraw on. The chances of your getting another big play for production in June are practically negligible. In fact, I wont let you throw away *Pygmalion* if Alexander will not play, and if you are free until September only. I have written to him to say that I cannot have so promising a potboiler used as a mere stopgap to tide him over a few weeks—for that is what it comes to, though he does not let himself see it in that indelicate way.

In short, sign on with Barrie and Frohman, and take your chance as to the interval. Remember that anything you do in the meantime *may* fail; and if it did, your stocks might fall, and B. and F. change their minds. Therefore, again, make sure of the Duke of Yorks. *Pygmalion* can wait. If you want a sentimental reason for that, to rehearse *Pyg.* now would probably kill me. (Alexander might stiffen his bill by putting on *Overruled* as an afterpiece, you and he playing Mrs. Juno and Gregory.)

G.B.S   I shall be here
until 3.30 (15.30)
8131 City.

10, Adelphi Terrace, W.C.
28th April 1913

——BUSINESS——

Attention !

Alexander says you have promised to sign for the run if he plays Higgins. This means that you love Alexander more than me, and your sudden fancy for an appearance at the St. James's more than either of us.

Now listen. You have the two best plays and parts in London in the hollow of your bosom. Nothing but your own extreme folly and wickedness can deprive you of both of them. They will provide for your old age. You are already a grandmother; and as such I shall regard you for business purposes.

Barrie's play is the surest and most lucrative. And Barrie is the author whom you can offend if you slight his offer. Well, if you sign for the run at the St. James's you will be unable to engage yourself for the D. of Y's. You will lose Barrie's play and he will never look at you again. And I will give you up as a poor creature with no character, who cannot wait as I have waited.

If you sign for the D. of Y's at once you secure Barrie's play and Barrie's regard; and you have *Pygmalion* to follow it up with or to replace it if it fails.

Therefore you must do as I order you. I am not, as an author, accustomed to argue with my stage slaves. Send for Boucicault and sign. And the other play shall be added unto you after the run of Barrie's.

In the meantime you can live on my adoration, on a sketch which I will write for you at the Palace, or on a retaining fee on a/c of *Pygmalion*, whichever you please.

In haste

G.B.S.

❖❖❖❖❖❖

The Barrie play is Leonora: *or* The Adored One.

Dion Boucicault was an actor-manager and the husband of the late Dame Irene Vanbrugh.

John Drinkwater, the poet and actor, founded the Pilgrim Players, which became the Birmingham Repertory Theatre.

This letter is not dated, but is obviously written in answer to G.B.S's of 28 April 1913.

33, Kensington Square, W.
[undated: April 1913?]

PASSIONATE LOVE LETTER.

You dont understand my way of doing business. What about your telegram and Alexanders letter last night signed by us both? a fine and witty composition that letter if you like!—

Now its up to you to make everyone happy. Persuade Lillah to play 'Eliza' when I am bound to go. Lillah can show the world how her husbands Reinhardt method enables her to play better than I—Alexander gets your play— and my Bank gets its money—I get hard work—no pence because all the pence I make are claimed.

—Send for Boucicault indeed—I have written to C. Frohman to say I am free for *Leonora* whenever he wants me.

Did you think I ever meant to let either part go if I could help it? its taken me 20 years to make you or Barrie think I was worth speaking to far less writing for—that fine play *Belladonna* at last convinced you!!!!

Barrie has promised me the Australian rights of his play— I would like the provincial as well as the Australian rights of yours—but these things dont worry me, its only other people who think it so *awful* that I have only a "housemaid"—and no motor etc. etc—

Alexander was very amiable to me and to Helen last night —I couldn't keep my 6.30 appointment—Drinkwater had sent me a box for the Kingsway—so we went to him afterwards he gave us wine and cake and showed us his picture when he was a baby!—

Do make me a present of a concertina at once! I would

like to play it *well*. I hope Georgina wont mind the noise, or Stella and her baby arrive until I am proficient.

My love to you
Stella.

33, Kensington Square, W.
30th April/13
Alexander has just read me your letter on the telephone. I hope it is not true you have had a "sort of nervous breakdown".

—It would have been quite wretched had you not felt happy over the management—conditions and rehearsals—

You know I wouldn't have suggested Alexander's doing the play had you not read it to him in the first instance, or indeed myself for Eliza had I not thought it your wish.—

I can understand other possible conditions may have cropped up more satisfactory to you.

Don't overwork and get ill.
Stella.

❖❖❖❖❖❖

In this same year the German theatre-managers, in despair at having to produce Shaw's plays after they had been reported from London as unpleasant failures, stipulated that in future the first performance should take place in Germany. Accordingly his Pygmalion *reached the Berlin theatre before its production by Tree at His Majesty's. After this it was Shaw's practice to give priority to foreign theatres whenever possible. The "one act play" is presumably* Overruled (*see G.B.S., 26 April 1913*).

33, Kensington Square, W.
Sunday. 4th May 1913
I hope your poor head is better—on the whole I think God lets you off lightly—

126

I told Alexander on the 'phone that you had arranged that the German nation should produce your play first—

I must say his merry peal of laughter shows he too has a sense of humour—that little one act play had better go to Germany too and then to Barker. Lillah can play the armonica-phone with its back to the audience.

These stamps are yours—you paid too much the day I played Eliza in the taxi.

Stella.

◇◇◇◇◇◇

By "we" Mrs. Campbell means herself and Sir James Barrie. When she speaks of "no rehearsal" she is referring to the revival on 4 June of The Second Mrs. Tanqueray, *in which she acted with Sir George Alexander.*

"Belvoir" is the home of the Duke and Duchess of Rutland. "Nina" is Mrs. Campbell's sister, and "Georgina" the dog.

"Cap and Bells" is a Barrie play, and "Typhoon", with Laurence Irving, began its successful run on 2 April 1913.

33, Kensington Square, W.
[undated; late April 1913?]

We didn't go to a Cinema. We talked until 11 p.m. and then I drove him home—I glanced at your windows—and marvelled at their quiet content.

Jim's going to see Frohman—he seemed to think my original demand *fair*—No rehearsal today—dressmaker this morning—then lunch at a restaurant with a man who doesn't mind being seen with me and doesn't think me undignified.

I cannot go to Belvoir, its too long a railway journey—so this afternoon and evening and tomorrow I am alone—letters, a little study—music—Richmond Park with Georgina and Nina.—

127

Jim has promised to take me to the theatre *Cap and Bells*
and *Typhoon* Ah ah ah ah a a a a a

Loraine will want you to let him put on *Pygmalion* at
once with Nancy Price and you'll get permission from
Germany—

Dearest take care of yourself—

Stella.

Open when alone!! [*written on the back of the letter*]

33, Kensington Square, W.

[postmark: 21 May 1913]

How I would love it—but its impossible—we rehearse
morning *and* afternoon.

So there's to be no theatre to-morrow—Coward!—

Last night I dined with Barrie and then to *Cap and Bells*—

Frohman wants to read your play—I said I couldn't let
him have my copy without your permission—what about
sending him one with a dedication—

My love to you

Stella.

10, Adelphi Terrace, W.C.

24th May 1913

I am all torn to bits: you dont know what it is to me
to be forced to act artificially when everything has just been
freshly stirred in me. It gives me a sort of angina pectoris:
all the fibres round my chest begin to sing and stir and drag
and pull in a way that would make anyone else wild, and
makes me set my face grimly.

But the worst of it is that all our conversation was over-
heard; and the effect was dreadful: it hurts me miserably
to see anyone suffer like that. I must, it seems, murder my-

self or else murder her. It will pass over; but in the mean-time here is a lovely spring day murdered.

Well, I dare say it is good for us all to suffer; but it is hard that the weak should suffer the most. If I could be human and suffer with a suffering of my own, there would be some poetic justice in it; but I cant: I can only feel the sufferings of others with a pain that pity makes, and with a fierce impatience of the unreasonableness of it—the essential inhumanity of this jealousy that I never seem able to escape from. And it is a comfort at least that you also have the unquenchable gaiety of genius, and can stand anything.

This much breaks out of me; I must say it. Now I can go back doggedly to work and write tragedies.

And believe that you cannot possibly have wanted a run through the lanes with me this summer day more than I. I throw my desperate hands to heaven and ask why one cannot make one beloved woman happy without sacrificing another.

We are all slaves of what is best within us and worst without us.

G.B.S.

◇◇◇◇◇◇

George West: George Cornwallis-West, whom Mrs. Campbell was to marry the following year. Evan Charteris: the Hon. Sir Evan Charteris. Playfair: later Sir Nigel Playfair, whose productions at the Lyric, Hammersmith—especially that of The Beggar's Opera—*were justly famous.*

33, Kensington Square, W.
[postmark: 3 June 1913]

Poor you. Its quite stupid nothing can be done to prevent your suffering—

Its not going to be a bohemian merry making. The supper

is now going to be given by Lady Wemyss, at 23 St. James Place, George West and his party come on then with Ribblesdale and the rest—so with the exception of my poor self the company would have been fit for your lady—If you won't come—it will make me unhappy—but that doesn't matter, does it?—Lady Wemyss was thrilled to the marrow when I said there was a possibility!—Evan Charteris had just read your one act play [about?] *D.D. and me* and said he thought it the wittiest thing you'd done!!—and the cleverest—I was disgusted.

Such a fool dress rehearsal of *Tanqueray* last night—Alexander played Macbeth—I a lively flea—Kate Bishop a serious chest-of-drawers—Playfair a publican—the young man—a jumping-bean—the girl quite good—

When it was over Pinero calling me "Stella" and I calling him "Arthur" gave imitations of my performances and I gave him a little straight talk on his "style"—the limelight man was amused—the others—serious artists—had hurried to their dressing rooms to get home to rest—Yes—you must be busy on *The Statesman* its a dull affair without you, and so am I—

Stella.

Ayot St. Lawrence, Welwyn.
9th June 1913

Ever blessedest darling

I write this (in shorthand which I must transcribe in cold blood tomorrow morning) in my lonely carriage on my night journey to Hatfield, where the car will meet me. On my way to King's Cross I told myself more than once that you were nearer than Hatfield; and certain enchantments that you wove in the manner of Vivienne with Merlin kept working. But with splendid common sense (now I am pulling out my literary stop: a great sign of self possession) I

reminded myself that visits are not really paid at midnight.
A wretched sophism, after all. How easy to call for you at
the theatre—a thing I have sworn never to do because the
commissionaire would not approve—and simply vanish with
you.

But that is not what I have to say. I want to implore you
not to rouse the family solicitor in me by talking of marry-
ing George (the other George). You dont know the treacherous suddenness with which I can switch off from one
character into another. No sooner do you mention George
than I see with a frightful lucidity all the worldly reasons
why you should marry him. I see myself putting myself
aside and driving you into his arms just as I put *Pygmalion*
aside and drove you into the engagement at the Duke of
Yorks. But that cost me nothing, whereas this would turn
me into rusty iron and cut me off for ever from what is
common and young in my humanity. Therefore, though I
like George (we have the same taste) I say he is young and
I am old; so let him wait until I am tired of you. That cannot in the course of nature be long. I am the most faithless
of men, though I am constant too: at least I dont forget.
But I run through all illusions and trample them out with
yells of triumph. And about you I am a mass of illusions.
It is impossible that I should not tire soon: nothing so wonderful could last. You cannot really be what you are to me:
you are a figure from the dreams of my boyhood—all romance, and anticipation of the fulfilment of the destiny of
the race, which is thousands of years off. I promise to tire
as soon as I can so as to leave you free. I will produce *Pygmalion* and criticise your acting. I will yawn over your
adorable silly sayings and ask myself are they really amusing.
I will run after other women in search of a new attachment;
I will hurry through my dream as fast as I can; only let me
have my dream out. And—here I am at Hatfield. How the
hours fly when you are concerned in them!

10th June 1913

What a night! The car didn't meet me after all: it broke a few hundred yards from our gate. I thought it was only late, and walked a mile and a half to meet it; then suddenly recollected that it might be coming the other way, as it had taken Charlotte up to London. So I turned back and retraced the mile and a half to the station. No car. No train back to London: the last gone. I went off to hire a car; but the place was dark and shut up, as was natural at midnight. To walk home was another seven miles, and I had risen at 6 in the morning and had a tiring day with only one delightful life-giving hour. It was windy and spitting rain and unquiet. So I roused the Red Lion and demanded a bed. The Red Lion barefooted, and with a hastily donned coat and trousers, knocked at the door of the landlady's bedroom and said "Here's a gentleman. Where shall I put him?" "Has he a car?" said the landlady. "I wish he had" I said. The landlady bounced out of bed; looked at my white beard through the crack in the door; and said "Put him in number four". What would you have said? And in number four, without enough bedclothes, I thought about you and then slept until 5 in linen sheets (I affect cashmere ones ordinarily) when I woke up very cold. So I had to resort to a quilt (I loathe quilts) until 7, when I got up and came on to Wheathampstead (our station 2 miles off) and thence walked home. Our wretched gardener, roused after midnight by the chauffeur, actually walked to Hatfield with 2 bicycles and then walked back—14 miles—neither finding me nor being able to ride one and push the other.

Such is life!

If the car had not broken a small bone in its body, I might —but you wouldnt have come. It is mended by this time.

I am crammed with Committees on Thursday and Friday. I shall not come up until Thursday. I was angry with myself about your dinner. I should have known, and made you eat

it in proper time. But how could I think of that, or of anything?

G.B.S.

◇◇◇◇◇◇

*Robert Hichens: novelist and dramatist (died 1950), author
of* The Garden of Allah, Bella Donna, *and* The Woman with
the Fan, *etc. Mrs. Campbell refers to the last-named in this
letter; the heroine suffers from a facial disfigurement, acquired
in an accident, and keeps her face hidden always. Later Hichens
wrote a one-act play for Mrs. Campbell called* The Law of the
Sands.

33, Kensington Square, W.

17th June 1913

Two railway journeys in one day—and such a day!
I never could catch a train—a station terrifies me and I
think only of suicide. I'll fly to you from Brooklands
rather—

—And now here's your telegram—there were days—and
evenings free! . . . Yes its just that foolish world that
Hichens is clever at, and I shall be able to show you what I
can do without a face!—

—Surely this is the sort of day the mountain came to
Mahomed! I've expected you since 2.30—

It was indeed a most dear afternoon—and your sister—her
delicious brogue—the pretty garden—and the unshut house
door—and you—and your severe face for your poor relation—what of London did he see with the £1 I wonder.

Such sweet remembering—When I was four one Christmas day a conjuror came—and out of his shiny tall hat he
brought a little soft bunny—oh the joy of the sweet surprise
and I feel like that at all the dear tenderness of your nature
—struggling about in your heart and eyes and voice—and

you holding it hard by the ears but I know it can get away with you in a moment—

—Did you write the enclosed letter—to try my vaunted and foolish ways! !—

It cant be cool anywhere today.

Stella.

Ayot St. Lawrence, Welwyn.

17th June 1913

The enclosed letter from Lucy, with its belated sisterly warning, may please you a little. This marble heart was most affectionately grateful to you for that visit. You are my friend and my darling; and I forgive you for not coming down today. The country was disappointed. The rabbits and field mice were waiting in the lanes for you; and when they saw it was only me on my reeking snorting bike, they scuttled away in disgust. The heavens were furious: they thundered, and hailed and hurled such mouthfuls of rain at me that the lanes became torrents in five minutes.

You cant come tomorrow because you have a matinee.

If you will come on Thursday I will not come up until Friday, though I ought to.

If you had come today you would have got damp; but we should have had tea *here*, perhaps. There is a little rift in the clouds at last.

G.B.S.

P.S. You brought out a nice side of Lucy that I havent seen since she was a girl.

◇◇◇◇◇◇

"Lena" is probably Lena Ashwell.

Ayot St. Lawrence, Welwyn.

18/6/13.

Dearest Sillybilly,

You need not be afraid of Kings X: I shouldnt have asked you to go to a confusing crowded place. The platforms are quite simple (the Hatfield Trains start mostly from No. 1), the passengers are all peers and county people, the booking clerks are venerable men with daughters of their own, the porters are most respectful and the air is excellent. I would go to Kensington Square with the car if it were possible; but it isnt. I am so full of work that I cannot get away from here before 2 or half past, and I must get in an hour more of work at least before dinner. And the country doesnt begin until Hatfield, where the immediate presence of Lord Salisbury in bronze and the proximity of Hatfield House gives the station a tone that makes it a positive privilege to alight at it.

Still, I have some qualms about your being in a railway carriage at the hottest part of the day even for 29 minutes (if you ask the engine driver not to stop until Hatfield he will touch his hat and obey). Perhaps you are right. After all, who am I that you should put yourself out to give me a couple of hours of pleasure?

But some people wouldnt think so. Lena, now: she is coming from Saturday to Monday. I shall photograph her. And then—ha ha—she'll have seen me in knickerbockers and you shant. "Well, if you come to that" says you; "*you* have never seen *me* in knickerbockers." Who said I had? I shall, some day. (You should not make such jokes).

I have put that most impudent professional begging letter into the waste paper basket. That woman must make about £600 a year by her pen—more than I used to at my best. The audacity of the thing is breath bereaving. And the prices—4/11! die rather than ask for the other penny, honest woman!

I shall give her address to all the beggars who write to me as that of a devout philanthropist who never turns a deaf ear to the cry of the needy. That will teach her.

Post hour—not time even to say how much I l. . . . . . .

G.B.S.

Ayot St. Lawrence, Welwyn.

25th June 1913

Tomorrow, oh treasurest, I have a committee at 3, another at 4.30, another at 6.30; and you have to go to D.D. at 6. So I shall not see you until Friday, I suppose. No matter: the sun will not cool in that time; and my heart is now a thousand times warmer than the sun.

For Friday morning I have been promised an invitation to a cinema rehearsal; as Gaumont et Cie want me to do plays for them; and I said I wanted to see how the thing had to be done—how fast they could move—what space the lens confined them to. I suppose it will be too early to rout you out of bed (I understand that it's to be at Ealing): but you ought to be there, as you must be my leading lady if I go into cinematography. I shall hear tomorrow whether Whelan has been able to fix it up.

I was in heaven yesterday. Spoke to the queen. A dear woman, and frightfully beautiful. She just slanged me in the most shocking way for a full hour; and I adored her and burnt endless candles to her all the time. In the end my prayers touched her; and she gave me a little blessing. And now I have a halo inside like this.

G.B.S.

◇◇◇◇◇◇

This "letter" is from a copy of four postcards from Dresden. The originals are not in the files, but there is a note on the copy saying "Mrs. Campbell has taken some of the postcards to

America (Dec. 1929)." The note is in the handwriting of Mrs. Campbell's secretary, Miss Morris (frequently referred to in later letters). Presumably the dots . . . represent illegible words.

"Richmond Park" is an allusion to the occasion when G.B.S. tried to teach Mrs. Campbell to jump from the ground onto a bench in Richmond Park when she was convalescing after her serious illness. John Burns, the Labour leader, passed by at the crucial moment. She tells the story in her autobiography. There is a further allusion to it in G.B.S.'s postcards of 1 July 1913.

Another revival of The Second Mrs. Tanqueray *had begun on 4 June at the St. James's Theatre.*

Hotel Bellevue, Dresden.

30th June 1913

I should have wired the above address if I could have persuaded myself that you would write. But intelligent people never write, and never think of the absent. I being infatuated, and therefore not intelligent, write to you instead.

And first I enclose a book for the education of your grandchild, which you please hand to Stella with my compliments, unless you would prefer to superintend the exercises yourself, in which case the photographs will tell you everything except that *fertig* means ready, *biegen* means bending, *Bauch* means—well, belly (young children are permitted to have bellies) *aufricht* means upright, *strecken* means stretching, *drehn* means the action of turning on a hinge like a door, *massieren* means to massage, *froschubung* means behaving like a frog, and *Kopfstehen* means standing on your head. All of which you know better than I do; but as you are always boasting of your ignorance I take you at your word and instruct you.

The Dalcroze school at Hellerau, which is what we came to see is very interesting. The theatre has walls and roof of white linen with the lights behind the linen. . . . Seventeen bob an ehr, lidy, is not the . . . to run; and the installation cost sixty something thousand marks. . . . The children can beat 4 in a bar with one hand and 3 in a bar with the other simultaneously, and they can change instantly in marching from 4 and 3 and 6 (and such rhythms as you and I can manage) to 5 and 7. . . . Tots as high as your . . . take a stick and conduct like Nikisch, only better, each making their own favourite rallentandos and rushes. There is no discipline, absolutely no nervousness, and no sulking when they cant pick up the rhythm though there are 700 strangers looking on. Costume is a blue bathing singlet without sleeves for arms or legs. . . . You should have come to see it instead of slaving at Tanqueray. We should have brought Pinero and then we'd have got you on the council of that silly Academy of Dramatic Art and revolutionized artistic education in England. Oh! there are lots and lots of things to be done in the world besides mingling with the elite of the *beau monde*.

I have never been in Dresden before; and my first glimpse of the Madonna di San Sisto was . . . (By the way, dont look at the obverse of this card: it is worse than your behaviour in Richmond Park) this morning at the age of 57. Santa Barbara is too awful; but the picture did not get its reputation for nothing: the babies, and the bits from the Virgin's waist up, with the floating scarf, is masterly if you can forgive the virgin being Maud Millet rather than my mother of angels.

Barker now demands that I shall go off again to Hellerau to see Dalcroze examining his grown up pupils and to have the wonderful white linen further explained to us. It is raining filthily: the sun we left behind with you; and the weather has been wretched ever—

Yes, coming, coming, coming—*teureste*.

G.B.S.

◇◇◇◇◇◇

The copy of this letter is described as "Set of 5 postcards from Dresden (illustrated). (4 costumes and 1 of house in the sky)." This explains the allusion to the "above voluminous costume."

Hotel Bellevue, Dresden.

30th June 1913

I was about to tell you when Barker snatched me away that the evening at Hellerau finished up with one of the best performances of Gluck's *Orfée*, one Leisner very good indeed (though she was too slow in parts of '*Che faro*'); and the production most remarkable: it only needed a few rehearsals by Barker and myself to be perfect. All the pupils at the school, heaped on the floor in a dim light and tossing their arms and legs about looked like heaps of snakes in hell. This afternoon we went again and saw the lighting installation—the acres of white linen and the multitude of lights behind and above it. It needs only a transparent floor with lights beneath it to make it capable of anything heavenly.

Also we saw an examination—two examinations. Both examinees confronted the examiners, a row of elderly gentlemen, not in the above voluminous costume, but in a bathing singlet without an inch of sleeve or leg drapery. Each had to take a class of other victims in singlets, and to play rhythms for them on the piano and make them march to it. Then they had to pick up impossible themes written on a blackboard, and harmonise them on the piano straight off. They had to improvise variations on them; to modulate into all keys on demand of the examinees then to listen to Dalcroze modulating wildly and name the key he had come into. Finally they had to conduct a choir, first with a stick in the ordinary way, and then with poetic movements of the whole body. This last was extraordinarily effective. I

foresee the day when there will be no more Richters and
Nikischs, but instead, beautiful figures bowed to earth or
raising their hands to heaven, and generally, as the wretched
William puts it "making their bends adornings". One of the
examinees, a Frenchwoman, began on her knee, with her
head bent to the floor. This produced a pp. When she
wanted a ff con esplosione, she shot up to her utmost reach,
tip toes on the floor, finger tips to heaven; and her crumpling
up for a *dim*, was lovely: the singers did what she wanted
without thinking of it. Yet I am told that this was a wretched
display of second raters, and that we must go again when
the examinations are over and see Dalcroze give a lesson.
They have 20 movements; and when they have learnt them
the first variation they are asked for is to give them in
canon; that is, when the right hand has finished No. 1, the
left hand begins it and accompanies No. 2 with No. 1, No.
3 with No. 2, etc., etc., etc. . . . All these games, instead of
driving them mad, seemed to come quite easily to them. I
shall try to learn some of them. Then I will buy you a singlet and teach them to you. Then we will give public dem-
onstrations of the new art. But for the immediate present I
must go to bed, having nothing more to say that can possibly be put on a postcard.

G.B.S.

◇◇◇◇◇◇◇

*John Burns (see page 137) lived at Richmond. Shaw was
later to caricature him as Boanerges in* The Apple Cart.
"Tintagiles" is Maeterlinck's play The Death of Tintagiles.

   *Sir Philip Sassoon's house was in Park Lane, and Mrs. Shaw's
attack of bronchitis was evidently the outcome of this party to
see* Tintagiles.

Dresden, Hotel Bellevue.

1st July 1913

It is now settled, oh loveliest, that we leave this place tomorrow (Wednesday) at midday; go to Leipzig; take a car there for Weimar and drive thence to Eisenach, where we will catch a train that will enable us to catch the Vienna express at Frankfurt at some unholy hour of the night—about 1 a.m.—and get to Ostend between 9 and 10 on Friday morning, which means getting to London late in the afternoon—too late, I fear, to save me from going distracted from privation of my soul's food. Charlotte, alas! writes that she has had a return of her bronchitis as the result of that evening at Park Lane, where we were roasted with closed windows until we grew desperate and froze ourselves by opening them and risking pneumonia. The papers here declare that Alfred Lyttelton is seriously ill and has to be operated on. This I saw just after I had seen the ill-used child in a cinematograph-play resemble D.D. so strongly that I could hardly bear her sorrows. It had not D.D.'s good looks, but it had her expression exactly.

The paper adds that the weather is delightful in England. Here it is grey, cold and rainy, a hideous contrast to Richmond Park. Oh to be in Richmond now that Stella's there, and to let John Burns see that I don't care except for Stella. Still there are things to be done in Dresden. Such Chinese porcelain does not exist in the world elsewhere. Amazing!

How did the dinner in Jermyn Street come off?

But what is the use of asking questions that you can't answer until I come back?

I have nothing whatever to say; but as I want to go on writing to you I will tell you about the festivity at Sir Philip Sassoon's. There were 95 people at dinner; a more vociferous mob I never heard. People used to say that Italians were noisy; but London society now shouts down every other sound on earth. The stage was in a room with a parquet

floor and the chairs were not felted. *Tintagiles* requires, first
an eerie silence, second that everyone should see the stage
and not see the audience. The chairs scraped on the floor
the whole time; and nobody could see the stage except by
fitful glimpses through armpits and under ears and over
shoulders and through feathers. Of the first act not a word
was audible; and when the curtain closed, the audience
roared that fact at one another and bellowed ribald specula-
tions as to what the show was about until they opened again
and Lillah renewed her struggle with adverse circumstances.
Everybody was there except you: would that everybody
except you had been at the ends of the earth. Smart ladies
hailed me as their oldest pal: I received them with enthusi-
asm, and wondered who on earth they were. Fortunately
my allotted lady—Lady Desborough—I knew. Charlotte fell
to the lot of Harry Cust: he didn't know her and had to
appeal to me to get him out of his difficulty. So he can now
tell you all about her. I tried to get a word with Lord Ribblesdale, but couldn't. Goodnight.

G.B.S.

St. James.
5th July 1913

I am sorry I missed you. My heart is aching intoler-
ably for my poor D.D. to night.

I am afraid Alfred is sinking, the children have been sent
for to the Nursing Home, I can do nothing to comfort or
help—she is brave and wise and good—and that thought
helps me . . .

I thank you for the pretty cards and all your dearness—
Perhaps you will ring me up—

Stella.

33, Kensington Square, W.

8th July 1913

I thought you would like to hear that D.D. said today "I think of all the letters I have received Mr. Shaw's
was the one that strengthened my spirit"—she looked for it
to show me but couldn't find it at the moment.

My love to you

Stella

I don't think you realized the other day how much I felt
my friends grief—

Ayot St. Lawrence, Welwyn.

9th July 1913

Stella: don't play with me. You know very well you
have only to look noble and hurt, the least tiniest shade in
the world, and my heart of stone turns to water; and this
you mustn't do merely for fun—cat and mouse—not in the
least that I grudge you the fun, but because you wouldn't
know what to do with me when I came back, and would
have to be horrid to get rid of me again.

When you shut the door on me the other day with a
forced smile, and said "Ouf!" when it slammed, I said "So
it has lasted only a month after all!" And then I remembered that it began in the middle of summer, and lasted a
whole year. I have been a saint for your sake for a whole
year. . . .

And not until the year was out did you say "Go and love
somebody else and don't bother me."

Not that I mind what you say. But you are such a born
actress that without knowing it you change yourself from
head to foot and offer somebody else to the amazed eyes
of your suitors. Before you tired of me, and plunged back
into that part of the theatre that *I*, madam, put in its place,
and into suppers and dinners with those dear pleasant spooks

143

of do-nothings to whom I am so kind for your sake, you
made yourself beautiful for me. When you had a good wallow and had washed me off, so to speak, and got comfort-
ably back to your old notions about me and everything else,
you turned a cold cheek to me, and with a most wonderful
pursing of your lips and eyes and wrinkling of your neck
and pouting of your bosom like a pigeon, made yourself exactly like a pork chop. I could not have believed it: it interested the critic almost as much as it hurt the man. But I am
a saint and a vegetarian; and I won't have pork chops, I will
have my own Stella and nobody else. I will have my harp,
and not the accordion you have substituted. Mind: I don't
blame you: I brought you a certain importunate mood at
an inopportune moment; but to whom else could I bring it?
Besides, that was not the first time: it was only the moment
when the change flashed on me, and I remembered all the
earlier symptoms. And then, with my magnified power of
switching off at a moment's notice when fortune changes,
I switched, and exulted in finding that the old metal still
kept its temper, and that I escaped the unforgettable pang
that rent me when I came upon Blake's drawing—"He shall
take from thee the desire of thine eye."

Nevertheless bless you, dearest, for telling me that my
letter to D.D. was right. And yet what a wretch you are
to have thought that it wouldn't be right, and driven me to
mockery! Shall I ever make a woman of you against the
time when you will be a whitehaired old lady and can no
longer live on love, gossip and mockery?

Always mockery! Stella: you mustn't deride: you must
remember that other people have souls as well as you, and
that if they hold them up before God with the scars of
wounds inflicted by you, He will not even throw you into
hell: He will stamp you out with His foot. Are you so
young that you can afford to sow dragon's teeth as you do?
Is it possible that you don't know that to treat B. as you did

was brutal and cowardly? The man's the most perfect little artist alive in his *genre*. That voice is like nothing on earth but itself; and its nuances of expression are worth studying for hours. The face, the figure, the eyes: all unique. Can't you *see* that? (Oh if I could shake you until you opened your silly prejudiced eyes and used them!) *I* can stop him with a turn of the hand. All you had to say was "Now, Dot: none of that. If you speak a line of my part or make a movement of it, I shall never be able to get away from it: I shall be a poor imitation of the inimitable". There! Isn't that simple? And he would have been pleased; and Barrie wouldn't have been embarrassed (by the way, it occurs to me that you are jilting me because you mean to be a baronet's lady); and you would have built in your rampart of friends instead of leaving a tactlessly insulted enemy in your rear.

You see, now that I am jilted, I can scold you. That is all the use I can be now that you say "Ouf!" when the door shuts. Oh, if you only knew how I've had to remind myself of your engagements, your future, your business! But for that—well no matter.

G.B.S.

33, Kensington Square, W.
14th July 1913

Mrs. Mervyn Beech is her name—she and Mervyn come here to luncheon at 1.30 today and then they go to *Blanco Posnet* with Helen. I cannot go—and I am very sorry. Your poor poor head—

Why do you go on scolding me because I am the woman I am and not the woman you would have me be—?

—I have felt very very sad all these days—D.D.'s misery is a great shock to me and I am not over it yet—

—I was glad to get a little message from you from Miss

145

Bishop—quite soon I am going to see your sister—I have just told Stella on the telephone about the tickets—she is delighted—I pray all Mothers don't feel as I do at giving their daughters up—Perhaps if I had had another to fuss over it would have been all right—

The baby comes at 3 o'c to play with me for half an hour—

My love to you,
Stella.

If my other appointment falls through at 3.30 I will try and get into *Blanco Posnet* somehow—

10, Adelphi Terrace, W.C.
14th July 1913

I have been worked like a galley slave all day. My secretary made an appointment for me late in the afternoon. I told her last week that she might do so *now*. Fool! I was entangled from 3 to 7.30. I rushed to the theatre after the committee, arriving just as the audience streamed out; but *my* Lorelei was not in that stream.

Tomorrow I shall be free after lunch to go down to Ayot. But it does not matter how late I go. This morning I had a little water in the desert; but I am still thirsty. I know I shall ring up tomorrow in spite of my dread of being unwelcome. I rang a second time today; but the answer was buzz, buzz; and I had to rush off.

G.B.S.

Ayot St. Lawrence, Welwyn.
15th July 1913

Something really important. Attend.

Egotist that I am, if you were my baby I should forget to feed you and see you dying of nothing but kisses without thinking why).

Stella: is that car insured?

If not, insure it *instantly*. Send up at once to the Car &
General Insurance Corporation, 1 Albemarle Street, Picca-
dilly, and say you want "cover" at once. It will be anything
up to £18 or so for a whole year; but you can insure for a
month or a week or anything you like. What is urgent—
what you must have above all is insurance against "third
party claims". If you get killed you are dead. If the car is
smashed, *it* is dead. But if it runs into a motor bus or a bean-
feast, everybody in it can take action against you, and even
keep on taking actions against you until the end of their
lives every time they have a fresh nervous symptom, and
get enormous damages. You may have to support them and
their children for ever. And you will have to buy a new bus
for the company. Your salary will be attached; you will be
reduced to beg on the streets. This always happens in the
first 5 minutes with an uninsured car. And you must insure
your driver. Otherwise he will sprain his thumb or knock
out his eye, and live on you for the rest of his life.

Of course if you are already insured I am wasting ink.
But it would be so like you not to be. The people who sell
cars do not always care to remind purchasers of the additional cost of insurance.

Mind: *at once*, before you let that car leave the garage.
If you grudge the money I will give it to you. If you
haughtily refuse it I will insure the car myself in spite of
your teeth.

Barker is going to grow a beard.

When I hear that you are insured I will take you into
favour again, and write you a nice letter.

Oh, why have I not a telephone here!

G.B.S.

◇◇◇◇◇◇◇

Prosser was presumably Mrs. Campbell's maid.

10, Adelphi Terrace, W.C.
18th July 1913

I got free from cares today at a quarter past six; but I didnt dare.

The faithful Prosser glared at me last time for depriving you of your rest and your dinner; and my conscience told me Prosser was right.

I went to the Russian Ballet and consoled myself with Karsavina and Charlotte with Nijinsky. That is how *we* should dance.

Bother Mrs. Tanqueray! There is an end even to my patience: I will someday take you by the throat and make you stop forgetting and coquetting and slipping back to old attitudes and old delusions. There is a woman there whom I love, a most wonderfully beautiful and utterly frank and simple woman; and I'll drag her out and adore her, no matter how many bundles of rags and bags of tucks you hide her in.

G.B.S.

◇◇◇◇◇◇◇

G.B.S. was staying in Devon with Dion Clayton Calthrop, artist and writer. "The Barrie play" is The Adored One, *and "Gertrude" is Gertrude Kingston, who was to play the name-part in G.B.S.'s one-act play* Great Catherine. *"His love letters" obviously refers to Patiomkine in that play—G.B.S. invariably wrote "P.T.O." on all his long letters to Mrs. Campbell.*

148

33, Kensington Square, W.

Thursday. [postmark: 31 July 1913]

I didn't like your letter—and now I haven't your address. I think you must be in a heavenly spot

—I envy you.

—I will hide in the sands somewhere for 3 days before I
start the Barrie play. So Gertrude is to have Catherine—since
I can remember people have promised me Catherine—Did
he have P.T.O. in his love letters too?—After my two performances yesterday I went to College St. D.D. showed me
your two gentle letters—I was glad to see them. . . .

People are to be envied great griefs—so much that is
worthless is swept away from the soul's vision—

This clown misses Joey—

Stella

◇◇◇◇◇◇

*Though this letter is headed 2 July, from the context (see last
paragraph) it should obviously be August 1913. Dion Clayton
Calthrop, in conjunction with Granville Barker, wrote a fantasy called* The Harlequinade. *This was produced in the same
bill as* Androcles and the Lion *on 1 September 1913.*

Torcross Hotel, S. Devon.

2nd July 1913

Today I motored all day over Dartmoor with the
Calthrops. I said that I would think out my Catherine sketch;
and lo! I could not think of it at all. I awoke at 7, having to
bathe at 8, and thus had an hour for prayer to the mother of
angels; and no saint ever had nobler, tenderer visions. The
sea was quieter; but an occasional wave was formidable; and
quite a giant rushed in when I was standing hand in hand
with Lillah. We both heard the kiss and surge of its crest at

the same moment. When we looked round it was rearing over us in the act of hurling tons of water on us. Lillah very naturally tried to run away from it, which would have resulted in its breaking her back possibly. I, knowing better, dragged her down with me and backed into it. What the next ten seconds were like I leave to your imagination; but Lillah thought I had tried to drown her.

However, that is not what I write to tell you. As we drove over the hills the mother of angels pushed Catherine aside, and reminded me of a thousand things that happened in my wonderful winter, of all the marvels and miracles, the happinesses and tendernesses, the intense gratitude to her, her inspired kindness to me. And on that past I built up a future with my imagination, and decorated it with hundreds of fancies on the way to its indescribable consummation.

And all this I tell you that you may know that I am not tired or faithless; that nothing is lost or forgotten that—oh, that I am scrawling this by my bedside, and stopping at every word to go off into reveries that come nearer and nearer to dreams and sleep.

Do you care to know these things?

You see, it is now plain to me that a bored man may be best for an active, enjoying woman. He seeks distractions, company, suppers, operas, outings, races, and all sorts of excitements to avoid being left alone with his burden. But the true lover is a gaoler to whom society is an intrusion and amusement an interruption. He is content with adoration, and adores adores adores until she yawns. He feels apologetic; but none the less everything but his adoration seems tedious and ridiculous to him, insipid, shallow, worthless.

Forgive, then, even if you must yawn and if you cannot recapture the first something something (Browning) rapture; for I recapture it again and again, sweeter than ever, deeper than ever, holier than ever; and yet not a bit colder than ever.

Witness my hand, this second day of August one thousand nine hundred and thirteen. Keep this: it is a certificate.

G.B.S.

❖❖❖❖❖❖

This letter (quoted in Mrs. Campbell's autobiography) refers to the occasion when she had to have a splinter removed, by surgical means, from under her thumbnail.

10, Adelphi Terrace, W.C.
6th August 1913

My dearest love: I think all that was good for my soul, because it tore everything that was selfish and imaginary right out of me, and made you a real fellowcreature in real pain (O Lord! my fibres all twist and my heart and bowels torment me when I think of it); and the more real you become the more I discover that I have a real real real kindness for you, and that I am not a mere connoisseur in beauty or a sensualist or a philanderer, but a—but a— a—a—I dont know what, but something that has deep roots in it that you pluck at. Only, why should you have to be hurt to cure me of selfishness and of little fits of acting? Why should it not be an ecstasy of happiness for you: that would move me too, perhaps still more deeply.

Are you very tired and low in the counter-reaction? for in the reaction after the pain I am sure you were wonderful. If I were with you, I would cheat that counter-reaction somehow—hide you from it in my arms—say all sorts of things (all true) to make you forget it.

Isnt solitude a wonderful thing? When I am solitary you are always with me. When you are solitary by the sea, where shall I be? Where, Stella? Where, where, where? You know dont you? Oh—! But it will be a holy, beautiful, noble solitude all the same.

G.B.S.

❖❖❖❖❖❖

"Sara and Molly" are the Irish sister-actresses Sara Allgood and Maire O'Neill. "Leonora" was the heroine of the new Barrie play.

33, Kensington Square, W.

Thursday 7th Aug. 1913

You were all kindness and sympathy yesterday and I am *sure* it would have hurt much more if you hadn't been there. I was soon all right. Sara and Molly came to the theatre and were mightily pleased with me—and we all three came back to supper here—

Oh you know I must be alone by the sea—how are strength and steadiness to come to me otherwise—and Leonora— This morning's letter is a most dear letter . . . when you are tender a thousand cherubs peep out of your purple and black wings—

Its getting difficult not to love you more than I ought to love you—Offend me again quickly to pull me together—But by the sea I must be alone—you know.

Stella.

The Guildford Hotel—Sandwich—10th August 1913

Please will you go back to London to-day—or go wherever you like but dont stay here—If you wont go I must—I am very very tired and I oughtn't to go another journey. Please dont make me despise you.

Stella.

152

◇◇◇◇◇◇◇

Copy of a coloured postcard from G.B.S. from Ramsgate.

The Guildford Hotel, Sandwich.
11th August 1913
"The Desolate Shore
and
"The Lights of Ramsgate".

The Guildford Hotel, Sandwich.
11th Aug. 1913
Goodbye. I am still tired—you were more fit for a journey than I—

Stella.

The Guildford Hotel, Sandwich.
11th Aug. 1913
Very well, go: the loss of a woman is not the end of the world. The sun shines: it is pleasant to swim: it is good to work: my soul can stand alone. But I am deeply, deeply, deeply wounded. You have tried me; and you are not comfortable with me: I cannot bring you peace, or rest, or even fun: there is nothing really frank in our comradeship after all. It is I who have been happy, carelessly happy, comfortable, able to walk for miles after dinner at top speed in search of you, singing all the way (I had walked eight miles in the morning, by the way, and written a scene of my play) and to become healthily and humorously sleepy afterwards the moment I saw that you were rather bored and that the wind was in the wrong quarter. Bah! You have no nerve: you have no brain: you are the caricature of an eighteenth century male sentimentalist, a Hedda Gabler titivated with odds and ends from Burne Jones's ragbag:

you know nothing, God help you, except what you know all wrong: daylight blinds you: you run after life furtively and run away or huddle up and scream when it turns and opens its arms to you: you are a man's disgrace and infatuation not his crown "above rubies": instead of adding the world to yourself you detach yourself, extricate yourself, guard yourself: instead of a thousand charms for a thousand different people you have one fascination with which you blunder about—hit or miss—with old and young, servants, children, artists, Philistines: you are a one-part actress and that one not a real part: you are an owl, sickened by two days of my sunshine: I have treated you far too well, idolized, thrown my heart and mind to you (as I throw them to all the world) to make what you could of; and what you make of them is to run away. Go then: the Shavian oxygen burns up your little lungs: seek some stuffiness that suits you. You will not marry George! At the last moment you will funk him or be ousted by a bolder soul. You have wounded my vanity: an inconceivable audacity, an unpardonable crime.

> Farewell, wretch that I loved.
>
> G.B.S.

> Sandwich. Darkness
> 11th August 1913

Oh, my rancor is not yet slaked: I have not said enough vile things to you. What are you, miserable wretch, that my entrails should be torn asunder hour after hour? Of that 57 years I have suffered 20 and worked 37. Then I had a moment's happiness: I almost condescended to romance. I risked the breaking of deep roots and sanctified ties; I set my feet boldly on all the quicksands: I rushed after Will o' the Wisp into darkness: I courted the oldest illusions, knowing well what I was doing. I seized handfuls of withered leaves and said "I accept them for gold". And now there is that desolate strand, and the lights of Ramsgate that might have been the camp fires of the heavenly hosts on the Celestial mountains. I said "There are seven stars and seven sorrows and seven swords in the heart of the Queen of Heaven: and for myself I want seven days". They began; and I held back: I was not greedy: for I wanted the last to be the best. And you yawned in my face, and stole the last five to waste in some desolate silly place with your maid and your chauffeur. Oh, may you be bored until in desperation you ask the waiter to walk out with you! You are worse than that fiend of a woman: she could at least hate and stick to it: you are neither love nor hate. Wretch, wretch, how will I, an Irishman, know this Roman Catholic product, this precociously forced erotic sentimentality, this narrow mind, this ignorance, this helplessness that longs to be forced because it can imitate nothing, will nothing, change nothing, that has no power except the power of endearment and no appeal except the appeal of beauty. These are the things you set up against me when I drag you out into freedom and fellowship. Give me, oh my critical mind and keen eye, a thousand reasons for treating this light creature as she deserves, if such a monstrous retribution is possible. Come round me all the good friends I have neglected for her. Even her slanderers shall be welcome: I shall say "Spit your venom; heap up your lies; vomit your malice until the air is poison: you will still fall short of the truth." And to her friends, her dupes, her adorers, I will say "All that you say is true and not half good enough for her; and yet it is all nothing: she would tear the strings out of an archangel's harp to tie up parcels: she has done that with my very heart strings." And this is the wretch whom I shall have to drive through a play which she will do her utmost to ruin, whom I shall have to flatter, to conciliate, to befriend, on occasions when she is about to run violently down a steep place into the sea. Stella, how could you, how could you? What micrometer could measure the shallowness that prevents you from knowing what you have done. Even if I had been secretly bored to distraction I would have stayed on in fire rather than have dealt you the enormous blow of deserting you. But at least the order of nature is restored to my imagination. It is I who cared, you who didn't. That is as becomes me. I no longer look up to the queen of heaven: I tower mountainous to the skies and see a pretty little thing wondering at me. How is it that this infinitesimal nothingness yet drags at my midriff and causes me strange pangs and makes me write wild nonsense? Oh, the world itself is too light to carry the reproach you deserve. You are more cruel than a child.

Enough. I will go to bed. I am still sleepy.

G.B.S.

Sandwich 12th Aug. 1913

Another day that might have been a day! What have I shrunk into? In all these years I have hurt many people as the Doctor hurt your thumb, sometimes sorely perhaps, but never maliciously, never desiring to hurt, never without such anodynes as my wit and address could devise. I have never said anything false or unjust or spiteful, and never wanted to. And now give me anything that is false, malicious, spiteful, little, mean, poisonous or villainous, and I will say it only if it hurts you. I want to hurt you because you hurt me. Infamous, vile, heartless, frivolous, wicked woman! Liar! lying lips, lying eyes, lying hands, promise breaker, cheat, confidence-trickster! Act I. Let us bathe before breakfast, at a quarter to eight. No, at eight. Too late: a quarter to eight. Please not before eight. Act II. Come and bathe. (Smiling chambermaid comes out) They're gone, sir. What? Today? I thought it was tomorrow. What a

charming voice and smile that old sport has! *He* dont care.
Curtain. He does care, though. How could a human heart
deal another such a—such a kick? This is what I have to
forgive. Stella: why did you do it?

Sir George Alexander desires to know where we stand. I
write God knows—tell him that there is Barrie, and *The
Woman With the Fan* that tempts and does not frighten
you. I think I shall stay here where my heart's blood has
been spilt in the sand. I walk well here. I sleep well here. I
suffer well here.

And you? Where did you go? Did you find rest and sleep
and happy days there? If you did, I forgive you and bless
you. If not—oh wretch, I could tear you limb from limb.

G.B.S.

Littlestone.
13th August 1913

You vagabond you—you blind man. You weaver of
words, you—and black and purple winged hider of cherubs
—you poor thing unable to understand a mere woman. My
friend all the same. No daughters to relieve your cravings—
no babes to stop your satirical chatterings, why should I pay
for all your shortcomings. You in your broom-stick and
sheet have crackers and ashes within you—

—I in my rags and my trimmings have a little silver lamp
in my soul and to keep its flame burning is all that I ask.
That I pray. My friend—my dear friend all the same.

Stella.

If you had'nt been so sleepy you would have noticed
my "goodbye". They have given me permission to stay
away until Monday. This heavenly place. I sat in the sea for
an hour this morning—not two dozen houses, not a hundred
people—The sea goes out miles and comes in up to the green

in front of the house, and as far as you can see to right and
to left just green and sand and glory—The peace is divine
and soul-strengthening and soul-resting. I and my part—and
Georgina to play with—the maid and the chauffeur at hand.

You with your eighteenth-century ribaldry habit. You
lost me because you never found me.—I who have nothing
but my little lamp and flame—you would blow it out with
your bellows of self. You would snuff it with your egotisti-
cal snortings—you elegant charmer—you lady-killer—you
precious treasure of friendship—for you do I keep my little
lamp burning for fear you may lose your way in the
dark. . . .

The drive to Rye and all about when the sun is low is
lovely.

Stella.

Your two letters—considering—are very well.
Do you think it was nothing to me to hurt my friend—

Littlestone.
13th Aug. 1913

I am sure you have done splendid work and have had
a divine rest.

You are trying to break my heart with your letters. You
know I did *rightly*. What other thing was there for me to
do? I had to behave like a man—and a gentleman hadn't I?
I will see you Monday or Tuesday.

Stella.

10, Adelphi Terrace, W.C.
13th August 1913

Back from the land of broken promise.
I might ring you up and say this; but I am too proud.
Oh shallow hearted thing!

The world has changed horribly since Sunday afternoon.

What did you want? Oysters and champagne? Why did you go? How could you go? This morning Brabazon accosted me in the hotel. He has a house close by. He said the worst of the place is that he cannot sleep there. My heart snatched at the excuse for you. But no, not like that. At the Great Judgment they will say to you "all your other sins are forgiven; but why did you do this?" There where I imagined heaven there is nothing. Oh mirage in the desert, I shall die of thirst after all, in spite of you.

I finished my play in time for lunch today, punctually at half past one. It is an old precept of mine: Do your work; and your sweetheart will never have too much of you. How I have thrust work between us lest I should plague you and tire you out! And now I am no better off than if I had thrown everything to the winds but temptation. Fool! Dupe! Dotard! Crybaby! Useless, these letters; the wound will not heal.

G.B.S.

Littlestone-on-Sea.
15th Aug. 1913

I looked about thinking I might see you to-day I missed a letter from you tonight.

Perhaps you are gone to Scotland—or to Ayot—or you are busy reading your play to your friends and my enemies.

When the man brought the ginger beer he said "You've paid your bill and ginger beer one shilling" I thought you would have guessed then but you were too sleepy—I owe you a shilling—

Whilst you were looking for me on the sands I was screaming for Georgina near the Hotel she had lost herself in the long grass. I lit matches and couldn't find her for ever so long. I expect you had got to the hammock by then—I didn't know you were looking for me. I thought you had forgotten all about me and you were finishing your play, and when I saw you you were too sleepy to understand—besides you had had my letter in your pocket all day—you *wouldn't* understand—

At 6 a.m. I was out of bed—so many years since I was up at 6. At 6.30 I called the maid, by 7.30 we were in the motor and had started—and it rained and rained and I was so sleepy and cold and hungry—and when we got to St. Margaret's Bay both Hotels were full. We had breakfast and then on to Hythe—it looked stuffy there—and then on here—the Hotel full but I found the nicest of landladys with rooms free until to-morrow Saturday 2 o'c. A large sittingroom with a balcony a large bedroom and a nice clean bathroom—a room for the maid next to mine and the chauffeur downstairs. . . .

Georgina is divine she smells of heather and the sea—she has made friends with a Pom and they play "catch me if you can" on the sands.

Your dear letters are not true—but they are wonders!—when I see you I can tell you what will make all clear—don't be hurt Joey dear—*please* PLEASE PLEASE

Stella.

Saturday.

I have studied—I have rested—I have slept I have thought a great deal—and I am ready for four months hard work. I leave at 2 o'c today and arrive at 7 this evening.—

10, Adelphi Terrace, W.C.
16th August 1913

I cant get away completely yet. I have only three minutes to scrawl this before dashing for the last train to Ayot. Tomorrow I bicycle to Essex to read the play to

Gertrude Kingston. On Monday I take the bicycle to Coventry for repairs and return to London by train; so I shall be in town on Monday evening and afternoon after all.

I am not tired of making excuses for you; but I wish I could stop doing it. You could not argue your case half as well as I have argued it fifty times. Did you ever meet so feminine a creature?

I will ring you up when I get back here on Monday—I know I will.

G.B.S.

33, Kensington Square, W.
Monday night 25th Aug. 1913

I feel quite unhappy at your going out into the night like that. Why didn't you take the car? I knew you detested the Savoy. Why didn't I hear that you hadn't left London? Write me a line if you have time.

Good night
Stella.

33, Kensington Square, W.
30th Aug. 1913

Barrie and I both rehearsing (not dress) at 8 o'c—first piece—2nd piece 9 o'c Monday night.—Boucicault says impossible to arrange otherwise. I am *sick*—I wanted to come so much. Barrie is at Killiecrankie—am going straight home now.

You are a giant, I am so thankful.

S.

33, Kensington Square, W.
30th Aug. 1913

I am not afraid—though its dreadful of you to say that, you turn all the blame upon me—

161

"Stronger than steel is the sword of the spirit,
Swifter than arrows the light of the truth is—
Greater than all is the love that subdueth—"

There is no air to-day. I am afraid you were tired out last night. It was the growls of the lion you heard—you dont growl—you *know* growls are nothing—and its the emptiness of the flat that freezes you—and you have no claws—because Androcles mended your poor hurt foot. So you have no claws for him—for her I mean—oh dear

Stella—

I am off to see the picture—to rehearsal—

◇◇◇◇◇◇

This letter is again from a copy. It was written on four illustrated postcards (see note to earlier postcards, page 136). It gives a fascinating foretaste of Saint Joan *(1924). J. W. Mackail, Professor of Poetry at Oxford, and his wife, Margaret (a daughter of Sir Edward Burne-Jones), were lifelong friends of Mrs. Campbell.*

Orleans, Monday night.

8 September /13

I am as punctual as Bradshaw so far. And as I fly thundering over these windy uplands my mind, contracted for a whole year to the petty corner of a Kensington square, expands to European dimensions with vast histories behind and huge hopes ahead. Like Handel's Polyphemus I sing:

Cease to beauty to be sueing
Ever whining love disdaining
Let the braves their aims pursuing
Still be conquering, not complaining.

That is how Jack Mackail ought to write. I do not yet wholly repudiate you; but I see you on pinnacles and in pediments in the glorious company of the apostles.

Strangely enough I have never been in Orleans before, though I have been all over the Joan of Arc country. How they canonize her you may see from the previous postcard. I shall do a Joan play some day, beginning with the sweeping up of the cinders and orange peel *after* her martyrdom, and going on with Joan's arrival in heaven. I should have God about to damn the English for their share in her betrayal and Joan producing an end of burnt stick in arrest of Judgment. "What's that? Is it one of the faggots?" says God. "No", says Joan "it's what is left of the two sticks a common English soldier tied together and gave me as I went to the stake; for they wouldn't even give me a crucifix; and you cannot damn the common people of England, represented by that soldier because a poor cowardly riff raff of barons and bishops were too futile to resist the devil."

That soldier is the only redeeming figure in the whole business. English literature must be saved (by an Irishman, as usual) from the disgrace of having nothing to show concerning Joan except the piffling libel in Henry VI, which reminds me that one of my scenes will be Voltaire and Shakespear running down bye streets in heaven to avoid meeting Joan. Would you like to play Joan and come in on horseback in armour and fight innumerable supers?

Now I have run into five cards; and I have only four stamps.

"E–   whi–
       ver   ning love
                           dis–
  "dai———
              ———ning!

So up to your pinnacle, and leave me to bustle, beanfed, on the ground.

G.B.S.

◇◇◇◇◇◇

This is from a copy of a letter originally written on two picture postcards.

[from Moulins Allier, France]
10 September 1913

If you look at this wretched card with a magnifying glass you will find that the two angels crowning the Madonna are lovely beyond words.

Also if you ever visit Cosne on the Loire you will find that the landlady of the Hotel du Cerf is the most dangerous rival you have in Europe. A dark lady in a rose du Barri blouse. She sat down at a table crowded with four officers, squeezing the forearm of the one on her left, overhand, with a seductive intimacy, radiating with beauty all over the shop (this was outside the hotel in a grove of trees in tubs) in such an irresistible manner that I should have ordered rooms for a week there and then had I not been dog tired with driving 65 miles in 2½ hours, which means breakneck speed when you get the chance. Doing this day after day is tiring me. Tomorrow I make a final spurt of 90 miles; and then the journey is over, and—but no matter.

The hands of this Hercules are very Rodinesque.

I must go to bed. We came 130 miles today. I have wandered about the town in the dark to digest my dinner, and found nothing but a café in which a very depressed and ladylike Frenchwoman was singing 'Yip Iaddy I Ay' like a hymn. She made me critical; and I came home elaborating a critical study of your character.

G.B.S.

◇◇◇◇◇◇

*"Not a sprite" is probably a reference to Mrs. Sidney Webb's
well-known epithet for G.B.S. in regard to his capacity for
love-making: "Shaw is a sprite in such matters, not a real person."*
The Adored One *had been produced on 4 September at the
Duke of York's Theatre.*

Hotel Croix d'Or, Valence-sur-Rhone.

17.9.13

I pursued the critical comparison of you with other
women for some time after I entered on them in my last
letter. I asked myself whether to be a frightfully wonderful
virtuoso in the old art of love was greater than to be a blundering beginner in new developments. I handled the subject
very coolly indeed. And then, in the evening I came out of
a high and windy region into evening and an Italian valley;
for though the long descent from St. Agreve to Lamestre is
in France, there is nothing more Italian in the world than
its color. At the first glance I melted and went to pieces; and
the Virgin's hood which crowned the mountains was *your*
hood. No; I am not a sprite—at least not always.

Stella: I am horribly unhappy every morning. *Now* I am
not particularly so; for this afternoon I came to a splendid
4000 foot mountain and had to drive right up it for eight
mortal miles, reversing at impossible hairpin corners, and
crawling so slowly that a good white horse which I passed
at the foot passed me at the top when we stopped to re-
plenish our boiled-away tank. Then came buckets of rain
and an interminable drive down again on a ledge along an
endless valley. After that, one is satiated with physical labor
& vigilance. But in the morning I shall be horribly unhappy
again. It is not wholly the lost-dog feeling of vagabondiz-
ing, nor the hideous vicissitudes of mood which make me
travel such a see saw. Oh I cant put it all down on paper:
I suppose I will tell you some day.

I must leave this letter unwritten after all. Send me a scrap of news: we shall be here for the rest of the week. What is happening to *The Adored One*? I send you many wireless messages: do you ever send me any? Goodnight.

G.B.S.

Hotel Croix d'Or, Valence-sur-Rhone.

21/9/13

I am no longer unhappy, though all sorts of unlucky things have happened—Charlotte in bed these three days with a bad cold, and the car disabled—its steel frame torn like a piece of paper. And I have an extraordinary feeling that you have forgotten all about me and vanished away into the distance. The compensations are that a mechanic here with something like an old acetylene generator as his sole machinery, says he can melt a lump of steel into my chassis in two days and make it as good as new; that Charlotte is happy in the prospect of joining Lena in Biarritz; and that after two perfectly frightful scenes with me, in which she produced such a case against my career and character as made Bluebeard seem an angel in comparison, she quite suddenly and miraculously—at a moment when murder and suicide seemed the only thing left to her—recovered her intellectual balance, her sanity, and her amiability completely, and became once more (after about two years) the happy consort of an easygoing man. Not even the discovery of some telegrams from Barrie about the first night of the A.O. has upset her. So I no longer sigh and drift before the storm close reefed, collar up, head bent, and hands in pockets. The relief is enormous: I have such infernal powers of endurance that I never realize the weight of a burden until it is lifted from my shoulders.

I have not seen a paper for a week. I do not know what is happening except that *Androcles*, though its takings are a record for a new play of mine, is doing only £850 a week at a theatre that costs £1000. Religious people write me wild letters about it, washing my feet with their tears and drying them with their hair. And Butt will not have *Great Catherine* because the cost of it would be too great; he says he cannot see his way out of it for less than £700 a week.

I should like to rewrite that trial for murder in Barrie's play. I see how it could be made to convince people for the first time that people really are hanged, and the tragic futility of the people that hang them, and the grounds on which they are hanged, just as I made Lena say after Androcles "I must realize now for the first time that the Christian martyrs were really killed". And I could make the woman crush the law and crush the judge and get her verdict without a single impossibility or real frivolity, making you do and be that great thing that people long for. I see my way better now that your magnetic poles are for some reason turned away from me than when I am foolish and amorous. So you see there *is* something left when that is gone.

G.B.S.

◇◇◇◇◇◇◇

The Adored One *was not a success, and attempts were made to improve it—without avail.*
The "baby" *was Mrs. Campbell's grandson, Patrick Beech.*

33, Kensington Square, W.
25th Sept. 1913
        Theres much to tell, heaps of happenings, but I don't feel like writing.
The Adored One has had a nightmare and a love scene added, the rehearsals were miserable—
Stella returns with her husband and the little one next week to Africa—I have worried about them a great deal. I

wish you had seen me with my baby at John Barker buying
him his first shoes and socks! it was fun—

I hope your honeymoon has been a success.

Write me some more letters—oh dear—

Stella.

It will be dreadful when you realize the commonplace
witless charwoman I really am! and you with so many
"great women" about you. . . .

◇◇◇◇◇◇

This is written on two postcards from Rouen.

[from Rouen]
16 Oct. 1913

Nearer, my goddess, to thee by another 120 miles.
We swoop up from summer to chill October very suddenly.
The first exhilaration of it is over; it froze a little last night;
and I had to put another blanket on my bed. And today the
sun retired vanquished after an attempt to reign; and with
the hood of the car up to keep off a half hearted rain I drove
along interminable stretches of straight road with two rows
of poplars stretching away to a point that never came any
closer, 85 miles of it, at mostly 40 to 45 miles an hour. You
should have been with me in the Le Mans cathedral yesterday evening. I wonder have you ever seen stained glass?
ever seen anything? or only imagined it all.

I wonder also whether there will be any letters for me at
Boulogne. I hold back that hope—it is my old habit to hold
back hopes—and await the event!

G.B.S.

33, Kensington Square, W.

19 Oct. 1913

I ought to have written for I was very grateful for the letters and postcards. But there has been much to do and to think over, and letter writing to you—seemed irrelevant—thats all.

I rang you up yesterday forgetting you would be in the country.

I am glad you are safely home again.

Stella.

❖❖❖❖❖❖

The veiled references are possibly to George Cornwallis-West. "Lucy" is presumably Shaw's sister. Denis Mackail: author and son of Professor J. W. Mackail.

33, Kensington Square, W.

4th Nov. 1913

Dear dear Joey,

I wanted you to come back to tea—for I wanted you both to meet—*really*, and to talk—

There are rocks ahead,—you are wise and clear sighted—

Life is difficult, and nature cunning, thank heavens if some sense of order grips one and helps one out—

—Do my feathers seem showy and expensive?—my mother looked a queen in black merino!

This house is grim with Beo and Helen gone—

I myself am the baby after all.

I go to see Lucy Wednesday afternoon, and she comes perhaps on Thursday to the play . . . be quite serious in your friendship for me—I am so so troubled just now, and must put aside trimmings and prettiness—

Stella.

Denis Mackail longs to do some work for you—and wants
to know if he may write to you—

◇◇◇◇◇◇◇

*H. Irving: Sir Henry's elder son, H. B. Irving, who died in
1919 at the early age of forty-nine.* The Grand Seigneur *is a
play in which he was to appear.*

Berkeley Hotel.

1/12/13

Yes I had a letter from H. Irving—he is delighted
with your play. We meet this week. *The Grand Seigneur*
goes over Christmas.

I am away to Eastbourne now with Helen feeling a little
anxious. I saw two acts of the play on Sat. without scenery
—and I wept like a baby when the new leading lady slim as
a pin with the personality of a school marm said 'Goodbye'
to her silly billy man—

To think—and think—ten years hence!—and realise *now*
is the golden hour—

The reality of life closes in upon one—suddenly and one
knows—*trapped*—

—Wings! Wings! Wings! we have our wings!—

Heres my breakfast. "Georgina" has jumped off the bed.
I'm sure thats bad for her.

Barrie dined with me last night and smoked his pipe and
talked and listened and talked. He was amusing and wise—
a little child whom the Gods have whispered to—

Grand Hotel Eastbourne.

You haven't told me of your interview with Tree I was
grateful to you for minding the "Stella Campbell"—how it
betrays him!—ugh—

Stella.

170

◇◇◇◇◇◇◇

The Wiborgs were American friends. Sarah Bernhardt's new play was probably Tristan Bernard's Jeanne Doré *(1913), in which, according to Maurice Baring, "she reached the utmost limit of quiet and simple pathos." This was the year before her leg was amputated.*

33, Kensington Square, W.

13 Dec. 1913

I have one moment to scribble a line.

Beo starts for New York tomorrow morning, as manager for the syndicate—to try and arrange for Kenneth Douglas —the company and the play, scenery and dresses to be moved over there at once—if he succeeds then Helen goes with the company in 10 days time, if he doesn't—well he looks around and comes back.

This reads easy—well it has *not* been easy to arrange!— I leave at 9 o'c. to-morrow morning with the Wiborg girls and their parents to Paris. I stay there one night and see Sarah's new play. I'd stay a week if I could find a friend, the Wiborgs go on to India.

I have had a strain upon me, and I wanted a day's break— Then when Beo and Helen are settled out upon their hard work—I'll turn to *my* venture.

So far this place is ready—its nice and clean. And for the rest—well the sky, the seeds in the earth and the wisdom of God—know about it!—

I think you're happy and well—I'm glad.

Stella.

In the New Year may you play with the moon and kiss the stars—and the earth lie in your lap—

◇◇◇◇◇◇

The Hon. Neville Lytton (who succeeded his brother as
Earl of Lytton in 1947) and his first wife, Baroness Wentworth,
were old friends of Mrs. Campbell. She was still staying at the
Berkeley Hotel.

20th Dec. 1913

I hope you'll have a lovely time—walk—and talk. I
stay with the Nevill Lyttons over Sunday and on here for
another week—the manager makes grand reductions but its
ruinous anyway.

You owe me a word for word repetition of the explanation of the face powder!—I know you made yourself out a
fine fellow—but what did you make of me?

I was told today you wanted me to play "Eliza" for the
joy of making a fool of me—

A Merry Christmas
Stella.

Ilfracombe Hotel, Ilfracombe.

31st December 1913

New Years Eve. O night of all nights in the year—of
my most immemorial year! Do you remember last New
Years Eve? I am actually asking you do you remember it?
Was it anything to you except that you were ill, and were
determined to prevent me from seeing the new year in with
Lillah and Barrie? *I* remember it: it tears me all to pieces: I
believe we were both well then, and have been ill ever since.
For what is this senseless walking about, this physical hardi-
hood, this business, this going to Paris to see the dead dance,
this cheese and ginger beer, this repainting and repapering
but disease and madness? On that last New Years Eve and
all the eves that went before it, there was Eternity and
Beauty, infinite, boundless loveliness and content. I think of
it with a frightful yearning, with a tragic despair: for you

172

have wakened the latent tragedy in me, broken through my proud overbearing gaiety that carried all the tragedies of the world like feathers and stuck them in my cap and laughed. And if your part in it was an illusion, then I am as lonely as God. Therefore you must still be the Mother of Angels to me, still from time to time put on your divinity and sit in the heavens with me. For that, with all our assumed cleverness and picked up arts to stave off the world, is all we two are really fit for. Remember this always even when we are grovelling and racketing and drudging; for in this remembrance I am deeply faithful to you—faithful beyond all love. Be faithful to me in it and I will forgive you though you betray me in everything else—forgive you, bless you, honor you, and adore you. *Super hanc stellam* will I build my Church.

And now let us again hear the bells ring: you on your throne in your blue hood, and I watching and praying, not on my knees, but at my fullest stature. For you I wear my head nearest the skies.

G.B.S.

33, Kensington Square, W.

5 Jan. 1914

Such a wonderful beautiful letter. Where are you? I will tell you how it was with me that New Years Eve.

If I could write letters like you, I would write letters to God—

Stella.

[Postcard]

Ayot St. Lawrence. Welwyn, Herts. 5/1/14.

WITH BERNARD SHAW'S COMPLIMENTS

I am back from my travels and hard at work. I come up to town late on Wednesday for an evening engagement.

I dont know which photograph of the bust you asked me for. I send all I can find. They may remind you of my forgotten existence.

G.B.S.

⬦⬦⬦⬦⬦⬦

Pygmalion—its first night was on the 11 April 1914 at His Majesty's Theatre—impends at long last. "He" in this letter refers to Sir Herbert Tree. The next few notes seem to imply that Tree knew how to be almost as difficult as his leading lady and his dramatist combined. "Dana" was Henry Dana, Tree's business manager.

33, Kensington Square, W.

10.2.14

Oh goodness we're in for it—and lets be *very* clever —he's fixed and you can manage the lot of us—and then indeed you'll be a *great man*! he wants to be friendly and his admiration for you and the play is *ENORMOUS*. I'll be tame as a mouse and oh so obedient—and I wonder if you'll get what you want out of me—I feel a little afraid—Your verses for my birthday didn't make my heart sing! I don't 'turn my face away for nothing!' *you* too have to be managed—oh dear—so you've missed [*word missing*] tomorrow and I too.

Stella.

33, Kensington Square, W.

(14.2.14.)

Of course I feel thoroughly uncomfortable—what with the thief in my house and Tree to be haggled with!—I am sure Tree thinks I am trying it on! and that turns my stomach.

I am sending him the enclosed note asking him the same terms I 'came down to' at the Haymarket.

I will try to be civil to Dana I see it will make it more comfortable all round.

Stella.

[Dear Sir Herbert,

You seemed very upset at my terms— £130 a week, full salary matinees and 2½ per cent with an eight weeks guarantee—

The best I could do is to make it 2% after the first £700—

Mr. Hawksley has returned from Africa if Mr. Dana would like to discuss further—With warm regards.

Yours sincerely,
B. Stella Campbell.]

◇◇◇◇◇◇◇

The "Duchess" was probably the Duchess of Westminster, George Cornwallis-West's sister.

33, Kensington Square, W.
(21.2.14)

Now I go upstairs to study to be a human Eliza for two hours. I am sorry you hated my most beautiful Duchess. Ah me! if you had heard the talk. How you would have thundered at our sentiment!

George only stayed a moment. . . .

You are wonderful at rehearsal, and we'll all shed our blood for you.

Stella.

33, Kensington Square, W.
(24.2.14)

It will be *AWFUL* if in the end I find even Boucicault easier to work with than you Joey!—

I am sorry I was severe.

Stella.

175

*This letter exists only in a copy made for Mrs. Campbell.
She has written in pencil on it "First Pygmalion," and the
context of the letter shows that its date must have been early
in March 1914.*

33, Kensington Square, W.
[undated]

Tell me what you think of these and please bring
them to rehearsal to-morrow.

I drew them whilst my thoughts were distracted by the
memory of your misery at our work to-day.

It needs a giants strength and great calmness but you will
pull us through with success I *know*.

I will help all I can for I realise what you want, and I will
give you a simple sincere and human girl.

I may make a few feeble remarks in the doing of it but
you must forgive me and I *WILL* have that seat if it has a
back to it!

For all my faults forgive me, and let Charlotte know you
are going to make silk purses out of sow's ears.

Stella.

I thought them the sort of dresses that men would have
chosen.

33, Kensington Square, W.
2.3.14

Could you come to-morrow afternoon late? I would
give you dinner and we could go through my part together
—that would help me enormously.

What pleasure could it be to me to make a success if I
hadn't done so faithfully?

For the rest—if you must say——things. I'll try and take them lying down.

Its splendid of Tree to accept with gentle indifference letters that would have made a frenchman 'call you out'— why did he? because none of us can spare the time to take that side of you that *hurts* seriously!—

I've learned my lesson—

Stella.

Send me a little message about to-morrow—

◇◇◇◇◇◇

"Merivale": Philip Merivale, the actor who played Colonel Pickering in Pygmalion. *He went with Mrs. Campbell to the U.S.A. in October of this same year and played Professor Higgins with her in the New York production.*

33, Kensington Square, W.
30th March 1914

Oh my dear—my dear how silly *you* are—

I told you that *I* was an utter silly-billy in that scene—you tried to help me with—slow—and quicker tempo—high and lower notes—(pianola effects)—but I couldn't be helped that way—I tried changing my seat—that was no good with the others where they were and the Dustman coming down where he did—so I remain—[1] and Merivale brings down the chair and sits opposite me—and I feel *comfortable* and *happy* and not as though I were in a railway carriage and I think you will be pleased with me. Merivale was truly grateful for the change of position—Tree thought it hurt no-one and that if it pleased us both, should be given to us, now I await

---

[1] A sketch of positions of the characters is roughly drawn here in the original.

YOUR APPROVAL. bless you for all your impertinence—and fun and wit and kindness and goodness—and charm and friendliness—Just sometimes I get a little tired—only because I have many worries in my heart—

What you think of me and my poor talent—I am not concerned with—just now—My affection for you is sown in my heart because its roots are planted in gratitude—I haven't forgotten your gentleness and hesitation as you offered me help when I was sick—bless you dear dear Joey—Stella.

All these words and dashes in your letter—are wind & the buzzing of bees.

◇◇◇◇◇◇

This letter was sent by special messenger. It has been marked, at a later date, by Mrs. Campbell in blue pencil: "Final Rehearsal Pygmalion."

Stanley Bell was then assistant stage manager at His Majesty's Theatre.

33, Kensington Square, W.
[undated]

You haven't hurt me at all.

You have only bored me by your ceaseless teasing and braggarting.

I wanted *you* to produce the play, and Tree not to be sufficiently insulted by you as to "throw it up"—in this I have succeeded—though there are a few more days! ! !

For myself the last three months and more particularly the last five days have been full of anxiety.

.   .   .   .   .

I expect I can act as easily in one place as another, once the time for choosing the more comfortable is over.

I have told you before, many actresses would play the part better than I.

178

What I bring to it that is my own, you could'nt give nor take away—

The accent will always trouble me a little I expect.

I hope you will make heaps of money Joey and keep your gay belief that you and your play alone did it and that without you there would have been but failure and fools.—Any more directions you have for me give me through Bell.

I am truly tired.
Stella.

10, Adelphi Terrace, W.C.
11/4/14

FINAL ORDERS.

The name Nepean is in two syllables, not three; and the first "e" is an obscure vowel, and is not to be pronounced "e", but as "a" in the phrase "a bean".

If you have ever said to Stella in her childhood "I'll let you see whether you will . . . obey me or not", and then inverted her infant shape and smacked her until the Square (not to mention the round) rang with her screams, you will . . . know how to speak the line "I'll let you see whether I'm dependent on you". There is a certain dragging intensity, also used in Act IV in "YOU thank God etc", which is wanted here to re-establish your lead after Higgins' long speech about science and classical music and so on. The author took care to re-establish it by giving Eliza a long and energetic speech in reply to him; but the ignorant slave entrusted with the part thought she knew better than the author, and cut out the speech as useless. Now she has got to do it the other way.

On the grand finish "I could kick myself" you retreat. The effect last night was "Now Ive spoke my piece; anitz your turn, Srerbert". You must plant yourself in an unmis-

takable attitude of defiance, or in some way or other *hold*
him for his reply.

At the end when Higgins says "Oh, by the way Eliza",
bridle your fatal propensity to run like Georgina to anyone
who calls you, and to forget everything in an affectionate
tête à tête with him. Imagine that he is the author, and be
scornful. All that is necessary is to stop on the threshold. If
you find it impossible not to come back, at least dont look
obedient and affectionate. And start going away on the cue
"Eale & Bimmans" so that he can shout the last sentence
after you and give you an effective cue for your last word.

That smile on "More friendly like" is developing to excess. It should be the ghastliest wannest thing, because you
are just about to burst into tears; and the smile must be that
sort of smile. What you have to express above all things in
that speech is the torment of the woman who wants to express something that she cannot (as she thinks) express
properly. Make that smile an inch wider, and you may as
well stand on the points of your toes and raise your arms
gracefully above your head.

I give up in despair that note of terror in the first scene
which collects the crowds and suddenly shews the audience
that there is a play there, and a human soul there, and a
social problem there, and a formidable capacity for feeling
in the trivial giggler of the comic passages. But until you get
it I shall never admit that you can play Eliza, or play Shaw.

The danger tonight will be a collapse of the play after
the third act. I am sending a letter to Tree which will pull
him together if it does not kill him. But a good deal will
depend on whether you are inspired at the last moment. You
are not, like me, a great general. You leave everything to
chance, whereas Napoleon and Caesar left nothing to chance
except the last inch that is in the hands of destiny. I could
have planned the part so that nine tenths of it would have
gone mechanically even if your genius had deserted you,

leaving only one tenth to the Gods. Even as it is, I have forced half the battle on you; but winning half the battle will not avert defeat. You believe in courage: I say "God save me from having to fall back on that desperate resource," though if it must come to that it must. I dont like fighting: I like conquering. You think you like fighting; and now you will have to succeed sword in hand. You have left yourself poorly provided with ideas and expedients; and you must make up for them by dash and brilliancy and resolution. And so, *Avanti!*

G.B.S.

◇◇◇◇◇◇◇

This note was written before the first performance of Pygmalion. *Mrs. Campbell subsequently wrote in her autobiography: "Surely no first night has ever gone with more success, and with such joyousness. The 'bloody' almost ruined the play; people laughed too much." "First night Pygmalion" is written, at a later date, in blue pencil in Mrs. Campbell's handwriting.*

Mrs. Campbell was now Mrs. George Cornwallis-West, having married George on 6 April 1914.

(11.4.14)

Dear Joey,
  All success to you to-night.
  Its nice to think of your friendship and your genius—I'll obey orders faithfully, I am so thankful you carried through your giant's work to the finish—

Stella.

33, Kensington Square, W.
[17 April 1914?]

  A thousand things to tell you.
Come soon—or you'll not recognize your play.

181

I hope you make £40 ordinary nights and £80 Wed and Sat—then perhaps you can accept the mushy show with some sort of tolerance.

Please come soon—and *DO WRITE*

I miss your letters and I want to know how much you are singing this divine spring.

My love to you,
Stella.

Tree takes 5 minutes between each word and each bite of the apple in Act 4. I have facial paralysis from trying to express some sort of intelligent feeling so now I hide my face until it is well again.

33, Kensington Square, W.
29th April 1914

Heavens am I really quite so hideous?

It was a great disappointment to me too yesterday—

I will keep from 4.30 Friday free.

Leave the leaf—dont turn over—just scratch out the errors and write sweeter words above—

I am very troubled, but wholesome troubles—

I should like you to take more pictures but to destroy the "wind and water" and "burst paper bag" faces.

Your play *goes* every night most wonderfully—

But Tree's performance is a most original and entertaining affair and most popular with his friends and admirers. Mine is a mere masquerade.

You are no shepherd—or you would have taken more care of your fold—

That is whats the matter with you—There is no shepherd in your heart—But then you never had any little lambs—to teach you—I wish you were a shepherd—dear Joey I send you my love.

Stella West.

◇◇◇◇◇◇◇

*"Grundy" is presumably Sydney Grundy, the playwright,
who died in July of this same year.*

33, Kensington Square, W.
11th May 1914

We tried the German bit of sentiment it went *wonderfully*—You must come again Joey dear. I am nervous
about my part for F. G. Smith and Sheldon said they liked
my *pathos* best thing in the play! !. God knows what maudlin stuff I have let into the part!

Tree and ——¹ supped with George and me at the Carlton
last night.

The managers association have written begging Tree to
leave out the unseemly word!—Grundy I hear has insulted
him and your play in the Daily Mail.

Tree has only one ambition in the world that you should
be pleased with his Higgins—he talks of Lucy with passion
—bless her heart she gave *two* kisses to the blarney stone!

Dont stay away too long—Tell Charlotte to be kind to
me—

I shall have had something to do with that lovely house
you are going to build for her—and the beautiful gardens
you are going to lay out!

My love to you
Stella.

33, Kensington Square, W.
17th June 1914

Oh dear that means you cant come to the matinee
I am sorry, but I daresay it will be pretty abominable.

Your letter—oh Joey Joey—if you could bring yourself to
smoke a pipe you'd see things differently—

¹ Name illegible (may possibly be Sutro).

Queen Alexandra and the Empress of Russia enjoyed your play mightily—and clapped and nodded with joy.

—You—promised *not* to show my photographs in bed—
Your promises are like piecrusts and sorry ones at that!

Stella.

⟡⟡⟡⟡⟡⟡

This letter was written on the very day of the momentous and ominous assassination at Sarajevo.
Norman Trevor: a well-known actor who died in 1929.

Hylands, Chelmsford.
28th June, 1914

Will you see Tree or Alexander please at once?—and me? It is quite absurd that the notice should go up at the end of a £2000 week! Alexander is willing to let me have the St. James, and we can move the play there at once at the end of the fortnight putting in the people I want for America. You will do a little work with them for me wont you—and with me too. I stand to make £600 a week for you in America so you must help me. What about Norman Trevor for Higgins? Tree will have to be approached very tactfully. I can have the St. James the 21st of Sept. and then I can have 3 weeks and then off to America.

I will keep 5.30 tomorrow for you—send me a telegram—Oh your last letter what a tragic resume of your experience! —George is more precious to me than my bones and we are bound together by a gentle and deep understanding of each other.

Lucy sends me a lovely letter—I see her a girl—my heart aches for her—go often to see her now—

Stella.

Bexley, Kent.

13th July 1914

I know all that—but had you bothered to come again after the first night I might have succeeded in pleasing you more. Anyway I would have had a good try.

Have you any objection to my taking *Pygmalion* to a few big towns in September?

George and I go alone to the West Coast of Ireland for 5 weeks with dogs fishing rod servants books and plays. . . .

I wonder how Lucy stands this heat.

I hope to get to her today.

No you dont wound me. I saw into your heart a long time ago.

My love to you

Stella.

◇◇◇◇◇◇

Mrs. Campbell left England in September 1914, and opened with Pygmalion *on 12 October at the Park Theatre, New York. She also toured America in the same play during 1915. She did not return to England until the beginning of 1916, when* Bella Donna *was revived in May of that year at the St. James's Theatre.*

Shaw in this drastic year published his Common Sense about the War *as a supplement to the* New Statesman. *This was regarded in some quarters as nothing short of treasonal propaganda, but time has shown that much of what he wrote was prescient and wise. For example, he wanted us (perhaps a thought prematurely!) to lend our minds to "the problem of how so to redraw the map of Europe and reform its political constitutions that this abominable and atrocious nuisance, a European war, shall not easily occur again." He said further: "It is not enough for the Allies to win: we and not Russia must be the decisive factor in the victory, or Germany will not be fairly beaten. . . . We must have the best army in Europe." This was his "great war article" referred to in this letter.*

185

"Lady Diana" is Lady Diana Manners, now Lady Duff Cooper. Elizabeth Asquith: later Princess Elizabeth Bibesco. Philip is John Masefield's tragedy Philip the King. *The courageous production of a selection from* The Dynasts *took place at the end of November.*

10, Adelphi Terrace, W.C.

6th October 1914

To save your eyes I shall scribble with the typewriter.

I came up from Torquay ten days ago, and have given two of my course of six lectures. The war has spoilt business for the poor Fabian Society cruelly; but the houses (slightly papered) look full; the last time smart persons of a soulful type—Lady Diana, for example,—began to appear among the dowdy real people whom you call, generically, suffragettes. On that occasion I had a ghastly headache, and have had to make such an effort that I spoke rather well.

Tomorrow (Saturday the 7th) my Open Letter to the President of the United States appears in *The Nation*, and will be reproduced, more or less, all over the American Press. If the President has seen *Pygmalion*, he will probably grant my petition if you promise to go and stay with him at the White House. Next Saturday—that is, the Saturday after next—(the 14th) my great war article will appear in England. Its enormous length and the impossibility of holding it back any longer has upset its American publication. The offer was £700 on condition that it did not appear in London until Xmas; but of course such a delay was impossible: the thing is stale enough as it is; so I have had to sacrifice the £700 and tell my agent he must get what he can for it at once or else publish as what the Americans love to call a Broshoor.

All this I tell you, not that it is of much interest directly,

186

but because I shall attribute all your success to the way I am advertising myself.

Forbes Robertson had a week of *Caesar and Cleopatra* in Chicago in competition with your first week of *Pygmalion* in New York, and beat you hollow. You drew only £2000: he drew £2500. This is the just vengeance of Heaven on you for that day when I read *Caesar* to you both, and you kept pinching the man's leg instead of letting him listen. You thought it so silly. And you ate a chop soullessly afterwards.

London is darker than ever. They are trying to frighten the men into enlisting. I am telling them not to enlist until their wives are properly provided for. At present they get sixteen shillings a week until the man is shot, when they get five.

The other day they brought me a card inscribed

STELLA CAMPBELL

I thought it was Mrs. Beech come to demand an engagement; but it was an impostor who said that was her real name and she had been on the stage before Stella was born. Capable looking person, too.

George called here when he got back from that hell; but I was in Torquay and missed him. Then the poor man wrote to me begging me to let him see the New York notices, as you had not sent him any and he knew nothing of what had happened. What a brute you are! He promised to return them with touching solemnity, evidently thinking that the damned things were precious beyond rubies. I was horrified, because I had chucked them all into the waste paper basket after writing my last letter to you with the improper drawing of your shockingly low necked dress which I sent to some other hotel than the one you now write from—the Alcazar or Plaza or some such nonsense. (I shall send this to the theatre). Well, as luck would have it, just then my publishers sent me another set of the notices; so I was able to make George happy, and to conceal my heartlessness in throwing away the others.

He says pathetically that New York is SUCH a long way off. . . .

Charlotte has gone to bed; and I shall keep her awake if I clatter the typewriter. I have, as you see, really no news. You must be frightfully lonely in New York: I believe you would give your soul for five minutes even with me, the cast-off. Or are you wallowing in infinite adulation? As for me—well, no matter about me. I am well and busy; and that is what I am good at and what I am for.

Have you restored Wu Pu to Helen; and has Helen married again? Of Beo I hear nothing. Barker has done a great production of Masefield's *Philip* at Elizabeth Asquith's Covent Garden matinee for the Arts Fund, whatever that may be. Lillah immense in impossible farthingales as the Infanta. Barker is also producing Hardy's *Dynasts* (!!!); but no doubt I told you this before; and anyhow you do not take a proper interest in that talented young man.

G.B.S.

◇◈◇◈◇◈◇

A day or two before this note was written, Laurette Taylor had made her first appearance in London in her husband's sentimental comedy Peg o' My Heart, *and repeated her huge American success.*

The Vanderbilt Hotel, New York.
14th Oct. 1914
The hot weather tired the public—last night they came and the play went gloriously. Dont believe any paper

that says I am sentimental. I'm *quite* simple—years too old—I *can* be heard—and its Laurette Taylor that should have played your heroine. I wonder if you have seen George and heard of his escape from Antwerp?—

I wonder what you are doing and saying. If it is possible for a human being to get any joy out of *living* just now—I hope some joy is with you.

Stella.

I have had the 'grippe'—the doctors attended me—I missed no performances.

◇◇◇◇◇◇

Denis Mackail was at this time working for Mrs. Campbell in connection with the American production of Pymgalion.

10, Adelphi Terrace, W.C.
13th November 1914

. . . I have had a long letter from Denis [Mackail] which I was very glad to get, as he told me what I wanted to know, and is moreover sane, which nobody else is at this moment. This war is getting too silly for words: they make no headway and produce no result except kill, kill, kill. The Kaiser asks from time to time for another million men to be killed; and Kitchener asks for another million to kill them. And now that they have settled the fact that their stupid fighting can't settle anything, and produces nothing but a perpetual Waterloo that nobody wins, why dont the women rise up and say "We have the trouble of making these men; and if you dont stop killing them we shall refuse to make any more". But alas, the women are just as idiotic as the men. Yesterday *The Times* announced that the Lambeth Guardians had decided to discontinue the practice of giving the workhouse children an egg on Xmas morning in order

to bring home to them that their country is at war and that
everybody ought to practice some self-denial. And yet no
thunder falls from heaven. Do we two belong to this race of
cretins?

G.B.S.

P.S. A man sent me quite a nice notice of *Pygmalion* the
other day. It read as if you were really beginning to move
people in Eliza. Denis says you have been unwell and that
you worry about the war. Dont. The real monstrosity about
the war is that, apart from its silly cruelty and destructive-
ness, it has no true importance and wont settle anything.
Put it out of your head; and stay in New York (or America)
until it is over, if you can.

I—but no matter.

G.B.S.

◇◇◇◇◇◇

*The Flag Lieutenant, which, with Cyril Maude in the lead,
first appeared in 1908, was revived (for the second time) 28
November 1914, with Godfrey Tearle as the hero.*

Ayot St. Lawrence, Welwyn.
20/12/14

The other day, having a headache coming on, and
feeling that I must sit down somewhere, I went into the
Haymarket Theatre, where there happened to be a matinee.
The Flag Lieutenant, which was new to me though a re-
vival, was on; and I struck it in the middle, with Tearle and
Aynesworth doing heroic deeds in battle. When we got
back to the inevitable drawing-room in Park Lane, with
Ellis Jeffreys and suite all complete in evening dress on
sofas, who should enter but Stella, now Stella Mervyn
Campbell, who set me wondering whether the others were

made all right and Stella all wrong, or Stella all right and
they all wrong. She looked a perfectly different animal anyhow; and if they turn up together as skeletons or fossils in
some museum in future ages she will be classed as a separate
species. Her arms start lower down; and she has quite a
devil of a lot of neck and sloping shoulder that they have
nothing at all like. They jack themselves up with corsets;
she wears hers below her waist. She was the sympathetic
heroine, and had quite the correct professional air of having her eyes full of blackberry jam and her heart full of
sorrow. She spoke her piece well, and is, I should think,
pretty sure of her livelihood, and the judgelike infant's, for
some years to come. Her part in the last act was so rotten
that she could hardly prevail on herself to come on the stage
and do it, and in some of her tricks and turns she is like her
Ma; but she has a personality of her own. She has quite lost
her old woodenness, and has acquired, instead, an odd resemblance to Lady Mary Murray: a sort of "I'm damned if
I'm going to be goodlooking: that does very well for actresses; but I am in earnest" expression. Nevertheless she *is*
very goodlooking and as distinguished as ever in spite of the
blackberry jam and the professional ease in an easy part.

Laurette Taylor is keeping the Comedy Theatre going
here. I havnt seen her yet.

On Christmas Eve I start on a walking tour with the Sidney Webbs until the 2nd Jan. or thereabouts. I have worked
continuously since the war began, and am exhausted for the
moment. My war pamphlet, which appeared all in one piece
here (they spread it over three weeks in the *New York
Times*) has put me back in my right place again. All the
forts opened fire on me; and they have capitulated one after
the other. The *Daily Telegraph* was so intimidated that it
cut my contribution out of King Albert's Gift Book. No
sooner had the book appeared Shawless than the Belgian
Minister appealed to me for a special article to help the

Belgian fund, and especially to influence America. All sorts
of little scores have occurred; and my enemies are my foot-
stool, and my swank colossal and intolerable.

And you?

Or do I simply bore you now? Have you found anybody
nice in America?

I have no address; so I will send this to Klaw. Tell Denis
to write to me again if he has time. I did not answer his letter, having no news for him; but I was very glad to get it.
He can tell me all about you.

G.B.S.

◇◇◇◇◇◇

*Ellen Terry's letter to Shaw, dated December 1914, began:
"Dearest G.B.S. (who is splendid about the war)." Christopher
St. John, editing their correspondence, points out that many of
Shaw's friends and admirers had joined in a "public chorus of
vulgar abuse" of him, and praises Ellen for having "the courage
of her knowledge." "Edie" was Ellen Terry's gifted daughter,
Edith Craig.*

*Robert Loraine was a distinguished airman and air-fighter as
well as an actor.*

10, Adelphi Terrace, W.C.

13th January 1915

. . . I have just received the returns for your Xmas
week: ruin retrieved by four mammoth performances in
two days. It is curious how steadily it averages out at £1500
a week.

Are they overworking you?

We are quite likely to have bombs dropped on us here as
the year goes on; so perhaps it is as well you are many million miles away. Ellen Terry, who is in New York, writes
to me to see that nothing happens to her Edie. Loraine has

just been describing to me how he dropped four monster bombs on a little town, two in the market place and one at each end of the main street. They shot him (on a subsequent occasion) in the small of his back, the bullet coming out of his collar bone after going through his lung and knocking his heart into his left elbow. The lung is still out of action; but he is fairly robust, and starts for Rio Janeiro the day after tomorrow on a recuperative voyage.

What I said in "Common Sense About the War" is nothing to what I will say presently if this silly business of feeding men into the machine to be killed, absolutely without any other result, goes on and on.

And that is all, Stella. Might be a scrap of newspaper, might it not? Do you never ask yourself what has become of my sonnets?

G.B.S.

The Blackstone, Chicago.
3rd Feb. 1915

Joey dear—

Its quite dreadful—6 more or less nice letters from you to me—and not one from me to you, and you enabling me to earn my daily bread! There's no excuse excepting the hard work of the tour—and three severe colds and a cough and three doctors and a nurse and two nights off— and more than once 9 performances a week and the last week in New York, *eleven* performances, ten of *Tanqueray* —and a tableau with a few words of *Melisande*, and eight of *Pygmalion*.

George is with me now on 3 months sick leave and so I am well again and happy. There was a horrid interview in the paper here the other day, the man, a friend of Robertson, told me Robertson had asked you to take less than 10% for *Caesar and Cleopatra* and you refused—and then

he (the man) made *me* say things about your percentage.
Should you see the interview please pay no attention its all
lies—never mentioned your % or offered any opinion—I
was afraid you would be shut up in the Tower only because
of the length of the article!!

I hear Lillah and Barker are doing splendidly—I am so
glad, they ought to have a brilliant season—You are very
much loved here—Only it *is* a bore how they will read the
deepest and eternal truths into your most topical badinage!

Denis found the hustling work on tour too much—so I let
him go—he has very little energy—and though he is a dear
boy and I am very fond of him—he couldn't be fitted into
the rough work—

George looks after me splendidly and the company and
the business—my side of it—George is an angel—he is a most
beloved man—I dont see how I can let him go back to that
crazy vulgar accursed war—its like a dream having him
here—

I wish you could have seen me play Paula—straight from
Eliza—I took a deep breath! —I send you a programme—

No I dont miss your love-making—and your sonnets! I
know you so well Joey—and just how much you appreciated
me—and how little—

I like Merivale's playing of Higgins immensely—its so
alive—He adores you and is faithful to all you said—I plait
my hair and wear it round my head in the first act and wear
a short jacket and a high neck! I am thinner and I dont look
dreadfully old for the part—Still it would be better if I were
25 years younger—if only you'd write the play I want! but
you cant and wont try—

My love to you and George sends his love too. . . . I
hope noone has disgusted Charlotte as much as you made
me—Such a pity that was—and I ready with a real affection
in my heart for her—but you with your infernal mischief
upsetting her—and betraying yourself hopelessly to me—

I am glad to hear Lucy is no worse—better you say—I send her my love indeed. . . .

Stella.

I am sure no letter at all is better than this vile scrawl! . . .

I would have been saved so much trouble and anxiety and time if in return for my showing *you my* contract with Tyler you had shown me yours!! I am sorry you lost money—I behaved bravely and well—I was sorry for Tyler . . .

10, Adelphi Terrace, W.C.
15th May 1915

Dear Mrs. Patrick Campbell

In pursuance of my conversation with Mr. Cornwallis West in London this morning, and in consideration of your undertaking a summer tour of *Pygmalion* under my agreement with Mr. M. W. Livingston dated 30th December 1914 I authorize you to retain for your own personal use as an addition to your salary one half of such author's fees as may accrue to me under that agreement from the 1st day of June to the thirtieth day of September in the present year in every week during that period in which the gross receipts for the week shall not exceed the sum of four thousand dollars.

Yours faithfully,
G. Bernard Shaw.

$4000:00

10, Adelphi Terrace, W.C.
15th May 1915

Bellissima Stellissima

I have just parted with George at Euston. Our meeting was delayed by my absence in Ireland. I went over there for Easter and returned to London yesterday after-

noon. If I had not forunately rung him up at the Club this
morning after my swim, I should have clean missed him.
He is looking very well in spite of his worries; and Georgina is frightfully fat.

that is her outline.

I enclose you a formal letter which you had better pre-
serve in case I should drop down dead and you should fall
into the hands of merciless executors. Please observe that I
have not reduced my fees: I have simply promised to give
you half of them during the summer when your receipts
fall to £800 a week. The distinction may not be important
to you; but it saves me from a flagrant breach of my Trade
Union obligations to my fellow authors.

Naturally, I have no news: George had to give the news
to me. In Ireland I stayed for a fortnight at Sir Horace
Plunkett's and then went on to Lady Gregory's, where
Augustus John painted six magnificent portraits of me in 8
days. Unfortunately, as he kept painting them on top of one
another until our protests became overwhelming, only three
portraits have survived: and one of these got turned into a
subject picture entitled Shaw Listening to Somebody Else
Talking, because I went to sleep while I was sitting, and
John, fascinated by the network of wrinkles made by my
shut eyes, painted them before I woke, and turned a most
heroic portrait into a very splendidly painted sarcasm.

Lillah is going on tour in America with *Androcles*. What
Barker is going to do I cannot say: probably he doesnt
know himself. He had a great success both as a manager
and after-dinner-speaker: but the expenses were enormous,
as he put up a repertory of four productions instead of wallowing in the success of *Androcles*; so except for the honor

and glory of it, he comes out of it not much richer than he went in.

I hope you got my last cablegram safely. My unfortunate reference to Jorkins and Spenlow roused the worst suspicions of the Censor, who concluded that these cryptic names concealed military secrets to be transmitted to Germany: and I never heard whether the message got through or not. Shortly before this they refused to let through a plain message on theatrical business to Gertrude Kingston because the address of her Hotel was a code word. As it ended with the letter "otel" that did not look very suspicious; but the Censor had apparently never heard of Gertrude Kingston and the message was stopped. Thus are we governed.

[*In Shaw's own writing:*]

I am so rushed that I had to dictate the above: hence its propriety, which belies my wayward heart.

G.B.S.

10, Adelphi Terrace, W.C.

14th June 1915

I have just had your cables about the payment of the royalties, and have replied to them. Also a letter from George.

Lemme explain.

Immediately after George's departure, and after I had written the formal letter to you which you have no doubt received, I got a letter from Livingston, in which, with the usual American theatrical innocence of law and business, he informed me that he had now nothing more to do with *Pygmalion*, and bade me a tender farewell. Thereupon I wrote and explained to him that under the existing agreement he was responsible to me for the royalties on all your performances; that I had no claim whatever on you; that I might drop dead at any moment and leave him in the hands of my executors, who could not recognize any informal friendly arrangement; and that I was quite ready to relieve him by cancelling the agreement if he wished, but until this was done he was responsible for the royalties and I could not recover them from you. On this Klaw and Erlanger cabled to say that it was all a mistake, and that they maintained their guarantee and Livingston's responsibility, which means that they think the play is good for another autumn season and will hold on to it. And this is why they want you to pay through their office, as otherwise they cannot obtain my receipts and be sure that the royalties have been paid. They may also want to know what business you are doing; but this I presume they can ascertain from the theatres.

When your second cablegram announcing the difficulty arrived, I cabled them that as there were some matters of account between us (you and me) it would be more convenient to me to receive the royalties direct from you, and that I would send the receipts direct to them in Mr. Livingston's name, notifying you at the same time that the remittance had arrived safely. I cabled to you at the same time that I had done this, and that the receipts sent to Livingston would be "in full". This means that in such accounts as you may send to K and E (if any) you must shew all payments made to me as at ten per cent. You should instruct Lewis Haase to make his remittance to me, not, as he has just done, in the form of a royalty, of five per cent due to me, but as a royalty of ten per cent, deducting from this half the total as due by the author to Mrs. Campbell. It is necessary to observe this form strictly not only because I must not appear in any theatrical accounts as accepting a royalty of less than ten per cent, but because payments as at five per cent would not discharge Livingston's liability to me under the agreement. Is that clear?

For the first time since you went away I have just met D.D. It was at the Albert Hall, where Beecham is giving orchestral concerts every night to console the unfortunate players for the suspension of the Opera. D.D. had a brother with her. My breast welled with affection for her after so long a separation; and she indulged me with a kind reception. Charlotte in the offing, studied her program, and, beyond an irreproachably bland Howdyedo, owed D.D. no discourse. D.D. is amusing herself at the old Vic Theatre in the Waterloo Road, which seems to be the centre of the dramatic movement nowadays. Her son is at Festubert, unhurt still, or was then.

The Augustus John portrait is at the New English Art Club. I returned from Ireland with the survivors of the *Lusitania* through millions of submarines (imaginary, as it proved) and immediately afterwards went to the lakes for a Conference on the War, followed by a week of walking over mountains. Am now at Ayot, finishing my second pronouncement on this monstrous war. The first one, by the way, is selling still vigorously. Whether it is extinct in America I dont know but when it was alive it was to be procured in the *New York Times* monthly—the number for January last, probably. This is an answer to something that George said about it.

At the Conference at the Lakes I had a good deal of talk with Philip Guedalla, who is a friend of the Mackails.

The latest and best story from the trenches is of two German prisoners. The men gave a little concert and asked that these two prisoners might be allowed to be present. The officer consented, and went off to attend to some other matter. On his return he found the two prisoners standing with a modest air before the audience, and the sergeant announcing "Ahr friends Hans and Fritz will nar eblawge wi' the Ymn of Ate." But I suppose this has reached you long ago. D.D. says that at Festubert there is an immense German who is so popular that there are loud cries of Ludwig, Ludwig, from the British trenches before firing begins. Ludwig takes his call solemnly by rising from his trench and bowing amid loud cheers. On his retirement firing begins in the usual course.

Barker, after colossal but ruinous successes with the Greek drama of Gilbert Murray in the stadia of Boston and Noo York, sails for England on the 19th. He has no prospects beyond a thousand pound lecturing tour next fall, and the tour of *Androcles*; so you will probably have the privilege of supporting him presently unless he is shot as a deserter. He seems to have joined some regiment here casually and then forgotten all about it and gone off to America. I trust it was not a serious unit of our forces.

Ann Elder will send the receipts to Klaw and Haase. I shall have to give her special instructions about them; so they may come a post later than this.

I have had no letter from you for fifty years.

G.B.S.

◇◇◇◇◇◇

Searchlights *was a play by Horace Annesley Vachell. Mrs. Campbell produced it in San Francisco in August 1915.*

Edward Sheldon had just made the success of his career with his play Romance *in 1913.*

Gurney: Edmund Gurney, an actor who died in 1925 (aged seventy-three).

Both Lillah McCarthy and Margaret Anglin had been acting in Greek plays in America this season.

The Washington, St. Louis.
20th September 1915

Joey my dear Joey,
    Here is a letter of mine written to you on July 25th. which was never finished. I am so ashamed of myself, and

the excuse is just fatigue, and the eight performances a week, and sometimes nine, since I started last year; we stop this tour on the 23rd of October, and then George and I go away to Florida for three weeks rest; he fishing. I will sleep under the stars if I can, I mean if the mosquitos don't absolutely gobble me up.

I was out of pocket $7,750:00 getting to San Francisco, in the sweltering heat and the one-night, practically empty towns. The people thought Bernard Shaw "high brow stuff" and would'nt come near him! *Tanqueray* had been done to death by every little Stock Company and on the Movies. In San Francisco we picked up splendidly for the first two weeks (they made a mistake in your percentage I hear—I am so sorry it was my fault, I had'nt given your letter to my business man and they only showed me Miss Elder's letter yesterday. I am having it put right and will send your check tomorrow). I had to have a cheap repertoire company for this summer tour.

The people in the one night towns expressed great disappointment that we never spoke the title of the play; they wanted so much to know how it should be pronounced, whether "Pig-ma-lion—or Pyge-malion"!

My business man "Hasse" told me I couldn't stay in San Francisco four weeks without a third play. George had seen *Search Lights* in London, and liked it and bought an option on it, so I got it ready. During my eight performances a week! It went without a hitch, but the role of the "woman" is too trifling. The public wants my guts, and then again the public here didn't understand the spoiled English boy, they called him a "cad", which upset what little charm there is in the play. I played it six times and give one more performance this week, then I drop it all together.

I propose starting another tour at the end of November playing *Pygmalion* with your permission, in all the towns we haven't visited before.

I wish I had the *Doctor's Dilemma*. I am then going to try two new Plays; one is practically finished, the other one half-way—One is by Miss Crowther and the other by Edward Sheldon.

George insisted on acting with me; he played "Orreyed" in *Tanqueray* and "Doolittle" splendidly, much better than Kent. I am sure Lucy would say "better than Gurney," and he played the lead in *Search Lights*. He works under the name of "George Frederick". Then he got very ill; he worked too hard. I had three good Doctors to see him in San Francisco, and they all said the same thing "brain fag". I was terrified; I felt it was all my fault; the Doctors said he must go into the mountains and sleep in the open air for six weeks; he went, but came back in two, much better, but not well; so then I sent him to Glenwood Springs, Colorado, fishing. He came back in ten days quite himself and looking splendid. Now he is playing again. He is so clever, I wish you could see him, and is adored by every one. He may return to England at the end of the year and settle up his financial difficulties and report to the War Office; I hope they won't want him, he looks so happy and well now.

I have grown quite plain and my hair is getting gray, but then the newspapers in this country are enough to make us all maniacs. A few Sundays ago in enormous headlines "British Navy Sunk".

I have been and am very anxious about Beo. He got ill in the trenches at the Dardanelles and was sent to Alexandria; they promoted him to the staff, making him Assistant Provost Marshal; so he censored his own letter to me; such a beauty, but it breaks one's heart to read; only three men left out of the platoon; only two hundred out of George's thousand; then a cable came from him saying—"the doctors had 'ploughed' him." Three days after another cable saying the "Board had 'passed' him", and then a cable from the Adjutant Paymaster Wilson, saying "he had returned to the front". No more news, except the big engagement of August 29th reported here and five thousand casualties. O the enormity and eternal bloody error of this war!

My English papers for the last four or five weeks have been stolen, or have gone down in ships, so we know nothing about the raid. I am hoping you will write to me. Do please! I thought Lillah and Barker seemed disappointed with their American Season. They should not be. They made a fine impression—and it's a pity they went back. If they had risked a summer tour as I did, I think if carefully managed, they would come out all right.

Margaret Anglin did wonders with the Greek plays. Many thousands at all her performances. I have not seen her. Her productions with Damrosch are very showy and concocted affairs I believe, but delight the public.

Hearst goes to New York today to oppose the loan, and one is wondering what will happen.

I miss you very much; I wish you were here.

I have cleared off the heavy debt to Hoare's Bank, that troubled me so when I was ill, and I have settled a thousand smaller things, and sent away a good bit to help people. I have let Stella and her baby and nurse go to Kensington Square, and my good servant is there with them. Stella is working hard and I should say by her letters is a little lonely and worried. You might ring her up; I am sure she would be delighted. I am sending you my latest portrait; it is not quite such a fool looking thing as most. George sends you his love and is so anxious that you should see him play. He wants you to write an Irish part for him; he is very set on his brogue!

Now I am going to look through a big packet of cuttings to find something to amuse you. Give Lillah and Barker my love. Tell him I got my chess men safely. I wonder whether I will ever see you again. My love to you.

Stella.

✧✧✧✧✧✧

"George Frederick Handel" was a Shavian nickname for George Cornwallis-West.

Ayot St. Lawrence, Welwyn.

19th December 1915

You sent me a long letter at last which was so welcome that I immediately resolved never to write again lest I should relapse into infatuation; for I would have you to know that I am now a reformed character; sing nothing but masses; and have consequently recovered my almost forfeited voice and got it into order like the voice of a priest, just as it would have pleased my mother.

However, the returns from Newark give me an irresistible opportunity to preach. I dont know what sort of place Newark is; but when it comes to houses of thirty pounds it is time to look for a new play or New York or London engagement at somebody else's risk. Enormously successful plays like *Pygmalion* are the most dangerous plays in the world. Nine times out of ten they are run on until every farthing they have made is lost again. That is what will happen to you with *Pygmalion* unless you stop in time. If you cannot find a new play, go and live in a cottage until you do find one; it will be cheaper than losing money at the rate *Pygmalion* will lose it once it begins to fall down hill. There is also the loss of prestige: all the New York people—the Shuberts and Klaws and Erlangers and the rest—know what business you are doing, and value you accordingly.

Besides, I have passed *Pygmalion* for press among the sheets of my new volume of plays; and it now has a sequel, not in dialogue, but in prose, which you will never be able to live up to. It describes in an absolutely convincing manner how Eliza married Freddy; how she realized her dream of a florist's shop; how neither of them knew how to keep shop; how she had to beg from the Colonel again and again to avert bankruptcy; how the wretched pair had to go to shorthand and typewriting commercial schools to learn; how they went even to the London School of Economics and to Kew Gardens simultaneously to learn about business and flowers and combine the information; how Eliza wrote such a shameful hand that she had to abase herself to Higgins to be taught his wonderful Italian handwriting; how Clara was converted by H. G. Wells and Galsworthy and went into a shop herself and saved her soul alive; how the flower shop began to pay at last when they tried asparagus and Freddy became Mr. Hill, greengrocer; how Eliza never got out of the habit of nagging Higgins that she acquired in the fourth act, and, though deeply interested in him, did not quite like him any more than she liked her father, who was rejected by the middle classes and forced into the highest society, where he was a huge success but poorer than he had ever been in his life before on his four thousand a year. The publication of that sequel will be the end of the romance of Sir Herbert Tree; and you will have to play Eliza properly and seriously for ever after, which is impossible.

Major Barbara has been produced in New York after ten years by Calvert and Grace George; and Mr. Grace George whose name is William Brady, wires me that it is an enormous success, which I do not doubt, though it remains to be seen whether it will last a fortnight. If it does, my stocks may go up to the point of making some manager mad to try *Getting Married*, which contains the most wonderful of all my serio-tragic woman's parts, suitable to a female of advanced years with the remains of irresistible beauty. The part of St. John Hotchkiss (Hankin) offers a field for the talent of George Frederick Handel which will test his skill to the utmost if he ventures on it. But how to get it produced unless I were there to stand over you with a broomstick (and I can bear no more than that) is an insoluble problem.

Barker lingers in New York at the Algonquin Hotel, producing endless literature in fulfilment of his solemn renunciation of the theatre. It was for him that I held up *Major Barbara* so long. Although he selected a financially disastrous moment to save his soul I cannot complain; for I have all along urged him not to waste his prime on the tomfoolery of producing. He got a job from the Red Cross people to report on the hospital arrangements at the front, and went over there in khaki and stood in Ypres with shells raining on him to sample that banal sensation.

I have not seen Stella junior, (who now calls herself Stella Beach Comber) I am by no means convinced that she pines to see me unless I have a part for her. To her I am, apart from dramatic authorship, only an absurd old josser whom her mother made a fool of, the old lady being incorrigible in that direction. Helen has written asking for news of you, and possibly wanting news of Alan.

I saw Lucy the other day and was told that it was my first visit for six months, though it seemed to me to be six weeks. She is in bed, frightfully ill; anyone else would be dead after such a relapse; but she will no doubt pull through. She always asks for news of you; and I supply as much as I happen to possess.

I appeared on the London platform at the end of October and lectured twice on the war. Riots were expected; but the result was three hundred people turned away, and only two questions, both about Jesus Christ. Similar results next time. Then I promised Sylvia Pankhurst a lecture; but when it was announced the proprietors of the hall, alarmed by the breaking up of a meeting the week before, cancelled the engagement; so I had to go to the Portman Rooms. Result: full house and thirty pounds collected for Sylvia's "Mother's Arms"—not Mrs. Pankhurst's but a public house which Sylvia has converted into a school for mothers.

Androcles is on tour in the States, doing just too well to be taken off, but not well enough as yet to shew much profit on its enormous expenses. Lillah would not go with it—calls the part supering—and is here looking round for work now that the family theatre no longer exists.

I note with satisfaction that you have at last realized that my regular terms are worth taking when the receipts are below $500 a night. I stick to these terms partly from greed; partly because I shall have to change for everybody if I change for you, as everybody demands a "most favored nations clause"; partly because the moment you feel those terms heavy it is time for you to drop the play; and partly because it is clearly the divinely appointed order of the Universe that women should slave for men. I hope *Barbara* will now come to the rescue of my American affairs; but if it had not been for you, last winter would have been ruinous for me. As it was, I could only scrape together £20,000 for the war loan, returning a mere £900 a year. You are, by the way, shewing the utmost practical patriotism in sending money from America to this country and thereby redressing the deplorable rate of exchange.

George Frederick's exploits on the stage, as to the complete success of which I have pledged myself, has created some sensation among his admirers here. Gurney, however, appeals to me to write him a star play; describes G. F. as "my lord"; and evidently regards him as a shameless blackleg doing a skilled workman out of his job. Wheater is still in business, and offers me blocks of Pinner Hall shares from time to time at knock-out prices, the war loan having made everything unsaleable of a steady kind.

This, I think, is all the news. Your photograph is too young and beautiful to be true: you should see ME: I look seventy. The theatre is passing away from me as a sort of wild oats; I go back to politics, religion and philosophy. They give me frightful headaches, but satisfy my soul.

G.B.S.

Mrs. Campbell returned to England early this year for Sir George Alexander's revival of Bella Donna *at the St. James's in May.*

Ruthin Castle, N. Wales.
[early 1916]

Oh Joey dear I owe you a letter—letters—I hope they cabled you from New York that this tour was over—

I could'nt go on. I was finished—I did'nt know one could be so tired and live—I had a masseuse in New York just before I left who said she could *feel* my inflamed nerves. When I lay down I could'nt get up, and when I sat up I could'nt lie down, and when I laughed I cried, so I thought it well to stop acting for a bit!

I hope you made £10,000.

I practically cleared all my liabilities and have a few pounds for a few weeks rest and I am very grateful—

George and I have had a fortnight's bliss here—1,000 acres of loveliness—Meadows and woods and singing birds and the young green on the trees, and the blue blue hills and lawns and old fashioned gardens and dungeons and secret passages and a soft green hollow where the moat was, and we sleep in a large room where my beloved George was born—and there's peace everywhere—a divine peace—

How to come back to London and the hellish brawl next week I don't know—

George says you have been so friendly and kind to him—there is no one like you when you are friendly Joey.

Of course *the* play has amazed me—he has worked on it here and made the love scene stronger—brought the Irish servant into it—it is new—a miracle of fun and feeling—the ease with which George writes and the colour is very astonishing. I am grateful he has this talent and I believe it will grow and be a fine amusement to us both—and who knows! perhaps pull up his fortunes a bit!—There is a great deal to hear and tell you dear Joey and I look forward to seeing you again with much happiness.

Stella.

Ayot St Lawrence, Welwyn.
14th May 1916

Stella

I have had influenza, and in spite of a fortnight by the sea, I feel suicidal. I dont believe all this about George needing a large room to be born in: he would have fitted into a small one just as well. My new volume should have been out a month ago, but there was no labor to print it, no labor to bind it, no ships to carry it to London, and no goods train taking less than three months to come to London from Edinburgh, where my printing is done. I send you an advance copy—the first that has left my hands—indeed the only one—but do not go dropping it about, as no one must see it until publication is at last achieved. The sequel to *Pygmalion* is on page 191. It will not interest you; but George will read it. I assume that you are in London; but I dont care: I never felt so morose in my life. Lucky for you to make money by *Pygmalion*. I must have lost by it; for my income is down by nearly half. I cant write: nothing comes off but screeds for the papers, mostly about this blasted war. I am old and finished. I, who once wrote whole plays *d'un seul trait*, am creeping through a new one (to prevent myself crying) at odd moments, two or three speeches at a time. I dont know what its about. I began it on the 4th March: and I have hardly come to the beginning of the first scene yet.

Barker is in America. He is only 39, and liable for military service under the new Act. Everything has gone to the devil. If you have begun rewriting George's play, God help it and him! I told you not to do those one-night stands: they are always the last straw; but when have you ever done what I told you except when I was standing over you with a poker? This is a rotten world. George looked tired when he came back: I do not think he has long to live. You must be feeling very old and feeble. Your handwriting is improved but there is always some little rally before the end. I wonder which is the easiest: charcoal, morphia, or prussic acid. Well goodbye: we shall probably never meet again. Lucy's address for the moment is 2 Grove Park, Camberwell Grove, S.E. Later on, The Crematorium, Golders Green, N.W.

G.B.S.

◇◇◇◇◇◇

Lady Alexander always supervised the dresses in her husband's productions.

[approx. June 1916]

Oh Joey dear do come along and see me—your nice letters and the lovely book—and not a moment for me to write a word—Trashy *Bella Donna* is having a success. I loved the Merci picture, and adored the Jackal and whatever that darling creature nosing about was. I wanted to go to Lucy this afternoon but Lady A. wants me to wear some other kind of gown.

I am bursting with news and questions. Come any time. I have tried to get you on the phone and so did George. You were away.

My love always,
Stella.

33, Ken S.

[undated; 1916]

Oh Joey do come soon—I think *very little persuasion* and Sir George A. will do *Pygmalion* in the Autumn. There is much to talk to you about—I am trying to get to Lucy this afternoon.

My love to you,

Stella.

I send you my Beo's last two letters—*do* send him a postcard of yourself wishing him luck.

Lieut. Alan Campbell

1st Anson Batt. Royal Naval Division

British Expeditionary Force,

France.

C/O GPO

⬦⬦⬦⬦⬦⬦

The movie was a (silent) burlesque film of a Western—with G. K. Chesterton, G.B.S., and Hilaire Belloc as cowboys fooling. It was specially taken for a charity matinée (for the Red Cross) and included in a performance of J. M. Barrie's Rosy Rapture, *with Gaby Deslys as the star.*

33, Ken Sq.

8 June 1916

Do ring me up when you are in town. You'll see by the enclosed I am not too fat and ugly to be spoken to. Charity recitation today—God what a fool I make of myself—and to-morrow an introduction before a movie of yourself rolling down a hill in a barrel to be spoken by me at the Coliseum and then I'll have a moment for dear Lucy.

My love to you,

Stella.

[approx. July 1916]

Joey dear you have two of my boy's letters, let me have them please.

I dont know *what* you have said to Alexander but it has effectively put him off doing *Pygmalion*—I am sorry.

Your man McDermot [*sic*] saw me and wanted me to do just the one week at Birmingham!! But it didn't seem worth-while.

It would be nice to see poor Lucy—he took care of her and was devoted I feel sure—She will miss him!

Stella.

10, Adelphi Terrace, W.C.
9th July 1916

On my way up today (to see a Stage Society show) I posted a letter to George about Australia—nothing important—only a formality. I have looked in for a moment before my train goes, and find your letter, which still pleases me from mere habit.

On the whole I think G. A. is right. Whilst the war lasts it will never be safe to have a play of mine running; for if I have another piece of my mind to give to this silly nation, nothing will stop me. Better wait until you can produce the play without risk.

You ask what I have done with Beo's precious letters. That is exactly what has been bothering me ever since I looked for them to put into my last letter and couldnt find them. For once I am really concerned and apologetic; but they will turn up presently: I know they are safe somewhere. Forgive me.

I must rush for the train.

G.B.S.

◇◇◇◇◇◇

Mrs. Campbell produced Robert Hichens's one-act play The
Law of the Sands *in October 1917 at the London Opera House.*

> 33, Kensington Square, W.
>
> 27th July 1916

Its your birthday today Joey dear and here's my love
to you.

I wonder when I shall see you again. My beloved George
is at Aldershot—he is writing to you.

Lucy has sent me a particularly charming letter.

Hichens has written an effective one-act play for me for
the Halls, and thats what I will be doing in a minute I
expect.

George will go to France quite soon with the 57th Division. Beo is still with his guns.

> My love to you.
>
> Stella.

◇◇◇◇◇◇

*Charles Macdona (frequently referred to in the letters): an
actor-manager who sent out touring companies of West End
successes (especially Bernard Shaw's) to the Continent and the
Near and Far East as well as round Great Britain and Ireland.
In 1920 he organized the Macdona Players in Shaw plays. Shaw
is credibly reported to have scouted Macdona's idea that he
should invest money in the enterprise with the words: "Thank
you, but I do not wish to spend the evening of my days in the
workhouse, and the fact that you would be there too would
not be sufficient consolation."*

10, Adelphi Terrace, W.C.2.

27th July 1916

Your telephone reports you out of town: why do you go away without asking my leave?

The other day a sacked Doolittle, seeking my intercession, and being apparently familiar with the private affairs of the aristocracy, informed me that you had inherited 10,000 acres and "chucked the stage".

Macdona, whom I met this morning, unfolded himself to the same effect, and wants to know can he have those towns N O W.

As the death of your father-in-law gives a certain plausibility to those rumors, I should like to know whether I am to regard you in future as the chatelaine of Ruthin, and have my love for you described as a scandal in high life, or as a mere professional slave.

Having had the misfortune to inherit a property myself, I shall not congratulate George until I know what it is worth. What came to me was a bundle of poor relations, a bundle of mortgages, and a bundle of pawn tickets. I experimented with one of the pawn tickets by releasing a gold watch for £3.10.0 I then went to a place in the city to which my solicitor directed me and shoved the watch in through a little window with my name and address. It was sold by auction for £3.10.0, which I received less commission. I put the other pawn tickets in the fire, and confidently advise George to do the same if his heritage includes any.

I paid off the mortgages, which were at 6 per cent, by borrowing the money from my wife at 4. I recommend this course to George. Later on I paid them off; but this I do not recommend.

For poor relations nothing is of any use but strychnine.

G.B.S.

Read the last line first.

The White Hart Hotel, Sedbergh.

4.9.16

I am wandering about, ostensibly to take a holiday, really to give the servants one. Charlotte is in Ireland. I went to Glastonbury for the musical festival; then came on here, where the Fabians are having what is called a Summer School. I shall stay here until the 16th with the Sidney Webbs.

If you ask me what the devil it is to you what I am doing or where I am, I reply that if you were told of the existence of a comet, you would want to know where it was and wonder what it was doing. Well I am at least as interesting as a comet. In fact I am a sort of comet; and I brandish my crystal tresses in the sky accordingly. Shakespear *that*. Anyhow, here is a letter; and if you dont want to read it you neednt, as there is business in it.

In Glastonbury I tried to fascinate a young provincial woman of twentyone, a mere local amateur prima donna, who will, when she is thirtyfive, fascinate the Empire, after leaving most of its households in ruins. When I arrived here, I struck up a precipitous flirtation with Rebecca West. Rebecca is an extremely clever young woman whose critical writings in the papers have been startling everyone for the last few years. Rebecca can handle a pen as brilliantly as ever I could, and much more savagely. We fell into one another's arms intellectually and artistically: and if I had not turned 60 and been afraid of being ridiculous, not to say disgusting, we might almost have fallen into one another's arms quite unmetaphorically. When we were wandering over the fells together, she suddenly began talking about you. She said you were perfectly beautiful, and she did not believe a bit of what people said about your being difficult or devilish (she had evidently met some poor

trampled author who *knew*) and didnt care anyhow; you
were just a delight to her. This, for some reason, was a
great comfort to me; and to show my gratitude I told her
that I quite agreed with her, and had in fact, at an advanced
age at which I ought to have known better, fallen head over
ears in love with you, absolutely like a boy of 18 and a baby
of 8 rolled into one. "Then why", said Rebecca wonder-
ingly, "did she marry somebody else?" I said I didnt know,
except that he was a nice fellow, and very fond of you. It
was quite charming of Rebecca to be surprised that any
woman loved by ME could ever be conscious of the existence of anyone else, and to doubt whether History would
ever forgive you. I said that she had better write a play for
you; and though she said she couldnt write plays she will
probably try. So if you come across Rebecca West (real
name Fairfield) speak her fair: she may be useful.

George wrote to say that he is now Assistant Provo-
Marshal in the 57th. As the Provo-Marshal hangs people, I
presume that the assistant cuts them down. He also shoots
Skeffingtons and other considered Irish persons. Why does
George take on these jobs instead of insisting of being at
least a Lieutenant General D.S.O. (Dug Solemnly Out).
Such modest devotion invites depreciation in this blessed
realm. . . .

And now, where are *you* and what are *you* doing? It
seems unnatural that I should not know—even still.

Forgive this small writing. Use a magnifying glass and it
will be quite legible.

G.B.S.

33, Kensington Square, W.

18th Jan 1917

I'm waiting D.D.'s answer. I cannot manage it here worse luck. My servant has been telegraphed for and you must be dined nicely.

My love to you,
Stella.

Ayot St. Lawrence, Welwyn.

7th March 1917

You have sent me half a letter, scrawled in a most uneducated manner. Send me the rest and I will answer it. What I have seems to be the last two sheets. Let me have the first six. There are four depths of illiteracy, each deeper than the one before.

1. The illiteracy of Henry Irving.

2. The illiteracy of those illiterate enough not to know that he is illiterate.

3. The illiteracy of those who have never read my works.

4. The illiteracy of Eliza, who couldnt even read the end of her own story.

There is only one person alive who is such a Monster of illiteracy as to combine these four illiteracies in her single brain. And I, the greatest living Master of Letters, made a Perfect Spectacle of myself with her before all Europe.

G.B.S.

❖❖❖❖❖❖

Mrs. Campbell had just appeared at the Coliseum in a one-act play by George West called Pro Patria (*February 1917*).

The "wedding gift" is a reference to the seventeen volumes of his works which G.B.S. gave her—twelve on 17 May 1914 and five more on 22 May 1914.

W. B. Yeats had written a play for her called The Player Queen.

33, Kensington Square, W.
[*circa* March 1917]

Joey dear would *How he lied to Her Husband* do
for the Coliseum? Would you let me play it there—I have
never read it—shame upon me. And now I have hunted
through your beautiful wedding gift and its not there!
Yeats reads me his play on Tuesday 6 o'c.

Both George and I hunger for you—George is silly about
you. I am wise.

My love to you,
Stella.

You really can write warm letters—I adore them.

33, Kensington Square, W.
11th April 1917

Joey dear I want to see you about *Pygmalion* I have
an idea which may or may not appeal to you. I shall be delighted if it does.

Yours,
Stella.

We are both starving for a sight of you. Any afternoon
and dinner will be a joy. I'll cook for you.

A vegetable soup macaroni salade cheese Devonshire
cream fruit, and brown good bread—Frid or Sat—Mon. Tues
or Wed. the sooner the better.

33, Kensington Square, W.
18th April 1917

Oh dear me, as though I didn't know *all that* years
ago! My weight—and my waist—have been outside magical
dreams for 20 years!

I don't think it would harm *Pygmalion* to be played for
12 weeks with the 4th Act omitted and a few lines cut—I
know it would be doing me a tremendous favour. You
might offer McDougall [*sic*] those 6 towns in return! Its
you and your fees I'm worrying about—these dark nights—
they won't give me more than £200 and the company and
dresses will come over that. *I* have to pay authors fees and
I can't give more than £25. You poor poor *rich* man, how
about *that*?

There is no reason why you should oblige me—saving me
risks and rehearsals—if I were your niece or Charlotte's
cousin it would be different!

I lean strangely towards the Yeats play in spite of my
sagging jowl!—I like these 'treading on air' parts. . . .

My beloved Beo is in great danger and my heart aches and
the hours are heavy.

> My love to you
> Stella.

> 33, Kensington Square, W.
> 9th June /17

Dear Joey,

Where are you these beautiful Summer days?

Do you think Mac Dona would like me to play Eliza in
the big towns with him?

It isn't worth while for me to enter a production for these
few weeks—and I should like to play them.

Write me a line or better still let me see you.

Theres the promise to Lucy—and I want very much to
see her new house!

> My love to you,
> Stella.

33, Kensington Square, W.

15th June /17

Dear Joey,

George insults me by saying "you had much better let Shaw approach McDona he will get you better terms!"

If you will write to him and not make me feel an absolute *brute* ousting the other lady whom I am sure looks and plays Eliza better than I did, or ever could—and get me enough salary to pay for Elizas two smart frocks—my hotels —keep 33 Ken S. going for the 5 weeks I am away and for 4 or 6 months afterwards—until Stoll gives me another 3 weeks at the Coliseum I shall be eternally grateful—

George and I are living for the 5 hours reading of your play. If on a Sunday, at any time and any place you say. If a week day it must be after 7 p.m. George doesn't get back from his A.P.M. duties until then.

Is there a part for an "inspired half-wit" that you can offer Tree then perhaps it will be done in the autumn at H.M.—

I could join McDona almost immediately if he wants me.

With love,

Stella.

◇◇◇◇◇◇

The play read on this occasion was Heartbreak House. *It remained unacted in London till 1921.*

33 Kensington Square, W.

25th June 1917

It was good of you beyond words to read to us and tire yourself as you did.

—I have *no* hesitation in feeling that I listened to a very fine play the first act delights me—you beget your dramatis personæ like a God—but as you went along you lost respect for their bones. They didn't always stand steady on their feet.

Your pen makes you drunk. You look for the keyhole with your hat!—You become unkind—you lose respect of persons—of your own dramatis personæ—and it gives a boneless locomote a-taxi [*sic*] effect—and the people become mere mouthpieces of the general scheme—without bones flesh or blood—I feel *disorder* where you would probably feel "there I was inspired"

Ah but you think me a fool.

I remember the diagram you sent—of my poor brain all black with only the smallest ray of light—well perhaps its this little bit of light which compels me to say, "Well-knit the bones of the people in your play and their words will be the words of a prophet".

—Ibsen's peoples bones are so magnificent that even translations cant give them the rickets.

But I am so grateful to you.

I wish I was a man and old enough for Shotover

Your affectionate goose,

Stella.

Ayot St. Lawrence, Welwyn.

1st August 1917

Damn your 6% I am not a money lender. Also you have *Pygmalion* reserved for *you* in 6 big cities, and not for anybody else. You cannot transfer the part, and therefore you have nothing to sell. If you wont make the tour, it goes to anybody who will, leaving you in outer darkness.

Of course you want to sell your power of hanging the play up. You wanted to do that for America; and where would you be if I had let you? It is a long time since you have been round the provincial capitals; and it is important that you should go with a sure success, and make the local managers anxious to give you dates in future. You *must* go if you do not mean to retire and leave George to starve. You ought to go to Macdona and get your £250 from him as an advance: he would be glad to secure you in that way. But as that would lame your power of bargaining with him, I will make you the advance myself. You must undertake to go on the tour, with Macdona or how you please, before the 30th June next, when I shall have to pay the second instalment of my income tax for 1917–18; for I may be penniless by then. The Americans have just come down on me for arrears of tax amounting to about £600; and what it will be next year Heaven only knows:

Talk of Jews: *I'll* Jew you. I'll drive you on that tour whip in hand.

In great haste: I shall lose the post if I try to answer the rest of your letter.

ever

G.B.S.

33, Kensington Square, W.

2/8/17

In bed acute tonsilitis temp 100° $\frac{6}{0}$ [*sic*].

How more than kind of you dear Joey I am really *very* grateful to you—

I hear Alexander is too ill to do his autumn tour. If this is true couldn't Macdona get those 6 towns and I will do them with him after my Coliseum engagement.

I have forgotten what you in one of letters seemed to suggest I might ask Macdona— £100 a week and what percentage?

I send you my love and thanks.

Stella.

◇◇◇◇◇◇

The play was Simaetha *at the Duke of York's. It appears to have run for very few weeks, as Mrs. Campbell's next marked success,* The Thirteenth Chair, *was produced at the same theatre in October 1917.*

33, Kensington Square, W.

29th Aug. 1917

Joey do come soon and see the play. it nearly killed me doing it. The first thing was to cut the stage in half which I did with a tent—the second to introduce a thrill which I did by introducing a fire and being burnt before the audience! its quite a little success.

I am always wishing I could see you. please manage something

My love to you,

Stella.

43, Savoy Court.

7th Jan 1918

My beloved Beo is killed—you have seen it in the papers. I feel he is asleep, and will wake and come to me if I am quite strong and calm—

I have your little letter—they gave me £275, and I paid author and brought actors but not scenery which they provided generously.—

Stella.

The chaplain writes that Beo and the Commanding Officer were standing at the top of the stairs of their dug-out and a shell burst and killed them both instantaneously—I would like you to read the letter it is full of tragic gentleness and praise of my brave son.

10, Adelphi Terrace, W.C.2.

7th January 1918

Never saw it or heard about it until your letter came.

It is no use: I cant be sympathetic: these things simply make me furious. I want to swear. I *do* swear. Killed just because people are blasted fools. A chaplain, too, to say nice things about it. It is not his business to say nice things about it, but to shout that "the voice of thy son's blood crieth unto God from the ground."

To hell with your chaplain and his tragic gentleness! The next shell will perhaps blow *him* to bits; and some other chaplain will write such a nice letter to *his* mother. Such nice letters! Such nice little notices in papers!

Gratifying, isnt it. Consoling. It only needs a letter from the king to make me feel that the shell was a blessing in disguise.

No: dont show me the letter. But I should very much like to have a nice talk with that dear chaplain, that sweet sky pilot, that—

No use going on like this, Stella. Wait for a week; and then I shall be very clever and broadminded again, and have forgotten all about him. I shall be quite as nice as the chaplain.

Oh damn, damn, damn, damn, damn, damn, damn, damn, D A M N

D A M N !

And oh, dear, dear, dear, dear, dear, dearest!

G.B.S.

❖❖❖❖❖❖

G.B.S. had an attack of ptomaine poisoning in February 1918.

15/2/18

Dear Joey
    I saw Barrie and was quite alarmed at his description of your illness. I thought you were joking a little. I can't believe it was the —— that we all drank so freely, but I hope it was—then it isn't anything more serious—Mind you come and see me soon.

                                                                            Stella.

                                    Egton, Grosmont, Yorks.
                                        16th Aug. /18

Dear dear Joey,
    How horrible it is not hearing from you.
    I have been at Ruthin N. Wales for 3 months. At first I loved the weeks of quiet. I wanted to think and think and realize what had happened to me—then the days were long and wretched in spite of the beauty of this place. George has now 14 days leave. We are here he murdering birds and trying to murder salmon—We go back to Ruthin on Monday.
    Please make some arrangement for me with Macdona. —On my way here I had my hair washed in Leeds—the girl told me *Pygmalion* had been there twice and was an enormous success. I thought Leeds was a first class town. I am sure a revival would be a fine thing though perhaps its a little cruel that I should spoil Eliza with my want of youth and slimness!
    Are you hard up? Let me know—*do* please write me a long letter and tell me how Lucy is and where.
    George sends you his love and so do I.

                                                                            Stella.

[*circa* September 1918]

Joey dear,

I wish you would come—
I am free on the 29th for Eliza if anyone wants me——tour or otherwise.

Yours
Stella.

43, Savoy Court.
Sept. 1918

Dear Joey,

Where are you? I am glad Barker is happy—he has suffered a good deal—and now the "stars have fallen upon him".

I have seen Macdona, and I have a heap to tell you.

I leave here for three dreadful weeks of the *13th Chair* Bir[mingham]—Man[chester]—and Liverpool, and then I hope *Pygmalion* in London!—but Macdona has'nt a brave enough heart, I am afraid—don't say I said so—

There is a dowdy wariness that makes me yawn. its born not of wisdom but of chicken-heartedness—however—come and call me a fool soon.

Yours
Stella

◇◇◇◇◇◇

Mrs. Campbell moved into her new house early in 1919.

Savoy Court.
[early 1919]

Thank you Joey for that stamped receipt—how funny of you—Do hurry Mac Donna.

226

I dont want to be idle a moment.

I have taken a house—15, Tedworth Square Chelsea. Quite nice and a room for George's big retriever "Sylvie" (poor Beppo has gone) and his golf sticks and fishing rods— and a marble floor to the drawing room—very low rent.

The Shooting Party fell through. I spent my Christmas with Stella and little Pat, George spent his in bed at New-lands, to his Mother's delight.

I had a nice dream about Charlotte, she shook hands with me warmly and smiled and said "I thought you were a bird of Paradise and you are only a silly goose"—it struck me as very funny in my dream but it is not so very funny on paper.

You might look in one morning and talk to me.

You promised to send me *Heartbreak House*.

My love to you,
Stella.

◇◇◇◇◇◇

Mrs. Campbell had been busy arranging and decorating her new house in Tedworth Square for the "last four months".

Judith: a play by Arnold Bennett, with Lillah McCarthy in the leading part.

15, Tedworth Square, Chelsea.
5th May /19

Joey dear do come and see me next Thurs. Frid. or Sat. and see what I have been doing for the last four months, and whether you think it worth while! often I have wanted to see you, but felt things must be a little more tidy first. I have been reading what you have been saying, and I have been smiling and wishing I had heard you speak.

George has been going on with the foolish A.P.M work —I wish he was doing something else.

—I see *Judith* on Wednesday and look forward to it.

My love to you.

Stella.

15, Tedworth Square, Chelsea.

13th Aug. /19

I wish you were near—perhaps soon I'll be going to Cork. George is A.P.M. there—and I believe loving it. He writes today he wants me to come—I'm too old for Eliza— I may go to America quite soon—I am not wanted here—I have offered to take 10% to 12%—they call me "Englands greatest actress"! but there it ends—

Couldn't I play Methuselah I am very old and very wise now—You often called me a fool but never told me how great a fool I was—

You with your "highbrow business relieved by dancing flirting and mixed bathing will be gay and fit for Paradise" I'm a dull dog.

Stella.

❖❖❖❖❖❖

Mrs. Campbell has written "5th Jan/19," but the postmark is 6 Jan. 1920—and this is correct because the revival of Arms and the Man *was in December 1919. G.B.S. makes a similar mistake the following year.*

15, Tedworth Square

5th Jan /19

Dear Joey

I meant to write to you some weeks ago, and tell you how delighted I was with *Arms and the Man* it went splen-

didly—heavenly chuckles all around me. I went with D.D.—
she spent four days at Christmas here. . . .

Someday when you feel inclined to come and see me. I
shall be very glad.

Yours
Stella.

❖❖❖❖❖❖

*Viola Tree started in management at the Aldwych in the
previous year. She revived* Pygmalion *there with Mrs. Campbell on 10 February 1920. Agnes Thomas was an actress of the
old school who had played in her youth with Ristori.*

Ayot St. Lawrence, Welwyn.
18/1/20

Your latest formula, as disclosed to me perforce under threat of instant withdrawal of the play, does not touch
me; and I have no objection to it; but oh! what a silly old
Mrs. Crummles you are to suppose that your name needs
those trimmings! I should like, by God, to see anyone dare
to decorate the name BERNARD SHAW with any im-
pertinences about special arrangements.

I also learn that you have "lost" your promptbook. You
think I should be shocked by all the cuts and gags. Nonsense! trot it out: I shant be surprised.

Poor Viola has already got that dreadful look on her face
that Boucicault had when you were rehearsing Barrie's play.

How *can* you?

She has engaged Aubrey Smith for Higgins, Doolittle is
still unsettled. I have demanded Agnes Thomas for Mrs.
Pearce: with her you will be like a poor little rabbit with a
stoat.

Now we shall quarrel for the next month. Oh Stella, Stella, Stella, why did God afflict us with one another?

in hot haste
G.B.S.

15, Tedworth Square, Chelsea.
19th Jan. /20

Dear Joey,

You make a fine mistake if you think I am out for quarrelling!

—I am grateful to be relieved from all responsibility of rehearsals, and I hope I am going to be excused from some of them, in view of my having played "Eliza" over 500 times!

You know I work quickly, didnt I arrive in New York on a Wednesday and produce the play on the Saturday without a hitch?—a brilliant success too! Now Eliza—and Eliza only is my business—

It was *Barrie* who changed the expression of Boucicault's face—when he said "she'll do better if you leave her alone".

The others who followed me in *Leonora* were not so happy.

My love to you,
Stella.

I don't mind a snap your interfering in my business—perhaps I think it would have been a little more English not to have done it behind my back—Viola is very young and might be easily frightened—to dress me up in bogey clothes wastes time—I would have been amenable to any frank, open and just amendment!

15, Tedworth Square, Chelsea.

19th Jan. 1920

Dear Joey,

I am afraid my letter was a little grumpy. Perhaps if you had NEVER made love to me I wouldn't mind your making disagreeableness.

Stella.

◇◇◇◇◇◇◇

Marion Terry, distinguished actress and younger sister of Ellen, played Mrs. Higgins in this revival. In one of his very last letters to Ellen—dated 1 March 1920—Shaw writes: "Marion did not arrive at the Aldwych until the production stage was over; so she had to produce herself, which she did very well, as she knew as much about it as I. Clever family, the Terries! When she found that I was not as detestable as my reputation (an impossibility) she was angelic to me. I needed kindness, as Beatrice Stella excelled herself in perfect hellishness."

10, Adelphi Terrace, W.C.2.

29th Jan. 1920

Belovedovedest

Viola will be the death of me. She finished up today by announcing that you are coming tomorrow at eleven to go through the whole play. Aubrey had previously explained that he must go filming at 12.30 (his third filming disappearance, though he was pledged to one only). Viola also declares that Marion Terry's movements are so beautiful that she must keep walking about the stage, which means that there is going to be a beauty and youth competition between Mrs. Higgins and Eliza. And finally she has cabled for Gurney, who is to come over and knock his way into the finished production with what he can remember of Doolittle after five years of plain living and high thinking in America. And I have to sit on the side and continue to smile.

Do not dream of coming until Monday at the very earliest, and not then unless I tell you it is safe. You heard for yourself today that they are still only gabbling their words in an agony of memorizing (except the short parts). Aubrey will drive you mad, and you will knock him silly, if you rehearse with him in his present phase. Even when he has mastered his words and business, you will have to put up with his incorrigible amiability, which the public wont dislike. But I will do what can be done to harden him up into a ringing anvil for your hammer.

I am most anxious now about Marion. She reads the part straight off with perfect accent and point; but she has not the slightest intention of playing a matron; and Viola will abet her. Viola is a darling unprofessionally; but as a manageress she is a spoilt child playing with dolls, and gives every reason for her whims except an artistic or business reason.

If you think it would do any good for you to come down and take a rehearsal in hand to explain what you want, then do it and warn me. I will stay away on some pretext. But I strongly advise you not to do so yet.

We shall not be ready on the 9th; but it may be possible to produce then, and leave the first ten performances or so to complete the production. Do not forget that the short date forced Aubrey to begin studying and trying to do without the book before he had the faintest notion of the part or the play. I should have liked half a dozen rehearsals seated round a table, books in hand, to get *the music* right before going on to the stage. But as that was impossible through lack of time, I have had to depend on the usual mechanical routine and start with the business and words, leaving the unfortunate victims to find out later what they are all about. The process is bewildering to anyone who knows the play; but it cannot be helped: I cannot apply a six weeks or two months method to a three weeks limit: that is the sort of thing that keeps the English theatre what it is. I know perfectly well what worries you about it; and you can imagine that it is not delightful for me; but my business is to get, not what I want, but what is possible under the circumstances. And I doubt whether I shall be able to do even that with Viola playing all sorts of tricks, and interfering on the stage at the most difficult moments.

However, it is no use plaguing you with all this. I do it to relieve my nerves. Just look at the effect on my handwriting.

G.B.S.

10, Adelphi Terrace, W.C.2.
[undated]

Belovedest

Quite seriously, do not come again until I tell you that the moment has arrived. You are all right. You look younger than in 1913, and your voice is better; but if you tire and worry yourself at the theatre, you will lose more than you gain.

The others are floundering for their words (Aubrey did not repeat a single phrase accurately today), and they dont yet know what the play is about, or where or who they are supposed to be. This does not worry me: I am used to it and know that it will presently come right; but when it worries you I simply want to cry in your arms or to shake your head off: I dont quite know which. When they are really at home in the play it will be quite easy to make any changes in the business that may be convenient. But I think I have got your movements correctly after this morning.

I greatly fear that the result of Viola's tricking me over Mrs. Higgins will be that we shall have to play with an un-

derstudy. Nothing that I can possibly do will make Mrs. H.
a Marion Terry part, or a part important enough to enable
her to do what the public expects from her. When she finds
this out, she will throw it over. Viola, poor lamb, forgets
that overcasting a part means undercasting an artist, and
that managing a theatre does not mean being kind to people
she likes. However, Marion *may* go on, in which case we
shall be a good deal held back, as she proposes to spend from
Saturday to Tuesday (both inclusive) in the country, and
memory is not a Terry strong point. But if she does not, the
mischief will be that we shall have to go on with whatever
understudy I coach in the next three days.

A quite likely matron called on me today with an introduction from Holman Clarke—Annie Esmond. Says she
played with you in a Frohman play in New York, and discussed Mrs. Cortelyon and Mrs. Higgins with you, though
neither came off. She is naturally loth to understudy; but I
think she will; and though she is not Rossettian, she is as
good, apparently, as anyone who would understudy on any
terms.

Do you remember her: and if so, is there anything against
her?

Later:

Viola has engaged her, and wants to change Doolittle for
some young man. But I shall get a real dustman out of that
ancient of days if his head will hold the words.

Goodnight. You convinced me today that you are still
capable of surpassing yourself if only you had the sense to
see your own values. You can go to your full range in Eliza
in the last scene, as I meant you to do all along. If I could
get you up to that you would no more be able to throw it
all away by that silly joke about the gloves than Hamlet
could end with a comic song.

The reference to "Miss England" is obscure.

> 15, Tedworth Square, Chelsea.
> 3rd Feb. 1920

O my dear Joey,

Of course I look 60—of course I have a hideous "gin and misery" voice, and of course I cant give any kind of a performance to compare with a pretty young girl's.

Be calm and try not to mistake my brilliant impertinence for insolence, or my desire for individual radiance even from Miss England for uppishness.

Please dont write me any more letters. I *have* letters from you that will be read out at my funeral oration, but these you are sending me render me witless.

> Stella.

> 15, Tedworth Square, W.
> 5th Feb 1920

Joey I'm dreadfully sorry but I just *dare'nt* read your letter. I'm tired and I think I feel a little afraid of the extra fatigue—

You dont quite grasp the other side—the side that is the breath of life to us inferior creatures—or perhaps I should say—to me—poor Fool that I am.

> Stella.

> 15, Tedworth Square, Chelsea.
> 23rd February 1920

My dear Joey,

I went to see Lucy today. I only stayed two minutes in her room, for she seemed very very ill indeed—Eva seemed to think it would give Lucy joy to see you for a minute. I have hired a car for four weeks so I could take you if you cared about my doing so. Tomorrow afternoon at 2.30, or when you say—Don't be angry with me any more. Life has taken some skins off me and I can't battle with your jibes and jests—though I admit the memory of your golden heart washes all away like waves of the Sea—and I do love you.

Lucy's little house is lovely—I hear you have it for 21 years—soon I will be too old and decrepit to act—perhaps you'll let me die there?

My love to you,
Stella.

15, Tedworth Square, Chelsea.
[circa 28 March 1920]

Dear dear Joey
Eva has just told me you were with Lucy and her hand in yours when she died. I am so immensely glad—for she would have loved that best—dear Lucy—

I send you my love
Stella.

◇◇◇◇◇◇

Lillah McCarthy married Sir Frederick Keeble. The second bride was Miss Ann Elder, Mr. Shaw's secretary.

Ayot St. Lawrence, Welwyn.
28th March 1920

My dear Stella
What a day—yesterday!
Bride's kisses at 11 (Lillah); bride's kisses at Eliza's church at 3 (my secretary); and at 5 Lucy died in my arms.

I tried to telephone you, forgetting that you were on the stage at the moment.

236

"My body to be cremated if possible and the ashes scattered. No funeral, no flowers, no mourning". That is from her will, dated 14 Feb. 1918.

The disease was no longer active. She died of starvation. The Zeppelins destroyed her appetite.

Oh Stella, Stella, Stella!

G.B.S.

15, Tedworth Square, Chelsea.
[circa 29 March 1920]

Dear Joey,

Thank you for writing to me—

I hope your lovely Lillah will be happy—

There's no doubt about it, its better to be loved than love!

Dear Lucy I am glad I saw a little more of her these last weeks—her suffering wrung my bosom—and how brave she was to be sure!

I thanked heaven you were with her at the end—What about Eva? What devotion—

Let me see you—and I want to arrange with you about the big towns—

I am sorry about the 'stays' it gets me off the stage and I can't "run about" in my kimono it shows my legs—

My love to you
Stella.

Ayot St. Lawrence, Welwyn.
31st March 1920

Belovedest

Lucy is now Cinderella. At 3 this afternoon I made up a little service of my own, and finished with the dirge from Cymbeline, which fitted miraculously, Zeppelins and all ("the all dreaded thunder stone"). By this time the ashes are scattered among the flowers.

237

On Friday morning I start in the car to go by easy stages to Holyhead. On Monday I cross to Dublin, where my address until the 10th will be C/O the Rt. Hon. Sir Horace Plunkett K.C.V.O. Kilteragh, Foxrock, Co. Dublin. I have been quite seriously ill (for *me*) for the last three weeks; and I must have a recuperative change.

As to the six big cities, lay them waste to your heart's content. If you feel too lazy to coach the wretched slaves in the antics you require from them, Reginald Fry will do it for you, no doubt, for due consideration. Anyhow, keep me out of it.

I can give you a much better gag than yours, and one that involves no words and therefore doesnt violate poor Viola's agreement. When you are listening with a rapt expression to the angels on high, change countenance suddenly and catch a flea in the top fold of your stocking. I guarantee the effect.

G.B.S.

❖❖❖❖❖❖

James Bernard Fagan: a well-known playwright who later founded the Repertory Theatre in Oxford (1923) and became director of the Cambridge Festival Theatre (1929). He was the producer of Mrs. Campbell's next play, Madame Sand, *and appears from this letter to have had a hand in producing* Pygmalion *as well. Lottie Venne was a delightful comedienne of tiny, plump build, who lived (and acted) till she was seventy-six. Kate Rorke was also a well-known actress of the period, who had played Candida in 1904.*

10, Adelphi Terrace, W.C.
15th May 1920

Belovedest

  I was in front last night. You have now got the play as nearly as you like it as you will ever get it. You are very much better than you were when I saw it before on the first night at the Aldwych. I dont know by what Irish charm Fagan persuaded you to give up that horrible American front spot lighting that made your face like a kitchen clock covered with make-up, and flattened out your figure to twice its natural width; but you now model beautifully (a thing you dont understand but I do) and look young and quite willowy and not at all like Lottie Venne. There was no use in telling you these things before, because you wouldnt have believed me and would yet have been unhappy about it; but now that the evil is cured there is no harm in letting you know how nice you look. Also you have got rid of that horrible third act dress; and though the fifth act dress is dramatically nonsensical, yet as you now really do act a bit, and relate yourself to Eliza, you are quite credible *as* Eliza, and no longer like Mrs. Cornwallis West in a very ill tempered and brazen mood (for that, dearest, is what you were like at the Aldwych).

You now play the second act (the first part) and the fifth act so very cleverly and nicely that I damned you up hill and down dale for doing it so badly for *me* when you could do it so well for yourself. It is now really good Victorian drawingroom drama, pleasant and sweet, and in what you (bless you!) call good taste. You are not a great actress in a big play or anything disturbing or vulgar of that sort; but you have your hearts desire, and are very charming. Kate Rorke at her best could not have improved on it. I enjoyed it and appreciated it in its little way. And that was magnanimous of me, considering how I missed the big bones of my play, its fortissimos, its allegros, its precipitous moments, its contrasts, and all its big bits. My orchestration was feeble on the cottage piano; and my cymbals were rather disappointing on the cups and saucers. Still, you were happy; and that was something. And Higgins was not brutal to you, as I was. A perfect gentleman.

Still, you have lost as well as gained. The fourth act was a failure. You really might have given me a turn there with advantage. You looked like the loveliest of picture postcards blinking there at the piano whilst Higgins was talking daggers—"Thank God its over"—"the whole thing has been a bore" etc., etc., etc.—without turning a hair, making your eyes twinkle like stars all the time— no shadows, no spasms of pain, no stabs, nothing but Stella. How carefully you avoided hurting him with the slippers; and how tenderly he raised you and reciprocated your gentleness! I almost slept. *"J'aime la musique qui me berce"*. You certainly can boil a scene in bread and milk better than anyone I know. But this, beloved, would be better boiled in brandy.

Your gag about the stays is a mistake. It chills the audience at the end of the act, because half of them know that it is a gag, and the other half are jarred by the inept attempt to repeat the effect about the nightdress. Also your "Dont e smell orrid?" is bad because Higgins has already got all the fun possible out of the dustiness of Doolittle. If these things had been needed I should have supplied them. Try a wild rush off the stage, Ahohooing for all you are worth, the moment Mrs. Pearce says the clothes have come, and you will get a much more cordial curtain.

The receipts, by the way, are so appalling that I doubt if the public knows that the play is on again. Or did Aubrey make all that difference? If so, let us turn our faces to the wall, and die. A procession of sandwich men might help; but we cant afford them.

Just off to Ayot until the 27th.

G.B.S.

15 Tedworth Square Chelsea
[between May and June 1920]

Oh you *are* a most horrible man—always gathering *information* and thinking thereby you are gathering knowledge!—

I take no percentage after the £1000 until the production is paid off and the weekly expenses—The production cannot be paid off at the Duke of York's as we have it only for 10 weeks so my salary under any circumstances will not amount to more than £150 for 8 performances—How much of that will *not* belong to me I will *not* say—and £150 is now worth £75! and I do all the work really—George Sand is thunderingly difficult—if I dont get stink bombs on the first night I will on the second!

Stella.

When will you read *Adam and Eve* to me? *do.*

◇◇◇◇◇◇

This note refers to Mrs. Campbell's forthcoming appearance in Madame Sand *by Philip Moeller. The play's success was an "artistic" though not a financial one.*

Ayot St. Lawrence, Welwyn.
2nd June 1920

Only to wish you luck, belovedest.

D.D., whom I met at Hatfield last Saturday, told me the part is a good one. Otherwise I should have sent for it and written it up for you.

G.B.S.

Duke of Yorks.

[undated]

Why Joey that was kind of you. I didn't expect your good wishes. To get out of Eliza into this minx in four days wasn't easy!

She has got some beauty about her—*any* night there is a box waiting for you—I would love to hear your fun about it.

My love to you,

Stella.

10, Adelphi Terrace, W.C.2.

18th June 1920

I went on Thursday night. I thought the British Public absurdly illiterate and stupid. After the second act I felt inclined to come before the curtain and explain to them that the Coliseum was across the road and that they had come into the wrong house. If they think that Alfred de Mussets part must be sacred music, at least Grock will make it clear that they are meant to laugh at him. Pigs!

What induced you to imitate Oscar Wilde? It was an inspiration, and amazingly like the original.

The third act is the weak spot. It is merely a repetition of the wooing of De M. and Pagello; and repetition is fatal on the stage. The author thinks that the repetition is the whole point of the play; but he does not know that every repetition must be a variation and a surprise. He is going to call on me; and I will try to persuade him to rewrite it for you, because your lovely performance is too good to be thrown away: it is a repertory part. Why can you not act as intelligently as that for me, devil that you are?

Do make the idiot who works the pianola take the slow section of the nocturne at less than half the speed of the opening. Properly played, it makes a divine accompaniment to your courtship of Chopin: rattled through in that soulless and blasted manner it spoils it. The change of speed is not marked in the music because Chopin could not believe that anyone *could* play the thing wrong: it plays itself.

This should have been posted last night.

G.B.S.

The project was a visit to Cologne to play Pygmalion *to the British Army of Occupation. Mrs. Campbell duly went, on 11 October. She describes the trip in her book as "an interesting fortnight—I was over-praised, over-entertained, and over-photographed."*

10, Adelphi Terrace, W.C.
24th September 1920

Belovedest.

I don't think there is anything in it but a busman's holiday, a change, a lark, and perhaps your expenses paid. If you want that at present, go by all means: I think you would enjoy it and be freshened up by it. But there is no big business in it: they cannot afford West End salaries. However, as you can play for the British Army of Occupation for half a crown and act without compromising your market elsewhere, you need not bother about the money if you want the holiday.

I have just returned from Ireland, where I did a great stunt of work, and got all the copy for my new volume of plays off to the printer.

Ever and ever,
G. Bernard Shaw.

James K. Hackett, the American tragedian, had produced Macbeth *in London with Mrs. Campbell in November. In her book she writes: "It was easier to act Lady Macbeth with Mr. Forbes Robertson than with Mr. James Hackett, with whom I played the part afterwards in 1920. Perhaps Mr. Robertson was inclined to look upon Lady Macbeth as the 'star' part, to use the word of the theatre. Mr. Hackett surely looked upon Macbeth as the Solar System. It seemed to me, he realised my presence only at his 'cues', and more than once seized the opportunity during a strong speech of mine to turn his back to the audience and clear a troublesome catarrh." But the whole passage is revealing and amusing.*

15, Tedworth Square, Chelsea.

20/12/20

Joey Dear,

They are at me again begging me to ask you to let them have *Pygmalion* for the Cinema. I have said you wont, but I have promised to make a fool of myself again and write to you for it—

It is a long time since I saw you! I want to tell you about Cologne, and to hear just how bad you thought I was in *Macbeth.*

Come someday soon—

If you let me have "Pygmalion" for the Cinema—(I am much too aged for Eliza on the Screen!) you will keep me out of the workhouse.

Stella.

◇◇◇◇◇◇

W. Bridges-Adams: producer, who did remembered work at Stratford-on-Avon. Massingham: H. W. Massingham, editor of the Nation *(1907–23). Archer: William Archer, famous dramatic critic, translator of Ibsen's plays, who had a great influence on G.B.S.'s early career.*

Ayot St Lawrence, Welwyn.

22nd Dec. 1920

Alas! alas! nothing will keep you out of the work-house. All the enchantresses end there. Serve them right, too, mostly!

My film business is too complicated to explain; and the explanation would not help you. But if I let *Pygmalion* go, it would be a big business—at least £10,000; and it would not be possible for me to attach the condition that you should be Eliza with Mary Pickfords and suchlike about. But I am not done with *Pygmalion* on the regular boards yet. It is still new in Spain, and has not yet been produced in Paris. Even here the play is not dead yet: you yourself have held up the six big cities and kept poor Macdona wandering in the number twos for six years.

No: *Pygmalion* is out of the question as yet for the movies.

Macbeth, as a production, was an ancient Victorian absurdity. Hackett is still in the XVIII century. He would have done just as well with Rhoda Symons; and you would have done just as well with Aubrey Smith: the intervals, with the *entracte* music played sixteen times over, killed the play; and the people know now that it is not Shakespear who is the bore, and that Barker or Bridges Adams could have made a success of it with principals at fifteen pounds a week. Hackett's game is as dead as Victorian croquet and archery.

As it happened, when I saw it you played Hackett off the stage, and made only a few blunders. Blunder 1. You should not have played the dagger scene in that best evening dress of Lady M's, but in a black wrap like a thundercloud, with a white face. 2. You should not have repeated the exit business by which Macbeth conveyed that he was going to see a ghost on every step of the stairs up to Duncan; you should have gone straight off like a woman of iron. 3. You should not have forgotten that there was blood on your hands and on his, and that you dared not touch one another for fear of messing your clothes with gore. 4. In the sleepwalking scene you should not have scrubbed your hands *realistically* (Drat the blood! it wont come off) nor worn an idiotic Handley-Seymour confection that wound your feet up more and more at every step, and finally pitched you off the stage on your head. That scene needs the whole cavernous depth of the stage, and the draperies of a ghost. If you are determined to be a Paffick Lidy all the time (Mrs. P. C's dresses by HS & Co) you cannot be Lady Macbeth or Mrs. Siddons. It was maddening to hear you deliver the lines splendidly, and be in a different class to all the others, and then throw it all away by half a dozen stupidities that the call boy could have corrected. I persuaded Massingham to go; but he came back chuckling and said you had sleepwalked all through the play. I could not understand this. I *did* understand when Archer told me that on the first night you twittered through the part and pecked at it like a canary trying to eat a cocoa nut. I knew that game: you were trying to make Lady Macbeth a lady just as you made Higgins a gentleman. But I couldnt understand the sleepwalking until D.D. told me someone had told you that Lady M. should be seen through a sheet of glass. I wish I had been there with a few bricks: there would not have been much left of your glass. Why do you believe every ASS who talks nonsense to you—no: why should I insult the asses?—every NOODLE who talks non-sense to you, and bite everyone who talks skilled common sense?

You might at least have made the scenepainter put in a martin's nest or two over the castle windows. You can bully effectively enough when you really want anything. Why dont you want the right things and bully to some useful purpose?

You see I have nothing agreeable to say: you have broken my nerve.

If Hackett and you would pay Bridges Adams a thousand pounds to produce *Macbeth*, and would do what he told you, you could go round the world with it. He is young, and doesnt *know*: not like Barker and poor me, who do know how impossible you are. It maddens me to see people blundering away thousands of pounds and the reputational chances of their lifetime through sheer ignorance, and imagining that those who know most about the production are those who, being on the stage struggling with their own parts, never see it and never see themselves.

However, what is the use of talking to you? Or at least of *my* talking to you? Something silly, like the *Thirteenth Chair*, will turn up for you presently. Or some nice man will come and talk about sheets of glass.

G B S.

P.S. You shouldnt talk to me about the theatre: it is my only sore subject; and it is you who made it so.

15, Tedworth Square, Chelsea.
11.1.21

What abominable letters you do write me Joey dear!—But you did *once* write me a letter that I am going to leave to the Nation!

Archer, and the other men never realize that I *chose* to be an amateur, and not a professional!—

I wish you would come and see me.

Life has been beating me, banging and bumping me this way and that and perhaps you will find me improved— Anyway you know I never was a whining woman, and I didn't squeal as you sat and grinned at my thumbnail being lifted whilst a long splinter was slowly pulled from underneath!

My love to you
Stella.

247

◇◇◇◇◇◇

This letter should be dated 1921. Bernard Shaw has made the same mistake that Mrs. Campbell made the previous year. Hackett's production of Macbeth *was in November 1920.*

Ayot St. Lawrence, Welwyn.

13th January [1921]

Belovedest

      I write you abominable letters because you are an abominable wretch. You dont want to be an amateur: you want to be a lady, like Eliza, only you have not the horse sense that made her go the right way about it by learning to behave herself. What with actresses wanting to be amateurs because they think it's ladylike, and amateurs wanting to be actresses because they think it's immoral, the theatre is no place for an honest workman.

      Mackail thinks that acting is unladylike, and that, like the celebrated decayed gentlewoman who had to cry laces in the street for a living but hoped that nobody heard her, Lady Macbeth should be unobtrusive and inaudible. Perhaps he thinks, too, that Macbeth was a strong silent man, and that Hackett should have cut out all his lines. That is, he doesnt think at all about it: no man ever really does think about a thing until it is his job, though he may play with it intellectually in a very pretty manner. When you play Shakespear, dont worry about the character, but go for the music. It was by word music that he expressed what he wanted to express; and if you get the music right, the whole thing will come right. And neither he nor any other musician ever wrote music without *fortissimi* and thundering ones too. It is only your second rate people who write whole movements for muted strings and never let the trombones and the big drum go. It is not by tootling to him *con*

248

sordino that Lady Macbeth makes Macbeth say "Bring forth men children only". She lashes him into murder.

And then you must modulate. Unless you can produce in speaking exactly the same effect that Mozart produces when he stops in C and then begins again in A flat, you cant play Shakespear. Ask Thoughtless Jack how he would say to the servant with the air of gratified hostess and gracious fine lady "He brings GREAT news", and then, when the man is gone "the raven himself is hoarse that croaks the fatal entrance of Duncan beneath *my* battlements". Unless you lift that to utter abandonment, how can you drop to the terrible invocation "Come, you spirits". Imagine an actress, instead of studying that until she had got it as safe as a pianola reflecting on what a perfect wife Lady Macbeth was and trying to imagine herself a sheet of glass!

If you want to know the truth about Lady Macbeth's character, she hasnt one. There never was no such person. She says things that will set people's imagination to work if she says them in the right way: that is all. *I* know: I do it myself. You ought to know: *you* set people's imaginations to work, dont you? though you know very well that what they imagine is not there, and that when they believe you are thinking ineffable things you are only wondering whether it would be considered vulgar to have shrimps for tea, or whether you could seduce me into ruining my next play by giving you a part in it.

The reported failures of *Heartbreak House* in Vienna and New York seem to be turning into successes. The Burg Theatre has NOT transferred it to the classical repertory (they are too polite to say taken the damned thing off); and New York has paid its thousand dollars a show regularly to see it since November. What is more, the Theatre Guild there is seriously proposing to produce *Back to Methuselah*, though each complete performance will consist of three

evening performances and two matinees. This will certainly
mean a production of *Heartbreak House* in London; and
you, ungovernable devil that you are, will be out of it,
though nobody could speak the lines as you could or give
the quality of the woman as you could if you would. So
Lillah, or Violet Vanbrugh, or some other hard-working
woman who doesnt want to be an amateur will play your
part and get your salary. Yet you wonder at my writing
you abominable letters. Oh, if only I could get a good grip
of your hair and drag you three times round Tedworth
Square by it, you would get a faint idea of how I feel about
you professionally.

I do not know what is to be done with you or what is to
become of you. Not that it matters: the whole world is
breaking up; and one tragedy more or less wont be noticed.

Gertrude Kingston, who is going to play Catherine at a
charity matinee, offered Patiomkine to Hackett. He didnt
see it. That reminds me of Laurence Irving, and of old
times. Lady Scott is always inviting me down to Sandwich.
Lady Bancroft has had shingles.

Avaunt, ye spectres!

G.B.S.

◇◇◇◇◇◇

*This is the first mention of Mrs. Campbell's projected auto-
biography,* My Life and Some Letters. *It was published in 1922.*

15, Tedworth Square, Chelsea.
18/1/21.

Joey—I have had a letter from a publisher that I
would very much like your opinion upon—*please let me
know when you will be in town?*

The letter is in the form of a contract and I am afraid of

it—Hoyti Wiborg writes from U.S.A. *most* enthusiastically about *Heartbreak House*—it *would* be a little unkind of you to leave me out if it is done here—Hoyti says it plays ever so much better than it reads! I wonder—

Please let me know about the publisher—I had the letter yesterday and he gives me two weeks to decide and I want to hear your views—These are some things you know more about than anyone else in the world.

Please be a little kind to me. I have stood your unkindness and your grumbling so bravely.

Stella.

Ayot St. Lawrence, Welwyn.
20th Jan. 1921

I shall be in town for a few hours on Monday (engaged all the afternoon) but not again until Thursday the 27th.

Therefore had you not better send me the letter at once? Let nothing induce you to accept a publisher's contract without expert advice: *all* publishers' contracts are booby traps. Giving you a week to decide—in other words, trying to rush you—is an ultimatum which you may receive with the thumb to the nose.

What have you written? Your life or mine or both?

This new stunt about you bearing my unkindness bravely takes my breath away. I am the greatest playwright in the world; and I have been treated by an actress as no dog was ever treated by the most brutal trainer; and she complains of *my* unkindness. Delaroche's Christian Martyr is not in it.

Belovedest: I *can't* put you into the cast of H.H. You have intimidated me far too completely. I had rather fight Carpentier. And the rest of the cast, the manager and the backers, would go on strike at once. What *I* dare not face, nobody else with any sense is likely to take on. You must

take a theatre, write your own plays, and train a company
of orphan apprentices to act with you.

Ever
G.B.S.

15, Tedworth Square, Chelsea.
21 Jan. 21

I send you the letter dear Joey. I wont insult you by
saying "Please don't mention it"—because of course you
wont—

I have written four chapters and I am afraid I have written
myself an ass!

I will never get over it if you dont at least make me an
offer to play in H.H.

You *know* I would not disgrace you.

You know you *teased* me at rehearsals. I cannot work
that way.—Besides my nerves are stronger now.

I enclose Hoyti Wiborgs letter. You know one of those
pretty girls I found you with lying on your stomach on the
floor doing swimming exercises.

Stella.

15, Tedworth Square, Chelsea.
[approx. 28 Jan. 1921]

Dear Joey,

I hear nothing will induce you to let me be in *Heartbreak House*, I expect you know best.

Thank you *so much* for this letter to Butterworth—you
do *know* about things—I am sorry I am such a bad and *impossible* actress, I expect you know about that too.

My love to you,
Stella.

Its such a pity I cant cry—I never could *after* my children were born!

If Macdona should want me, tell them to let me know—

10, Adelphi Terrace, W.C.

29th Jan. 1921

Belovedest

Put H.H. out of your head: nobody in it will get more than £40 a week. With the strictest economy, beginning with 12 matinees in Hammersmith and transferring to the Kingsway for the evening bill, it is just possible that the £1500 a week which is the best I can do may suffice. I cannot afford to repeat the double catastrophe of *Arms and the Man* and *Pygmalion*: two brilliant revivals which might have been running still but for Loraine and you and the theatre landlords. I have no use for stars: *I* am the star this time: a poor one, but the best we can afford.

Besides, H.H. must win—if it does win—on its production, and, as I practise it, it is not compatible with your presence within a mile of the theatre. I know already what happens when an irresistible force encounters an irremovable obstacle; and so do you. You dont want to try again, do you?

I shall tell Macdona that you will tour the 6 cities with him for £100 a week. I doubt if he would give you that as a minimum guarantee for a percentage of the gross receipts: at least I shouldnt in his place. I should offer £50 with a percentage on the gross, or £100, with a percentage on receipts in excess of £1000. But of course I shall not prompt him in any way. You know how scrupulous I am about interfering in your private affairs. I only mention the figures to prepare you for the sort of reply that Mac. might make if he were as intelligent as I.

Yes: it is a pity you can't cry. Any actress could. Crocodile!

G.B.S.

15, Tedworth Square, Chelsea.
18th Feb. 1921

Joey, I have been ordered to lie up for 6 weeks, I am in the sitting room, I couldn't face an illness in a bedroom again.

Wont you come and see me before I am dead. Forgive me my sins at rehearsals.

Stella.

15, Tedworth Square, Chelsea.
Feb. 1921

I think it is something like this—I injured my ankle, knocked it and bruised a vein. Then I wore silly cris-cross [sic] elastic shoes, and now if I put my foot to the ground for more than a few seconds I collapse. I have a silly doctor who comes now and again. I cannot afford doctors.

There's no such thing as falling in love. Joey dont be silly. I hope you will come. I will keep Thursday free from 3.30 onwards. Don't make me cry.

Stella.

◇◇◇◇◇◇◇

"Confidential" is a reference to Mrs. Campbell's autobiography and the title she proposes. The "Biblical film" was a film called The Dawn of the World.

15, Tedworth Square, Chelsea.
[*circa* Feb. 1921]

Dear Joey,
There is nothing "confidential" of any kind. Just things that are amusing or show interest in me and my work. You will see and not let me be careless.

I got up for half an hour and felt very queer. I had to get into bed again.

I hope I'm not fretting and that its only my silly ankle.

I don't quite trust myself.

I have asked £200. for making a fool of myself 3 times a day with the Biblical film for four weeks.

I understand a clergyman will write the words.

The Life of Mrs. Patrick Campbell

by

Beatrice Stella Cornwallis West.

There is no doubt you are the kindest man in the world—when you feel so disposed.

Stella.

◇◇◇◇◇◇◇

The handwriting of this note is very bad, and the transcription necessarily tentative. By "notation" Mrs. Campbell presumably means "punctuation."

15, Tedworth Square, Chelsea.

23/2/21

Do come when you can tomorrow—

This book business worries me—you know I can neither write nor spell—neither can I spin, nor act—my wedding of words is un-moral and my only idea of notation is a hyphen. True I have some "pabulum"—I dont know if that is the right word—and the workhouse so near is an incentive.

I am sorry about the poor dogs ear—

I am rather German in my views about people being run over—

One is fined there for not "looking where you are going" —and if you're killed, your relatives are fined.

My love to you

Stella.

◇◇◇◇◇◇

*"Ph. B.J." is Philip Burne-Jones, son of Sir Edward. Some
twenty-five years before, he had painted an easily recognizable
portrait of Mrs. Campbell and called it "The Vampire." Otto
Kyllmann was and is a partner in the publishing firm of Con-
stable & Co.*

Ayot St. Lawrence, Welwyn.
26th Feb. 1921

I have settled that the book is to be called *The Autobiography of an Enchantress.*

I think you must obtain Ph. B.J.'s permission to publish
his father's letters. Otherwise he might possibly have the
edition confiscated and ruin you and Constables. Here is a
quotation from a Law-book.

"The position of the receiver of a letter is that in the absence of some limitations imposed either by the subject-
matter of the letter or the circumstances under which it is
sent, he has an unqualified title to the material upon which
it is written, and he can deal with it as absolute owner, subject only to the proprietary right retained by the author and
his representatives to the publication or non-publication of
the ideas in their particular verbal expressions." And again—

"Ordinary correspondence will generally be conducted
on the understanding that it shall not be published, and, if
it were published, the writer of the letters would not require
to rely upon his copyright at all, but could restrain the publication as a breach of confidence." B U T again:

"It would seem that letters may be published if the object
of doing so is to vindicate the character of the receiver." [1]

The last may be useful in the Vampire matter; but your
best course is to ask Phil's permission to use his father's letters (and perhaps to reproduce the Vampire as an illustration

[1] Acknowledgment is due to Messrs. Sweet & Maxwell, Ltd., for
kind permission to quote this extract from Copinger on the Law of
Copyright.

if you feel mischievously disposed). If he refuses, you can
paraphrase the letters (copyright is only in B.J.'s exact
words, not in the meaning) and explain that Ph. has made
himself disagreeable. But it would be hard for him to justify
a refusal; so the danger of it is much less than that of pro-
ceeding without his consent. I am writing to Otto Kyllmann
by this post.

G.B.S.

15 Tedworth Square, Chelsea.
[approx. April 1921]
I hear of you speaking in Chelsea—I wish you would
come in and see me. I have caught a chill but am better—not
able to accompany the great Hackett to play "Lady Macbeth" and he is in Paris.

We have got something to talk about—you and I.

Stella.

◇◇◇◇◇◇

*"Pin": Sir Arthur Pinero. "Gerald": Gerald du Maurier,
who was knighted in the following year. He had been Mrs.
Campbell's leading man in several plays.*

Ayot St. Lawrence, Welwyn.
27th June 1921
Belovedest
I did not send anything to Tedworth Square except
the new book, *Back to Methuselah*, which should have arrived there before this; but I was moved telepathically to
scrawl the following, which my secretary Miss Patch has
just typed for me to spare your eyes.

You remember what I said to you about autobiographies

being unreadable when childhood and apprenticeship is over, and the career set and started. I think you will get under way again quite easily if, after chronicling *Tanqueray*, you draw a double bar and say "From this time onward my history is to be found in stale press notices, which I know better than to inflict on my friends. What they want to know is not what plays and what theatres I appeared in. They can get all that from *Who's Who in the Theatre*. They want to know what I have to say about it all; how I justified myself for being so mad a thing as an actress at all; whether I was able to keep my real life and personality through so much mumming; what I made of the many interesting people I necessarily met; whether I would do it again if I could begin again; why everybody adored me and nobody could stand me; why, though I have Italian thrift in my blood and could live on next to nothing if I were put to it, I could not be what I was on the stage and keep out of debt"; and a great deal more which is no business of theirs but which they nevertheless want to know. And there are your chapter headings for you. For instance, you can have a chapter on authors, beginning (after Pin) with Henry Arthur Jones, who said that you had an extraordinary sense of everything that was within ten inches of your nose,—and ending with the author who tried to seduce you when you were an unprotected widow, and treated you on the stage with a brutality and savagery which you can never forget. You might even write a chapter on stage lovers from Tree, whose evening suit you stroked with passionate embraces of your heavily made-up arms until the poor man was like a zebra, to Gerald, whose outpourings of adoration on the stage you punctuated by such asides as, "Good God, to have to play a scene like this to a face like that!"

If you will take it in any order that occurs to you, and never forget that biographies are dull, especially autobiographies, but that Confessions are interesting (think of how

Rousseau shamed himself into immortality) you will not have the least difficulty in making the book three times as long as at present.

I have sent you a copy of my new book to humor your fancy for having books that you never read.

Somebody—it must have been Lady Horner—told me you were not as well as you expected the change to make you. But a break-down is a very queer process. I had one myself in 1898. Instead of getting down to the lowest depth and then gradually recovering, you begin to recover before the break-down has completed itself; so that for some time you are actually getting worse and better simultaneously. You are half well by the time you have stopped breaking down. It is all right when you understand what is happening, but very bothering and discouraging if you don't.

I must go back to my business now; I have snatched a while from it in the hope that I could perhaps set you going again at the book and amuse your solitude—for I suppose you are carrying out your Irish doctor's instructions and not seeing more than 30 people every afternoon.

G.B.S.

P.S. I believe Miss Florence Jackson (the provincial Liza) will get the six towns after all; for if Macdona is really going to take the Shaw theatre seriously and plunge into a big touring company with a repertory of half a dozen plays it is not humanly or commercially possible to deny him the big cities. He has waited eight years for them, and lost eight harvests of *Pygmalion* in them. No success that you could possibly make now would make up for that. Besides, you will never go. You could have gone any year since your return from America just as easily as—*more* easily than—you can ever go hereafter; so what reason is there for us to delude ourselves any longer? Let it go. I shall.

◇◇◇◇◇◇

"Sally" was another Belgian griffon. Mrs. Campbell's second marriage ended in failure and she and George West parted finally about this time. A few passages on this subject have been deleted from the correspondence for obvious reasons. Most of them are obscure and not very characteristic of the writers.

Rusper, Sussex.
29th June 1921

Dear Joey,

My secretary, Miss Morris tells me she forwarded a letter on to me from you—I haven't received it. Was it important? please write it again. I am much better—and being alone is doing wonders—and then so many books—Schopenhauer *Studies in Pessimism* to make me laugh—Nietszche to shake hands with—Bergson to remind me by 2 a.m. its time to go to sleep—and Samuel Butler to make me say "dear Joey"—and novels galore—and there's Bach's Brandenburg 5th Concerto to play on the Pianola—

Hutchinsons cheque in advance to steady me up and feel the book *must* be finished by December.

Pray for my poor little "wits"—and that those who have hurt me will hurt me no more—Dont take my Pygmalion towns away, but *make* that silly MacDona play them with me.

Stella.

Georgina and Sally and the large Bull dog have much to say—and lying out in the garden is a joy for all four of us.

Hotel Belgravia, Victoria.
2/12/21

Two things I wanted to ask you Joey and forgot. Will you please tell Miss Elder to find me a photograph of you. **D.D.** wants one of you sitting down looking up with a paper in your hand—or a book, that I liked very much. She might send me two to choose from.

Your kindness is beyond my thanks.

Stella.

◇◇◇◇◇◇◇

This is the letter referred to later by Mrs. Campbell as "the gentleman's agreement"—when G.B.S. refused to allow her to publish her selection of his letters in toto. (See page 273 et seq. Also page 322 et seq., and page 341.)

10, Adelphi Terrace, W.C.2.

2nd Dec. 1921

I have sent the letter to Hutchinson, saying that I leave the matter to your judgment and that he may take it that there is a gentleman's agreement (the usual phrase) that I am not to raise the question of copyright in respect of anything of mine in your MS.

You ought to read *The Doctor's Dilemma*. Indeed now that I think of it I dont see why you shouldnt play it: Jennifer is a part that you could play rather well. It's a warning, that play. . . .

G.B.S.

Hotel Belgravia, Victoria.

5th Dec. 1921

Dear Joey,

Send me *The Doctors' Dilemma*.

I have all your books at Ashfields. . . .

Stella.

*The reference is to the final separation between George West
and Mrs. Campbell and the former's financial troubles.*

Ayot St. Lawrence, Welwyn.
6th Dec. 1921

I am writing to Constables to send you a *Dilemma.*

The difficulty about not telling is that Nature abhors
a vacuum; and if people dont know the truth they fill up
with inventions. I couldn't bear to make you tell me before;
but I have sometimes had occasion to wish that I knew. I
nearly asked D.D. once, but couldn't quite bring myself
to. . . .

I'm sorry: I ought not to be the sort of person that it's
painful to tell such things to; but I suppose I am.

And yet perfect strangers write me letters ten pages long
about the most private affairs. My Secretary reads them for
me.

By the way, Ann Elder, that Secretary who never opened
your letters, got married, like Lillah, the day Lucy died; so
I began that experience with two weddings.

Ann's successor is Miss Blanche Patch. My correspondence is so astonishing that nothing that you could possibly
write could produce the slightest effect on her.

ever and ever
G.B.S.

10, Adelphi Terrace, W.C.2
7th Dec. 1921

I sent the letter to Hutchinson & Co., Hutchinson
House, Friar St. E.C.4. Possibly Sir G's office is at 34, Pater-
noster Row. Or perhaps, like most modern publishers, he
never goes to his office. Anyhow, it will reach him before
he dies.

As you are pretty sure to pull your proofs about a good deal, make them send you the first set in "galley proofs"— long strips unpaged. If they send paged proofs, then every addition or deletion (omission) will involve over-running: that is, alteration of every page to the end of the chapter (sometimes to the end of the book), which is costly.

As I shall have to read the book anyhow you had better let me read it in proof. I could do the more obvious "literals" (corrections of spelling, punctuation, etc.) for you, and might perhaps spot some dangers that you may not have thought of. When you are writing about living people you have to be very circumspect; for though the most violent vituperation is priviledged as "vulgar abuse", a very mild and well intended remark may carry some commercial or legal implication that is libellous. . . .

I shall be in town from Thursday morning to Saturday.

G.B.S.

Ashfields, Lathom, Lancs.
16th Dec./21

Dear Joey,

I hear Charlotte is distressed—I hope this isn't true—

You never told her I was a gentleman or that I was merely swan-singing?

It is a pity I ever read these letters again and its a pity they are so lovely. And I am *glad* I never destroyed them.

Only *you* seem to have considered the fact that my reputation might be injured!—

Did D.D. tell you that she said "I wish he had written *me* letters like that".

People talk so big, and they act so small—and they move sideways like crabs.

Its divine down here—and theres no believing I am an actress.

The earth is my Mother's bosom and I am of no more account than a worm.

Let me know what you think, now you have spoken of the letters.

I shall never have the courage to send you the proofs of my tosh.

My love to you,
Stella.

❖❖❖❖❖❖

Clemence Dane's Will Shakespeare *had been produced by Basil Dean at the Shaftesbury Theatre on 17 November. Philip Merivale played Shakespeare, and a notable cast contained Mary Rorke, Haidee Wright, Mary Clare, Claude Rains, Ivor Barnard, and Flora Robson.*

Ashfields, Lathom, Lancs.
17/12/21

Your card has been forwarded to me from the Belgravia Hotel. I am not interested in Satyrs—only in Angels—I think you were foolish not to have come to *Will Shakespeare.* I am glad the critics havent killed the play.

Such a day it is here today. The sea-wind blowing in from Southport. I have my sick brother with me.

I have given him a spade to dig up the earth with and a chopper to cut up wood. But back he goes to his chess problems—What a world—What a silly joke!—

I hope Clemence Dane will soon have a play ready for me—With a woman—as a woman should be—to play.

I could have played any part in *Heartbreak House*—The girl in the hammock and the Adonis in the toga are the two that should have been blown to smithereens in the dynamite pit.

Bless you,
Stella.

264

◇◇◇◇◇◇

The following letter is typewritten, but the words "and that never did I think your love making other than what it was—sympathy, kindness, and the wit and folly of genius" have been inserted afterwards in pencil (possibly at a later date?).

Ashfields, Lathom, Lancs.
21st December 1921

There is no mistake about it you are an extraordinary man.

Miss Morris is making a copy of the letters that I propose publishing if you agreed and consented.

I will send them to you to-morrow.

It is quite easy for me to come down from the clouds and realise there are other points of view than my own.

I did indeed hate speaking of George to you.

What I wanted was your clever opinion how to get just enough truth on the written page.

I thought you knew he left me two years ago.

You know you always thought me a fool, and that you never even pretended unfaithfulness to Charlotte and that never did I think your love making other than what it was—sympathy, kindness, and the wit and folly of genius.

What you sometimes think ignorance in me is often deliberate—Perhaps I see what I choose to see—I look at what I want to look at—a joy and a tragedy that—

Don't mix up your genius and your clay, which is what you will do if your lovely letters are tampered with now—

I am glad you both felt as I did over *Will Shakespeare.*

There was nothing wrong excepting the bridge of Shakespeare's nose—he may have altered it since I saw the play.

I could have played Mary Fitton with more subtle danger—

Clemence Dane is a most dear woman and superlatively

clever—Please send me your letter to her, it would interest me tremendously.

My love to you. If you had a good memory you would recollect that I always wanted to send my love to Charlotte. *You* led her to see me all askew.

I alone kept my head and saw you both as you are without any help from anyone—If you dare to pretend it is otherwise, you will assuredly boil in hell.

Stella the peasant
(Italian)

If you want to hear something out of the common, hear Renata Borgatti play Bach—

Such a face too—Her art is absolutely impersonal—and her passionate love of music sings and sobs and blows a gale about her—She is very wonderful.

◇◇◇◇◇◇

"The Goosens": the Goossens family of musicians. Lord Lathom was a young dilettante (in the word's best sense), playwright, and patron of the fine arts.

Blythe Hall, Ormskirk, Lancs.
24th Dec /21

Here are the dear letters.

If I inspired a little of the tenderness of their genius I am proud, not vain.

Have you forgotten I asked you to read the letters the other day you refused.

Both D.D. and Barrie said the letters were wonderful—and that it was generous of you to let me publish them.

Of course, there is always the "baker's boy" point of view, and if it came over D.D. when she was talking to you, God help us, for it never lasts long with her. I fancy it was she who said I was generous and brave to risk the criticism that might fall upon me!!!

People talk carelessly, but nobody will *think* anything but what lovely letters and what a dear man you are.

I do not fancy that Charlotte will misjudge me, or that she will see that permitting the letters to be published is other than a *panache* in her bonnet. Otherwise why read them?

I am telling no 'untruths', Joey, when we gather roses, we don't touch the roots, or the clay about the roots. We nip off the thorns, our intelligence does that—and its just the lovely blossoms with their scent and their colour that we love.

Some day I will take "clay" for my theme—if only I could write.

I am here at Blythe for Christmas. The Goosens are here and others. Lord Lathom is pleased about something you wrote about the Goosen Concerts. They cost him £600 I believe.

My cottage is almost two miles from here over the fields. So there is much gaiety for the moment.

Don't please misjudge me, or allow others to.

A lovely peaceful Christmas and joy in the New Year.

Stella.

❖❖❖❖❖❖

The Countess of Cardigan, at the age of eighty-four in the year 1909, had published a volume of reminiscences, My Recollections, *which scandalized society with their frankness.*

Ayot St. Lawrence, Welwyn.

30th December 1921

In vain: you cannot evade your doom.

Listen. Have you ever read the Confessions of St. Augustine? And have you ever read the memoirs of the Countess of Cardigan? St. Augustine immortalized himself. The Countess wiped herself out of the visiting book of good society for ever (not that she had been much in it; but still—). Nobody without seeing what your memoirs are like, can possibly tell you how much you dare put in them if you wish to keep your standing.

Take that terrible wadge of letters, and put it into the hands of any court of honor you can induce your fittest friends to form, or submit it to the judgement of any capable and experienced woman of the world, and both will tell you without a moment's hesitation, and with considerable surprise at your having any doubt on the subject, that their public exposure is utterly impossible, except in the physical sense in which it is materially possible for you to undress yourself (or me) in the street.

You say that you will behave like a perfect gentleman. Well, a gentleman does not kiss and tell; so that settles *that*.

I am writing some autobiographical sketches for the proposed Collected edition of my work. Suppose I put in your most intimate letters! Would any plea that I had your leave to do it save me from being put down as an inconceivable cad and coxcomb, without any sense of your old pet virtue: good taste? Would it be any use my calling the public the baker's boy for not appreciating my super delicacy? Not a bit, belovedest—Yet I could plead Hazlitt's *Liber Amoris* (about the lodging house keeper's daughter) as a more respectable precedent than the Cardigan Book. But D.D. would spit in my face. Another hypothesis. Round about 1895 or so, I wrote a wonderful string of love letters to Ellen Terry, and got a wonderful string of replies from her.

268

Ellen afterwards wrote her memoirs, and wrote them very well. Ellen must have bushels of love letters; and she has been adored by all the poets of her day. There is not a line in her book that was meant for her eye alone, or that could make mischief in any household. Do you prefer Ellen's way or the Cardigan way?

Do you ever read breach-of-promise cases? Or divorce cases? Do you ever shudder at the way in which the letters of the parties are served up cold to the ridicule or the pruriency or the simple scandalous curiosity of the person you call the baker's boy, and feel ashamed of profaning love by reading them, or resolve to ask your member of parliament to bring in a Bill to assimilate our law to the French law, which makes such publication a misdemeanor? If you have, can you bear your memoirs to read like a breach of promise case?

Besides, I should play you off your own stage: the memoirs would be the Bernard Shaw memoirs; and you would be only the woman I wrote the letters to.

There! I cannot go on saying nasty things; but neither can I leave these unsaid; for it takes an extraordinary heavy hammer to knock anything into you that depends on your seeing yourself as others will see you. What I have said is all that can be said on the strength of the letters alone. I quite understand your intense reluctance to let me see the whole book. You are quite right in foreseeing that I shall ruthlessly tear it to pieces, cutting out all the notices with which actresses plaster their books (not a line in Ellen's except the Oscar Wilde sonnet), all your little snobberies—"Darling: come to tea at Marlborough tomorrow: Alexandra: P. S. Edward sends his love" and so on. I shall have to connect your titbits into dignified paragraphs, and, where I happen to know the truth, to substitute it for your dramatizations. In short, I shall probably have to rewrite the whole damned thing. No matter: you must face it; and nobody can compel you to adopt my suggestions if you dont like. Then, if you send me *all* the letters that survive, it may be possible to work in quite a good deal of them harmlessly and amusingly. But you cannot do that yourself or you would never have sent me that budget (the cruelty of making me read it!) and proposed to insert it chock-a-block. Why, there is one passage on which George could get a divorce, though it is really quite innocent. And several perfectly uninteresting things about hours and appointments which would nevertheless give the greatest pain to Charlotte for nothing.

I must break off here, or I shall miss the post.

G.B.S.

Ashfields, Lathom, Lancs.

2nd January 1922

Joey—I am going to take your letter seriously:

"Suppose I put in your most intimate letters! Would any plea that I had your leave to do so save me from being put down as an inconceivable cad and coxcomb, without any sense of your old pet virtue: good taste?"

Any letters of mine you may publish, if you will correct the grammar and see to the punctuation.

". . . . . D.D. would spit in my face." D.D. writes: "Don't cut out G.B.S. letters. I think it would so easy just to take out one or two little phrases—nothing—without spoiling them at all—I do really. As for C. she knows they are going in—"

"Another hypothesis, round about 1895 or so, I wrote a wonderful string of love letters to Ellen Terry, and got a wonderful string of replies from her . . ."

Cannot you get Ellen Terry to let me publish her love letters from you, with mine?—

"I quite understand your intense reluctance to let me see

270

the whole book. You are quite right in foreseeing that I
shall ruthlessly tear it to pieces . . ."
I *long* for you to see the "whole book" and to damn it—
only not at Ayot, or 10 Adelphi Terrace.

It would not take you more than two hours to read. I
would come up to London. Shall I?

"I shall have to connect your titbits into dignified paragraphs, and, where I happen to know the truth, to substitute it for your dramatisation".

That's a silly word "dramatisation".—I have done my best
to be truthful and non-theatrical.

I cannot write paragraphs—or those glorious long sen-
tences of yours where, when I have arrived at the full stop,
I have to begin all over again to get my brain's balance! I
murmer "Back to Methuselah"—Yes, you are naughty in
this weakness in the beginning of *that* book especially.

"Why there is one passage on which George could get a
divorce, though it is really quite innocent".

Let me know the passage which could enable George to
get a divorce.

"And several perfectly uninteresting things about hours
and appointments which would nevertheless give the
greatest pain to Charlotte for nothing."

Cut for me uninteresting things about hours and times that
could hurt Charlotte, and return the "wadge"—

Please Joey don't put on your suburban cap. You first
said "I leave the publication etc. to Mrs. Campbell's judgment", which is the *real you*, and has won you fresh honour.

"The cruelty of making me read it! and proposed to insert it chock-a-block".

Are you right about the whole "wadge", chock-a-block?
That way I think shows you *did* care a little, but of course
not enough to sacrifice one hair of your own dear head: and
it certainly shows you did feel real unhappiness over the
suffering even your genius could not lift.

"There I cannot go on saying nasty things; but neither can I leave these unsaid: for it takes an extraordinary heavy hammer to knock anything into you that depends upon your seeing yourself as others will see you . . ."
Say as many unkind and cruel things as you like—hit me with a thousand hammers—nobody can hurt me any more: is that not wonderful?

My love to you
Stella.

Ayot St. Lawrence, Welwyn.
5th Jan. 1922

Now God defend me from idiots!
I might just as well write essays on Relativity to a female Kingfisher.
Send me your proofs when you get them. I will then tell you, brutally and dogmatically, what you may say and what you may not. The situation is new to you. You have been before the public for sixty years or so; but during that time you have never uttered a word to it that has not been put into your mouth by somebody else. You have therefore never learnt the rules or acquired the sense of responsibility of authorship. And, owing to abysmal deficiencies in your nature, you never will. So you must do what you are told.

Out of all patience—G.B.S.

Ashfields, Lathom, Lancs.
7th January 1922

Dear Joey
I may be an ignorant "Kingfisher", but nothing will induce me to send you my proofs to Ayot or to 10, Adelphi Terrace. But I will go through them with you *anywhere* you like.

I have the proofs here, and I must admit your letters in print seem more of a joke against me than ever, but delightful reading. My book is obviously the work of an inexperienced sentimental, elderly lady—with gentlemanly feelings —and it is a little interesting and unusual. Your letters are of course its illumination.

Please return the wadge with all your "cuts" of those things that would "hurt Charlotte" and "give George reason for divorcing me."

Why do you lose patience with me?

I wonder how you would have liked to send Shakespeare your first manuscript for him to damn, and his wife and typist perhaps to criticise, when he *could* have talked it over with you? Now, don't lose patience, but do be *young* and *kind* and help me without scoffing and teasing. Please.

As to "Relativity", I read somewhere that it is a philosophy that "empties the baby out with the bath water"—that's what you'll do with my book.

My love to you.
Stella.

P.S. If I am "difficult" it is a little your fault: you don't tell me exactly what is the matter. I can't be quite the fool you would make me out to be surely.

Ayot St. Lawrence, Welwyn.
11th January 1922

Stella, Stella,

This tomfooling is no sort of use: if you persist in it you must give up the idea of making any use of the letters once and for all.

Remember: you start from the position that the publication of intimate letters that were never intended for publication is not permissible among persons of honour. If they

are love letters the difficulty is decupled, centupled, miltu-
pled. If they are love letters from a married man to a
woman who is not his wife, and who is engaged at the time
to another man whom she has subsequently married, the
difficulty becomes a wild impossibility: if the man publishes
them he is a blackguard: if the woman publishes them she
is a rotter and a courtesan.

In the face of this obvious state of things, you keep asking
me why you should NOT publish the letters. You might as
well ask me why you should not pick pockets or sell yourself on the street.

What is possible is the publication of amusing scraps of
correspondence, not excluding such gallantries as need not
be taken at more than drawingroom value, and such serious
passages as are entirely fit for publication. The selection
would have to be made with tact; and one of the tests would
be that neither my wife nor your husband could be made
ridiculous or feel slighted by it.

However, I dont think the matter is really practicable.
It is very nice of you to want to come and argue with me
for six months about every comma; but you know that I
havent time for that, and that it cannot be done in that way.
I should have to take the MS on as a professional job is taken
on. When I had cut out what I found impossible, and fitted
in the rest suitably, I should hand the thing to Charlotte and
ask her to read it for me and say whether there was anything offensive to her in it, or anything that in her judgment
you ought not for your own sake to divulge.

But this is exactly what you (very naturally) do not want
to do. To have your own story of your own life censored
by another woman is just what your sort of pride and mis-
trust cannot stomach. But the alternative is to do the perfectly correct thing, which is undoubtedly to abandon all
notion of publishing her husband's letters. The effect of my
action in the matter is to put you on your honor; and you

see how that ties you up. The worst of it is that you dont understand me, and think I am joking when I am most in earnest.

G.B.S.

Ashfields, Lathom, Lancs.
12th January 1922

Dear Joey,

I send you the letters in proof, more has been deleted.

To put them into the middle of the book breaks its rickity spine, and they won't sprinkle as I have constructed it.

The beloved "wadge" at the end with your photograph and a really lovely one of mine seems best.

Please be young and give me my own way.

You *know* how honoured and proud I would be for you to look over and help me with my twaddle.

But somehow I cannot send my first born out in the cold.

My love to you.
Stella.

Ashfields, Lathom, Lancs.
13th January 1922

Dear Joey,

You will see by the enclosed that I have been trying to get out of the letters with Hutchinsons.

So you see that as soon as I saw your attitude was changing I behaved like a gentleman.

My contract with H., which you read, was "second £500 on delivery of MS"—there was never a mention of your letters until after you gave your permission—

There are two letters on "Beyond Human Power" and one on "Macbeth" with Hackett—with letters from Mackail, Yeats etc.—A goodly company—still in the book. I suppose this is all right.

Tell Charlotte not to worry. I am sure Mr. Chantrey—
my business man—will manage Hutchinson, if not there's
young Hawksley—and I will go to America and pay
damages!

Stella.

Ayot St. Lawrence, Welwyn, Herts.
16th January 1922

Stella,

Did you ever read Kipling's story of the three jour-
nalists at sea who actually saw the sea serpent, and thought
their fortunes were made? When they got back to New
York they realized that their tale, though true, was too
good to be published, three or four hundred years hence
perhaps, but not in our lifetime. All you can do with them
is to sell the actual letters themselves to an American millionaire collector of manuscripts. You can sell him the paper
they are written on, and the inkstains, but not the copyright; so he cannot publish them. Except for that, they have
no value for you, heartless wretch that you are.

Their omission will not hurt the book nor affect Hutchinson's contracts. What remains is ten times more than he
has any right to expect. Do not forget that the letters, being
very flattering (God forgive me!) are more interesting to
you than to the baker's boy, and that you got them at long
intervals in small doses. If you cram them all down the reader's throat at one go, without any explanation of the circumstances which led to them, he will be fed up. And you
must not leave yourself open to derision for having swallowed them greedily without any wit or power of judging
them. They must have a certain quantity of connective tissue; and you must make it clear that you were perfectly
conscious of their extravagance. I shall be laughed at; but
that is Joey's metier.

276

But it is no use bothering you with instructions as to what you ought to do. I have done it. All you need do is to read through the proofs to see whether you can do it any better. You will find you cannot; so send the proofs back to the printer marked REVISE to Mrs. C. W. (address) and he will send you a clean copy with all the alterations made. I have spent two days on the job, and have very carefully considered every point. Nobody can reproach you for publishing it as I have left it; and there is the requisite touch to set Charlotte right without which I would have seen the whole universe damned before consenting to the publication of a line. It will be hard enough on her as it is to see her husband as the supreme ass of a drama of which you are the heroine.

Pity that it must be dramatized; but the thing in itself cannot be put into words at all.

I think I shall drop a line to Hutchinsons telling them not to fly into a state of shell shock. Heaven knows what you will do if they begin worrying and trembling for their serial contracts. . . . Just you don't mind them: they will get what they want if they behave themselves.

G.B.S.

P.S. Haven't you a letter from Pinero or any other of your authors? They will be furious if you leave them all out: that is, if they have written you any nice ones. You *must* have some more love letters. You cannot appear as a famous beauty who had only one catch: an old idiot of 56. Will there be nobody to keep me in countenance?

"Stolen your fig-leaf": see Mrs. Campbell, 14 June 1931.

Ashfields.

[undated: Jan. 1922?]

I burn so with blushes at your confounded impudence, that I dont feel the cold.

You have spoilt my book.

You have spoilt the story.

You have hidden from the world the one thing that would have done it good: Lustless Lions at play—

May you freeze in that sea of ice in Dante's Inferno—I dont care.

"Stolen your fig-leaf" indeed! You wear no fig-leaf in your letters.

Wait until you read Pinero's letters, Maeterlinck's, Barrie's, Edmund Gosse's, Mackail's, Burne-Jones', Pembroke's, Wemyss' etc. etc—you will be *sincerely* sorry you were 'second best'.

It is really sad: you creep on the ground, instead of flying in the air—through taking away those delicious letters.

Only one thing hangs up in my wigwam—a charm to keep off Satan—my Mother put it there.

"Hutchinson—money—"Rot"—Ugh!

Stella.

Since August I have been working 12 hours a day. Since your murdered bundle came—eighteen hours.

3, Deanery Street, W.1.

1922

What a pity that you "dare not"! If I "dared not", it might be reasonable—and we could both have enjoyed the concert and had a happy afternoon.

Only God can interfere on my behalf. He knows I cannot last much longer at this pace. Do you know of an inexpensive tutor, not too old—not over 70, neither too young —not under 20—a scientific mathematician, and a bit of a poet too? I am out of my poor depth with some writing I am doing, and I want a tutor to live in the house with me to help me—

What a pity it was you made Charlotte dislike me. I would have done for her friendship's "glory-hole", to be pulled out perhaps when she was a little tired by you.

Try and arrange that when we next meet it shall be in a church, otherwise I am sure to rush into your arms, and to throw my arms round your neck.

My love to you.
Stella.

Albany Hotel, Hastings.
24th Jan. 1922

I am down here until next Sunday afternoon, when I return to London.

It is slightly colder today than the North Pole, or your heart.

G.B.S.

Ashfields, Lathom, Lancs.
2nd February 1922

I am afraid Joey, your explanation does not hold water.

It is just this epileptic revulsion that keeps you from being the "Superman" you would be—and that you think you are.

When you stand on your head, and are upside down, you think you are superior to your fellow men, silly creature that you are—and at your age too!

As the letters are now, they are twaddle—for of course I have been obliged to cut out more. As you sent them, they misrepresented both me and my feelings.

Now, even the "crackle, crackle, crackle" reads as dm . . . d but very kindly impertinence.[1]
I "flirted" with no "super-philanderer". That is all lies. I was attached to—with my silly childish heart—what has turned out, a very ordinary individual—a man who cannot realise that, what he considers his "folly", is his "honour". Only the sweep knows *all* that is up the chimney.

Stella.

I cannot bear your letters when they touch upon the gross, and in an elderly manner! dont please write me any more of that kind—

◇◇◇◇◇◇

"Beb Asquith" is Herbert Asquith, who was then reader for Hutchinson & Co., the publishers.

Ashfields, Lathom, Lancs.

19th February 1922

Dear Joey,

I am sorry not to have answered your letter, but I got it three days late. I was in London visiting and saying "Goodbye" to a dying friend, and my Secretary thinking I would be home earlier, did not forward it.

On receipt of your telegram, I took your cut letters to Beb Asquith. When I got home, I felt out of sympathy with the whole matter so I did not write in a hurry.

I have not told D.D. what you have done with the letters, and yesterday I received the enclosed from her, suggesting I should put them in the book.

I think my nose makes a very good periscope, for there is no doubt I realised before many people, just how big a

---

[1] See above, letter from G.B.S., 10 Dec. 1912, page 70.

fool Henry Arthur Jones was as a writer of plays: and that I never, for one moment, failed to see through your bluff, or allowed myself for one hundredth part of a second, to fall in love with your pretence.

It is a supreme pity that you have massacred the letters as you have done; they are now the only insincere thing in the book.

If you are very anxious about anything, had you not better write to Hutchinson yourself? I do not relish looking a bigger fool than I do already.

I saw Pamela, Lytton's sister the other day. She told me that you had praised my book and said you were picking out some letters.

I told you, I think, that I am putting in your letter about Hackett's acting and mine; I hope this will be all right.

You cannot criticise my writing in spots. Of course it is amateurish and not professional—thank God.

My love to you.
Stella.

◇◇◇◇◇◇

The letter from G.B.S. giving permission is dated 2 Dec. 1921.

Ashfields, Lathom, Lancs.
24th February 1922

Well, there is nothing left for me to do but to hit you back with the poker, holding it with both my hands—having no respect for your few remaining transparent hairs—and to hit you flat dead.

I *am* going to publish exactly what I like—if you didn't mean what you wrote about *Macbeth*, you shouldn't have written it.

These two letters you wrote to D.D., make *all* the other letters *quite right*.

Be thankful if I cut enough out, and leave enough in, so that you dare face the public again. Start saying your prayers.

I have your letter giving me *absolute permission*—and I have all the hundreds of other letters and postcards.

So you be civil.

Its no use being a gentleman with you—

You are one of those who only respect people who behave worse than you do yourself—I am *ashamed* of you—and the AWFUL thing is, you have ceased to amuse me.

You have *revoked*—that's your game always—so you must now start writing to Hackett and Hutchinson—Your letter to Hutchinson made no impression.

Its a dreadful thing to have a vaulting mind that o'er leaps itself and goes "potty"—thats what has happened to you.

I read in a paper yesterday, that you had ceased to be popular. Had I had my way in the beginning, you would have been as popular as Lord Byron, and Joseph!

Next time you try and fascinate an actress, don't use her as a means of teasing Charlotte—*that* was the ugliest thing you did.

You don't amuse me—"We are not amused".

A man who *revokes*—and then uses the poker on the other man—is . . . . . . well . . . . . . an *Irishman*.

Stella.

◇◇◇◇◇◇◇

Ethel Irving successfully sued a newspaper because its critic, describing what he considered to be her overacting as Julie in Brieux's play The Three Daughters of M. Dupont, *departed so far from the literal truth as to say that she rolled on the stage and bit her own toenails. Mrs. Weldon has not emerged from her "total obscurity," so far as the editor of this correspondence is concerned. Lottie Collins: the music-hall singer who made the song "Ta-Ra-Ra-Boom-De-Ay" world-famous.*

"Those letters to D.D." were two notes written in December 1912 by G.B.S. They are not reproduced here for the reason that they are, in his own phrase, "eyewash," and would needlessly confuse the story. One contains the passage: "It was clear, wasn't it, when she had nothing to do but lie there staring at the ceiling, that nothing could occupy and distract her and give her an interest in life but a thrilling love affair—and you will admit also that a more desperate enterprise for an elderly gentleman of 56 than to make himself the Romeo of such an affair could hardly be imagined. It was like Richard III and Lady Anne."

Ayot St. Lawrence, Welwyn, Herts.
25th Feb. 1922

You mustn't slaughter Hackett for this reason. A criticism of an actor in the ordinary course of press criticism, is virtually privileged, because, though he can always get damages if he takes an action (like Ethel Irving the other day), he will frighten the papers out of mentioning him next time. Mrs. Weldon passed the last 20 years of her life in total obscurity because she had set up a Terror by her litigiousness. Much the same thing happened to Lottie Collins after she sued a critic. Ethel Irving will probably be forgiven because the critic made a false statement which amounted to an accusation of professional incompetence and misconduct; but as a rule it is an extremely ill-advised step to sue a newspaper for a criticism which is current news.

But no such privilege attaches to an unprovoked publication of a disparagement *à propos de bottes*. If you publish anything damaging to Hackett professionally, he can sue the publisher for damages (and you have signed an agreement indemnifying the publisher), and not only suppress the book but have it struck out of the catalogue of the British Museum Library.

Besides, it is unprofessional; and the social feeling against that is very strong.

I dont really like those letters to D.D., because they are eyewash in spite of their superficial accuracy. I hate the whole thing, because it is impossible to present it in its simple truth to the public, and it is dishonest to disguise it, and disloyal to pretend that it was all playacting. I felt a great deal more than you did; and I still feel a great deal more about it than you. You are doing—if you only knew it—a dreadful thing; and someday you will say "I had better have tied a millstone round my neck and cast myself into the sea: why did you not warn me?" You must have about a ton of letters that would interest the public (not those that interest *you*); and if you were wise you would use them, and stick to your dignity with iron tenacity. You *can* be dignified sometimes—beautifully dignified. Why do you want to be ridiculous and scandalous?

G.B.S.

Ashfields, Lathom, Lancs.
6th March 1922

Dear Joey,

You needn't be nervous. The love letters are now no more like love letters than my hat.

I have had a millstone round my neck and been to the bottom of the pond a thousand times since last August—metaphorically.

And now that my book is finished, do for heaven's sake suggest a play and give me a chance to use my old age and little talent—or else to the workhouse I must go.

What nonsensical things you write about me, about life,

and about the world. If you are wise, then thank God for my ignorance.

I wonder that any one who knows you does other than hide under the bed with blinds down; for to face the light of day with all the terrors you set grinning at one, is enough to scare the wits out of . . .

I am in London tomorrow, staying at 1 Lowndes St. Please write me about the enclosed, c/o Colonel Guy Wyndham C.B. (George's mother's sister was his wife— she is dead). To quote a famous man. God and I know what my book means now, but the day will come when God only knows.

My love to you
Stella.

8, Carlton Mews, S.W.
3rd April 1922

Well Joey I arrived in this horses house on Saturday. Mrs. Benjamin Guinness has let it to me cheaply.

Though I have not forgotten your abominable and most vile letters to me, I would like to see you. I think it is good for your soul to know that I forgive you and my affection remains.

My love to you
Stella.

I see blasted cuttings about Bernard Shaws love-letters. Hutchinsons way of trying to advertise my book which is all about myself—such crass trash it is too—my enemies will giggle—its *your* fault.

Ashfields, Lathom, Lancs.
1922

I am glad to get your letter and the silly cuttings. I cannot afford to subscribe.

I am wondering what you will say when you see that all the "wadge" is in—Oh dear, oh dear—I dont mind, but if it is going to hurt you—I *do* I *do*.

—Perhaps after all you wont mind and you will give me the permission for "Dearest" in the "crackle crackle" letter,[1] and for the beloved New Year letter putting Swift to shame.

I am truly dreadfully sorry if Charlotte is distressed, if only she had been kind to me we could have selected the letters together—

If only she would pity—instead of despising actresses for not being as well educated and as well behaved as herself—

A serious man stopped me out of doors and thanked me for having shown the world the real human Bernard Shaw: "Your courage makes the whole world understand him and love him" I didn't like to say you were pulling my leg, and it was *I* who was full of deep affection for you—

Stella.

Please write.

6, Carlton Mews.
9th April 1922

Dont be devilish Joey. You know quite well what I mean.

I longed for you to look through it all and guide and chide within reason. You insulted me, and flattened it into a pancake—And I wished you and your letters in hell—I have dozens of your letters that no-one has read. I was far too proud, after your madness to show you the book,—and I hope you will never read it! I have never said you were in love with me, for the good reason that I never believed you were. In love with making a fool of me yes.

---

[1] See above, letter from G.B.S., 10 Dec. 1912, page 70.

I wish I could make you change your mind about the "New Years Eve" letter—it is so lovely and good for the world—and for all the Jackanapes that live in it—to read.

Dont forget when you are accusing me that I sent the letters for Charlotte to read. And that when I heard she was distressed I tried to get them back from Hutchinsons.

And never forget they are not *love-letters* at all—you have only pretended they were to frighten me into not publishing.

I am here until the 1st of May then if I can get no work I must sell or let "Ashfields" and live in one room. I have a seven years lease at £75.

I do hope Joey when the poor book is published you will behave like a gentleman, you could of course behave disgustingly.

Don't write any more "Confidential" letters to my publishers, it isn't seemly, and please get out of your mind that I am going to cheat you in any way over the letters.

Have you heard of the new disease "perfection"?

I have not expressed *my* feeling for you, nor my delight in your company—it didn't come naturally after the letters were massacred.

I wish you were as stable in friendship as I, and had more of the right kind of courage.

My love to you,
Stella.

◇◇◇◇◇◇◇

Me and My Diary *was a curtain-raiser by Gertrude Jennings, and Ellis Jeffreys was a stylish and pungent comedienne, who died in 1943, aged seventy.*

8, Carlton Mews S.W.

25th April 1922

Dear Joey. My ignorant, illiterate, ungrammatical, and probably illegal book would not have been *so* disgraceful if you had'nt "hit" so hard that I did'nt dare have your help. I needed it, and do need it dreadfully—

Last week I went to the Everyman Theatre. *Misalliance* is surely out and out the best you have done, and that I suppose means the best modern play. Do the public and the critics appreciate what a splendid bit of work it is I wonder?

It was acted extraordinarily well and sanely. The clerk and the Polish girl were particularly good—

I wonder if they would give me a job at that Theatre, and salary enough to buy sandwiches and pay my tube fare? I offered myself at the Box Office.

I am not quite "tabooed" by the London Managers they wanted me to follow Ellis Jeffreys in *Me and My Diary* and then Harrison found he did'nt want it for the Haymarket after all.

I leave here Saturday—I would like to see you if you could spare a minute.

Stella.

◇◇◇◇◇◇

"Mr. Walkley" was the distinguished critic of The Times, *who died in 1926, aged seventy. "MacDermot" is Norman Macdermott, a manager of taste and enterprise, who founded the Everyman Theatre in Hampstead. He presented many plays of interest, including eight of Shaw's. Mrs. Campbell's second book was sketched but never completed.*

5, Carlton Mews.

27th April 22

Dear Joey—

Your letters are not kind, aren't you tired of knocking me about?

I met Mr. Walkley at the Ivy Restaurant he has never seen *Misalliance* I told him to go *at once*.

I believe on May 20th I open at the Everyman Theatre in *Hedda Gabler* for a fortnight: so I shall have £3 a week for a fortnight—thank God!

Don't write to MacDermot [*sic*] saying I am an impossible woman, and that I will smash his Theatre at the first rehearsal—I mean his enterprise—I need that £3 a week sorely.

To-morrow I go to 3 Deanery St. Park Lane for two or three weeks.

I have a strong desire to face your taunts and jibes and show you my silly book in leaf form—and yet!—

I have started another book *Some sense and much nonsence* it comes easily—the nonsense part of it. I like your idea of Grocks assistant—but the idea I like best in the world is the idea of eternal sleep.

I am grimly grave—and most seriously sincere if you only knew! I fool at times to keep my heart from freezing—
(*Contd. on May 1st at 3 Deanery St. Park Lane*).

I play Bridge quite well, it pulls me together like Bach.

I wish I could trust you not to offend me.

I like your answer to those questions—I read them in the *Observer* yesterday. Our soul is our prayer house always—the rest is begging we know—It is only because I have conjured with your name I suppose that I feel you ought to see the book—

Please don't do me out of that £3 a week engagement.

I greet you with a kiss of charity Joey.

Stella.

3, Deanery Street, W.1.

5.5.22

Oh Joey—oh lor! oh Hell! I have just seen the *New York Herald*, they have put in all the letters uncut, this in spite of all their promises and the enclosed. What can I do now. And they have put in my uncorrected proofs.

Please send me word what I can do?

I feel *very* unhappy because I know how much you will mind—for myself, well. . . . . . .

Stella.

3, Deanery Street, W.1.

9th May 1922

I expect I will get the letter, I didn't understand the telegram.

Everyone says the same thing: "You have shown us the real Shaw—the human Shaw—the divine Shaw—"

You see I was right and you were wrong.

Please write and say I may put the New Years Eve letter in the book and the "Dearest" in the "crackle crackle" letter.[1]

You write "nothing matters now" so I suppose I may. I see *Misalliance* again on Wednesday with Mrs. Guiness and others. I *do* like that play.

Stella.

3, Deanery St, W.

10th May 1922

Dear Joey.

Please write me a line saying I *may* put the New Years Eve letter in—and the "dearest" they wont do it at Hutchinsons they are *afraid* of you, and I want it in the

[1] See above, letter from G.B.S., 10 Dec. 1912, page 70.

book dreadfully—the letter has not come here that you posted to Lord St. it is rather important!

Yours
Stella.

We went last night again to *Misalliance* that is a good play if you like!

Pitt House, Hampstead, N.W.3.

19.5.22

The Hutchinson's letter I sent you has not been returned to me, it is rather serious what are we to do—

I did not photograph it!

Errors of many hideous kinds are appearing in the serial rights grammar, words, names etc—a nightmare—

Did you object to the funny silliness of the world in a hundred years saying I was your mistress and G.B. our son?

Have Hutchinsons sent you the M.S to read?

I wish I could see you.

This lovely place is opposite Byrons cottage and it's a joy in the garden—the flowers and birds, and my hostess is a beautiful Irish widow.

Yours
Stella.

Pitt House, Hampstead, N.W.3.

19th May 1922

What did you mean by: "I am glad Hutchinsons has some common sense"—

There are two important things I want to speak to you about do manage it after *Hedda*. I looked in last night and heard a happy audience laughing at *You Never Can Tell.*

Stella.

Cadogan Hotel, S.W.1.
26th May 1922

. . . Yes indeed that was damnable, and I have written to Pinero. It was most carefully 'cut' in my galley proof.

I read it in the train back from Paris, and I went from the station to Hutchinson and behold it was *not* 'cut' in their proof.

The *New York Herald* evidently found my stuff dull, and they have enlivened it with a nightmare of lies and vulgarity.

The fault of the whole affair is yours because together we might have managed something a little respectable, and yet foolish enough to give some sort of a portrait of me.

Indeed the company acting at the Everyman is just as good as mine, only they dont *think* before they speak, and that funny rattling away of words is quite dreadful—You think for us. Ibsen gives us just a little chance to think for ourselves—besides I am very much on my P's and Q's. I need that £3—Yes I do sweat visibly—my hair is so heavy—

It will be nice when I see you—will I ever again—unless I bribe you with the packet of all the letters that I have not published and only your eyes and mine have seen!

Stella.

Only here and there do I do anything nicely as *Hedda*, and I look a freak on that little stage—I love the theatre—all but the spiral staircase after a tragic act to the dressing rooms.

3, Deanery Street, W.1.
11th June 1922

Dear Joey,
        Hasn't the letter been returned?
Its odd that it should have disappeared altogether for it is very important. Sir George Lewis wants it. I would like you

to come and see *Hedda Gabler*—it would be nice to hear all the abominable things you might say.

Some say I "walk through".

Gosse is very flattering, he says I get nearest of all to what Ibsen meant.

Denis Mackail declares it is a bad play and that I put worlds more into it than Ibsen ever dreamed of!

Am I never going to see you again? How stupid it is, you are not a super man after all—but I knew that from the beginning.

My love to you
Stella.

◇◇◇◇◇◇◇

"Gosse" is Sir Edmund Gosse, the littérateur, poet, and critic. He was the literary critic of the Sunday Times. *He was one of the first to introduce Ibsen to English readers in* Studies in the Literature of Northern Europe *(1879). He died in 1928. G.B.S. was, of course, only joking because of Gosse's early enmity towards him. Later in life they became friends.*

3, Deanery Street, W.1.
16th June 1922

What a bore it is. I do want that letter. *EDMUND* Gosse, "Who he is God knows" you say—Fie!

How dare you say *I* have created a delicate situation you know perfectly well—it is all your fault from beginning to end.

Its a pity you dont see *Hedda*—It would be good for you —I mean, inspire you one way or another.

I go on the road on Monday—South Coast—and try and pick up a shilling or two.

My love to you
Stella.

Ayot St. Lawrence, Welwyn.
17th June 1922

A notice has been stuck up in the hall of that confounded lodging house proclaiming a handsome reward for
the finder of the letter. If that fails, I am done. It is thought
that the charwoman may have been attracted by the strip
of pictures of Stratford-on-Avon on which I wrote my letter and in which I enclosed Hutchinson's.

Didnt know Denis was married. He is right enough about
your extraordinary virtuosity in phrasing. If it were not for
that— ! ! !

G.B.S.

Alexandra Hotel, Eastbourne.
20th till Wed—then
Brighton 22nd
Bournemouth 23rd
Westcliffe-on-Sea 24th
[between July and Oct. 1922]

I wish you would make a clean breast of it to Charlotte and *tell* her I sent you the wadge of letters to show her
and to 'cut' as she liked.

I don't like hurting her.

You do make your friends get into ugly places to be sure.

I always have been able to act—and to speak—it is all of
you that have been so unkind to me.

It is very wicked of you to lose important letters. I
thought you were much too business-like.

I am "on the road" for the rest of my life. I started the
tour at Macdermott's £3 a week—

I hear he has made his first profit out of me and that his
affairs are in the receiver's hands. So we could'nt join up
and start a repertory together, I doing a new part every
four weeks and starting with *Getting Married*. My love to

you—how I can go on sending my love to you I cannot imagine.

Stella.

Frank Schuster told me you were so funny about Tree—and so splendid about Elgar—

Ashfields, Lathom, Lancs.
24th Oct. 1922

Bless you I knew you by your colons! I confess I laughed heartily—

I want to hear from you and see you—and tell you about *Hedda Gabler* at the Potter's own Theatre. I play at Wimbledon next week, and will be staying at 1 Lowndes Street, c/o Col. Guy Wyndham, C.B.

My poor effort has been shockingly overpraised.

If only the letters had been published as *I* wished them to be we would have both been crowned Saints.

My love to you
Stella.

Ashfields, Lathom, Lancs.
9th Nov. /22

Dear Joey,

These are the two cuttings I like best. Your letter is sad—66 indeed!

I know a woman of 40 who married a man of 84 and was blissfully happy with him for 12 years—he is dead, and now she sleeps with his dressing gown on her bed over her feet—a clever woman, and he a man full of wisdom and tenderness—

So dont you say you have lost all interest in women—

I have bought a play—so expensive, too—and I, 50 years too old for the part and 3 quarters of a yard too broad—pray for me.

295

My financial affairs are clearing up, but they'll smash up again in a minute no doubt—

I thought the semi-colons were colons—I suppose I am going blind.

I am surprised it wasn't your doing. Some other fellow has mistaken real tragedy for sentiment.

This week Manchester, and living here. Next week Derby —in an Hotel; then Hammersmith living at 1 Lowndes Street.

The sooner I see you the better.

My love to you.
Stella.

10, Adelphi Terrace, W.C.2.
3rd January 1923

You must be wallowing in wealth to send shilling telegrams instead of three-halfpenny letters. I hope the book heaped gold on you. I, too, liked the *Spectator* notice best. It was funny how few people knew.

When I told you of my sudden loss of all *specific* interest in women you did not notice the adjective. I see women as I see other people. I always did, but with one eye only: the other eye was enchanted. Now the enchantment is gone; and I can no longer tell myself love stories.

I forgive you the letters because there is a star somewhere on which you were right about them; and on that star we two should have been born. I told you you had never learned to live in this one; and the Titanic slavery by which I have learned has separated us.

Not a day too soon, perhaps, considering my dotage.

I made you pretend; but do not ever let yourself suspect that I have pretended or denied. And now I am going to Bournemouth for a week for a change.

G.B.S.

◇◇◇◇◇◇

This letter was written the day after Saint Joan *was produced for the first time in London (at the New Theatre, on 26 March 1924). [It had been produced by the Theatre Guild in New York in December 1923.] Lyall Swete was an accomplished actor and Old Bensonian who was to give the most striking performance of his career as Warwick. Sybil Thorndike was the Joan, and has never been surpassed. Edith Evans had originated the Serpent and the She-Ancient at Birmingham the previous year. She was to play both again in London the following September.*

During 1923, 1924, and 1925 Mrs. Campbell toured Great Britain and Ireland with her famous parts in The Second Mrs. Tanqueray, Magda, The Thirteenth Chair, *and also with a "new play" called* The Adventurous Age.

10, Adelphi Terrace, W.C.2

27th March 1924

Then you still live! After reading your telegram I went to Lyall Swete's dressingroom to give him a final word before the curtain rose; and he began to rave about you as the greatest actress in the world, swearing that you are as beautiful as ever, and that you had trained a perfect company to support you in perfect performances of Hedda and other plays; he having seen you lately. The man must be crazy.

God intended you to play the serpent in *Methuselah*: I wrote it for your voice. When I told Edith Evans that she would have to enter baldheaded, old, half naked, and in rags, in a bevy of youths and maidens made as pretty as the stage could make them, and that in that ghastly condition she would outfascinate them and play them clean out of existence, she believed, and did it. Sybil Thorndike for a whole month never let me doubt for a second that she regarded me as far superior to the Holy Trinity as a producer. And now Siddons and Rachel were never so praised and exalted as these twain. If you had only had faith as much as a grain of mustard seed!

Well, are you quite well? and are you making plenty of money? and have you still the cottage at Ormskirk? and has your virgin loveliness really come back? and do you remember Tristan and Isolde and forget all our stupid conflicts? and did the book get you out of debt? and—and—and —and—what sort of life are you having generally?

I shall be 68 in July: that is about all MY news, except what you may read in the papers.

G.B.S.

3 Deanery Street, W.1.
30th March 1924

Dear dear Joey,

Your letter at the theatre gave me strange pleasure— all the dreariness vanished.

I have owed you a letter for a long long time—I did write to you very many months ago, but never sent it.

Its two years next June since I started to clear £6000. Its nearly cleared up now, but it has been a mighty, an almighty job!

The book brought in about £2500. I believe, and there is still more to come in.

I started my tour on £15 with *Hedda Gabler*—

Then I produced Bernstein's *LÉlevation*, translated by Jack Mackail's daughter, she did it well. The play was a success, but too sad, so I dropped it.

Pinero then let me have *Tanqueray*, I am playing it at Croydon also *Magda* this week, and living here with friends.

I have a car. I couldn't stand waiting about in cold stations, and I must have air—a bedroom in station hotels couldn't be borne for nearly two years. I spend most of my day in the car, that is a joy. Next year I mean to drive it myself. It is a six cylinder Buick, that can be shut or open, and has done 24,000 miles without a rattle.

Yes, I still have my cottage at Ormskirk, with its lovely garden. I have it on a twenty years lease. Ned Lathom is no longer my landlord, the local grocer is.

I have an excellent cook-housekeeper, a gardner with one leg and four fingers—blown up in France—I was persuaded by the local clergyman to take him—for my sins!

I wonder if you remember my brother Max, who was very strange. I have taken care of him for over three years, and he is now quite well which delights me.

Ashdown, the Publisher, took six pieces of his music and published them and they are now publishing some more. They thought very highly of them, as did Sir Landon Ronald, who has promised, to use his influence to get them into the School Syllabus.

Dear Lyall Swete loved me when Beo was four years of age, and wrote pretty poems to me, one entitled "The Child of the King". He would have me believe I haven't disappointed him, but I daresay you are right in saying "he must be crazy".

Will you take me to a matinee of *Saint Joan* this week? That would make up for a great deal. I have read your praises with so much pleasure—dear Joey—that you go deep deep down into the human heart, that it is far the finest thing you have ever done, and you are compared with Mr. Shakespeare of course and in one paper all they said of the *youth* of you!

How lovely it would be to see the play with you. You won't refuse me will you. I'll soon be dead, and the "grocer's boy" died years ago.

Sixty eight indeed? Twenty two—and I your grandmother.

I never forget *Tristan and Isolde*—and you twenty one—
I seventeen—harps in the air—

My love to you
Send me a message.
Stella.

12 Dec. 1927

Dear Unforgotten
        . . . If you knew the trouble those unlucky letters
made for me you would understand a lot of things. I don't
regret it; and it doesn't matter as it got you out of your difficulties for a moment; but O Lord, Stella, it mustn't happen
again until we are both dead. Then we can be added to
Heloise and Abelard and all the rest of them.

I pick up what news I can of you from D.D. and Lady
Horner and Mrs. Dorothy Cheston-Bennett and the rest.
They say you are recovering your good looks. When did
you ever lose them? By the way, dont discard the gramo-
phone business. It is very difficult, being as much the opposite of stage declamation as movie acting of stage acting; but
it can be done; and your voice and articulation—!!!

G.B.S.

❖❖❖❖❖❖

In June 1926 Mrs. Campbell appeared at the Savoy in What
Might Happen, *and in February 1927 she went to the U.S.A.
in* The Adventurous Age. *Except for one letter from G.B.S. in
December 1927, there now occurs an interval of more than
three and a half years in the correspondence. The interim was
for Shaw somewhat eventless, and for Mrs. Campbell not no-
ticeably happy. He wrote no new play and produced no major
work of any sort. By July 1927 Mrs. Campbell was back in
England, and for a time gave a series of talks on "Diction in Dramatic Art." She is more happily glimpsed in Arnold Bennett's*

300

Journal. *In the entry for 27 September 1927 we read: "Mrs. Patrick Campbell and Komisarjevsky came for lunch in order to meet each other. Komi said very little. Stella talked tremendously, and very well. Her ideas are exceedingly sound, and in spite of all that I have heard about her naughtiness, she seems to me to be fundamentally good-natured." And again on 7 December of the same year: "Mrs. P. Campbell came for tea at 5.30 and made a terrific outpouring. She said: 'If you want to keep me quiet give me a cigar.' So I gave her one. Later, she went out into the Square smoking it. Her energy seems quite unimpaired. She now wants to produce and play* Flora. *She arrived with a great scheme all complete. She read the play about a year ago or more, and saw nothing in it. Now she reads it again and sees everything in it."*

"Arnold" is probably Arnold Bennett, who about this time wrote or translated a play called Don Juan de Mañara *(privately printed). But this is conjectural. (The play referred to is obviously* Flora—*mentioned in the following letters.)*

4, Whitehall Court, S.W.1.
14th January 1928

I did not mean *that* way: of course I know as well as you that it added a star to my (our) halo; but all the same, dear Stella, on the terre-à-terrestrial plane it tied my hands cruelly, and does still to some extent. If I have to hurt somebody I had better hurt you, who are made of iron and can stand it.

Arnold will not consider you authorized to shew me his unpublished work; but do it all the same: he will forgive. I know a little Spanish: enough to make out a play in the original with a dictionary at hand.

On Monday I have to be a pall bearer at Westminster Abbey for Hardy; and I havnt any proper clothes.

G.B.S.

Flora, *the play by Arnold Bennett, seems to have been acted only at Rusholme (Lancashire) and generally to have had a hapless existence.*

Mrs. Charles Calvert played as an infant with Charles Kean. After a long and distinctive career she died in 1921, aged eighty-five.

4, Whitehall Court, S.W.1.

18th January 1928

My dear Stella,

I do not see any room for hesitation about *Flora*. Either you are in business as an actress or you are not. It is now, I take it, a case of "Mrs. Patrick Campbell at liberty. Matrons, heavies, comedy, character: 64 Pont St." Well, here you are offered a leading part in a play by an eminent author. Of course you take it without any fuss, as a taxi driver takes a fare, and glad to get it.

It is of great importance to you to get into the routine of the theatre as leading Old Woman, and break with your starry past. It is very difficult: Ellen Terry, like Kate, failed in the attempt; but Mrs. Calvert, once a beautiful Myrhha Myrrha? (that can't be rightly spelt; but let it stand) in Byron's *Sardanapalus*, rose from utter extinction to play the mother in *Arms and The Man* in 1894, and finished the century as the greatest draw on the London stage in old parts with Hawtrey. It is by taking ordinary jobs as they come that you will have to repeat that success.

From this point of view I think it is a pity that your part is the title part. The play should be called *Was she right?* or something of that sort; and you should resist all attempts to star you in it as the famous and beautiful Mrs. P.C. You have a *new* reputation to make; and the old one will make your task a hard one. Tell them that they must do nothing more than they would for Ellis Jeffreys. If you hold on to the old wreaths, you are lost.

And if it comes off, *do* behave yourself, dear Stella, if you can. Dont begin to do everybody's business except your own, especially the producer's. *That*, as you very well know, is what is standing in your way.

I have to rush to catch a train. I will take the book of Benavente's plays with me, and write again.

ever
G.B.S.

◇◇◇◇◇◇

"Dorothy" is Dorothy Cheston-Bennett.
Jacinto Benavente's play The Passion Flower *had been successfully produced at the Everyman Theatre two years earlier.*

64, Pont Street, S.W.1.
19th January 1928

Dear Joey,

I understand, but the position is like this. Four years ago Arnold B sent me *Flora*—I only saw it as a commonplace, ordinary and good sort of working vehicle, or whatever the right word or expression is for that kind of play. I returned it to him. The other day Dorothy brought the play to me again.

On re-reading it I thought if I bring to this play an imagined radiance and vibration I could make the audience expectant and alive and Flora might become a romantic and interesting figure—

If I may make an excuse for my bad name it is this—I am—in a small way—an imaginative artist, and there is my difficulty—Sometimes I cannot learn my words until I know what the others are bringing to or taking away from their words . . . I search for the spirit whilst the producer is struggling with the letter—this reads as *banale* but it is simple and true for me.

Miss Ellis Jeffreys is not an imaginative or romantic artist, neither I suppose was the late Mrs. Calvert. It is so much easier for the producer when the artist is just very clever obedient and amiable. . . .

You should have seen "Eliza Doolittle" in America! and my God the poor Dustman with his face to the audience and Pickering and Higgins many feet behind him! . . .

I have'nt been asked to play *Flora* I have been asked whether I would get the necessary backing and do the play myself.

Now in the Jacinto B play all the imagination the romance and loveliness are *there*—I have only to interpret faithfully.

It is stupid of me that I cannot as you do realise I am an old lady who has arrived at 'Heavies, Matrons etc.'

I see myself an unwanted child just as I see you, not as an old gentleman, but as a brilliant adorable Irish lad whom I love with ardour.—

Stella.

64 Pont Street, S.W.1.
27th January 1928

Dear Joey,

What a scorcher!—perhaps from some angle true.

D.D. said after *Pygmalion*, "Does Shaw realise what you have done for him, you have made Eliza a human being!"

Sybil Thorndike was here the other night. She recited some Browning—She said she would like me to produce her in something. I had scolded her a few days before for her want of 'legato', turning out her good things to the audience like potatoes out of a sack! I tried to explain how the audience must be drawn to the artist and filled with a little wonder now and again—She listened as one doesn't listen to 'noodles'!

Be an angel and send me back the Jacinto Benevente. Somebody will steal my lovely role if they get the idea, and that will break my heart.

I know where Satan has gotten you Joey, you are *brain proud!*

Bless you, write again.
Stella.

P.S. I have written the Synopsis of a play—how I would like to send it to you, and have all my "noodledums" pointed out to me.

64, Pont Street, S.W.1.
3rd Feb. 1928

Oh Joey dear you are potty—I "staccato"—the idea! My synopsis is in the hands of Mary Borden. You are the only one who could have done it—D.D. said Tchehov!

Well, you will go to Westminster Abbey, believing me an affected ass and then the angels will tell you something you have passed by in your whirligig of fame—

Bless you for ever.
Stella.

Ayot St. Lawrence, Welwyn.
6th Feb. 1928

Petty! Woman: you are profane: the prophet speaks not without weighing his words.

I said *that* because you are trying to teach (being incapable of learning, which is sometimes not a bad qualification); and the first thing you have to knock into a stage novice is

305

staccato alphabet so staccatissimo that every consonant will put out a candle at the back of the gallery. Not until her tongue and lips are like a pianist's fingers should she begin to dare think of speaking to an audience. I do not know who taught you to articulate; but whoever gave you your staccato gave you the power that, with your unaccountable fascination, enabled you, until you were found out, to persuade people that you were the supreme actress of your generation: no small feat for a woman who could not act at all except in fantasies of her own, like Irving. *His* elocution, by the way, though so pedantic that every slovenly tongued cockney ridiculed it, was half the secret of his illusory distinction.

Such music as your pupils may have must come from within them; all you can teach them is the value of your *martellato molto*. That is the foundation of my platform effectiveness. The laugh comes from the back row of the gallery as heartily as from the front of the stalls.

Only, if your pupils want to be trained for the phonofilm or Movietone, they must after learning the staccato, renounce all its *sforzandos,* and learn a delicacy of touch and subtlety of nuance which could never "get across" viva voce, but which the microphone and the wireless amplifier will carry to the remotest cheap seats of the world.

Oh, if only you could learn—but I waste words. Farewell.

G.B.S.

64, Pont Street, S.W.1.
[undated]

I wrote you were potty not petty!
God taught me to articulate.
Oh dear. I cannot stand up to life much longer. . . .
What a wonderful thing it would be if great thinkers and

great talkers understood the human heart was of more con-
sequence than the human head——

Surely both you and Tolstoi *knew* and know God is the
Holy Spirit that dwells—or should dwell within each one of
us. Epilepsy is an accident caused by wrong living somewhere or somehow.

Nobody really believes in a personal God—I cant understand why you wrote of Tolstoi like that.

Oh those ten children of yours you never had, and all
their teachings you have missed. And my love is taken from
you by your—or someone elses—fear of a policeman.

Stella.

64, Pont St., S.W.1.

20th February 1928

Dear Joey,

They have asked me to play "Mrs. Alving" for the
Ibsen Centenary, and I have accepted. You have bashed me
and beheaded me so often, do do it once more if you think
I should ruin the play—I could get out of it.

I feel rather like the little black girl who after the Englishman kissed her, ran to her mother and said "Englishman
eatee me upee" and the next day crept back to the Englishman and said—"Eatee me upee some more".

I have all your books except *Translations and Tomfool-
eries*—make me a present of that please. I returned Dorothy
Cheston's copy to her.

My love to you

Stella.

◇◇◇◇◇◇◇

*The original of this letter is in typescript, excepting the third
word, "Joey," and "oh lor! my French!" and the final "Stella,"
which are in Mrs. Campbell's handwriting.*

She played Mrs. Alving in Ghosts *(for the first time) on the occasion of the centenary of Ibsen's birth, a single matinée performance on 27 March 1928.*

64 Pont Street, S.W.1.

23rd February 1928

You know Joey it was'nt nice of you to say I could'nt produce! I realise all too well plays *as a whole*—though I try not to when it is not my business!! *Pelleas and Melisande* was my production—Forbes Robertson and his brother only damned and said what rot it was! Sarah Bernhardt followed every detail of my production—with one exception—Sarah asked my permission (I nearly died of shame)—to stand with her back to the wall so that Melisande's hair fell over her face. I took all rehearsals for her and her company without question—and oh lor! my French!

Then look at *Beyond Human Power*, I did that entirely alone without a direction in the book—and it was'nt so bad!

I wish you would'nt judge people's brains by their expanding or elastic reach. There is a power of subtle understanding and sympathy, and taste—that have often passed by you—unrecognised.

You have done me out of my job my boy, and taken it *yourself*. And there is 'Mrs. Alving' carrying no salary—all her rehearsals and luncheon expenses—and I with a hearty appetite and no funds!

Does'nt your conscience prick you—you with your daily fortune pouring in—and I a beggar—I cannot think how I can go on loving you as I do!

Stella.

◇◇◇◇◇◇◇

Another complete silence, lasting nine months. In October Mrs. Campbell played another great Ibsen part, Ella Rentheim in John Gabriel Borkman.

308

Shaw's letters to Janet Achurch have still to see publication. She was a powerful Ibsen actress. Charles Charrington, the actor, was her husband.

The widowed Mrs. Alan Campbell married the Marchese Ugo Spinola.

4, Whitehall Court, S.W.1.
22nd November 1928

My dear Stella

Gabriel Wells is an American-Hungarian bookseller, publisher of collectors' editions, and dealer in manuscripts, who has made a special business of buying up Shaviana. His operations have raised the market against himself, though of course this only advertises his treasures for subsequent sale to the lunatics who collect such things. He paid £10 for two postcards which he might have had for ten shillings, and he has just bought 130 letters of mine to Janet Achurch which were sold as waste paper after Charrington's death.

I have been recommending all my friends to sell every scrap of my writing they possess whilst the craze lasts. I mentioned your name to him (of course without special emphasis among others) as "possibly" having letters of mine. *All* my letters to you cannot have been unfit for ex-hibition; and with my usual want of delicacy I did not see why you should not get *some* good out of them at last.

Selling letters has nothing to do with their publication. The copyright lies with the writer or his heirs, but the sheet of paper belongs to the person to whom they were written and is saleable.

I had a letter the other day from a Spanish Marquesa with a resounding title, to whom Lee Keedick had offered £1000 if she would persuade me to visit America. She turned out to be Beo's widow re-married.

I have 230 letters from Ellen Terry out of which Edy Craig might make some money with Gabriel's assistance.

Ever	When I am dead, my dearest,
G.B.S.	Sing no sad songs for me
	But cast my spells on Mister Wells
	And ask a handsome fee.

64, Pont Street, S.W.

25th November 1928

Oh my dear Joey what cruel ill luck that I was out, and on a horrible errand too—with lawyers!

No. No; I just could'nt bargain with your lovely letters. The really ladylike thing for me to do would be to hand them back to you.

Have you forgotten how gay and sweet and fit for Paradise you were—they are?

I wish Lucy would lean out of Heaven and nudge your elbow for me—To think of it—twenty minutes—20 pages and you would make yet another fortune—and enable me to live in peace!—

I am free Thursday, Friday, and Saturday next at 4 o/c. come and say "goodbye" to me—I think I am going to die soon.

It was nice to hear from the girl who does odd jobs for me that you looked so amazingly young, and "barged out into the rain without an umbrella or taxi, and it didn't seem to matter."

My love to you

Stella.

◇◇◇◇◇◇

"Jitta" is Jitta's Atonement, a play adapted by Shaw from the German of Siegfried Trebitsch.

The new play was The Apple Cart, which had its first production in this year (1929) at the Malvern Festival with Cedric Hardwicke and Edith Evans as King Magnus and Orinthia.

64, Pont Street, S.W.1.
12th February 1929

Dear Joey,

It doesn't really seem fair to expect an answer to my letters when yours can fetch anything from £15 to £50.— if only "tapped out" and initialled!

I wish I could have been of some use to you at Malvern!

I was under the impression that the great battle of life was fought in our youth—not a bit of it—its when we are old, and our work not wanted, that it rages and goes on—and on—and on—

My landlord won't allow pupils here, and to take a place to teach in—well, its too much of a venture: and when I think *Jitta* would make my fortune, and yet another one for you, I feel I must have courage and yet more courage not to curse you that you do not pull it off somehow!

I wonder if you will come and read the new play to me, as you half promised me you would.

I hope you keep fit in these Ice-Age days.

My love to you.
Stella.

4, Whitehall Court, S.W.1.
19th Feb. 1929

My dear Stella

I can't read plays to a starving woman. What are we to do about you? I have a financial partner who won't let me throw money into the sea. Your objection to having your affairs discussed avails nothing: we never do anything else.

What about a Benefit? Sybil Thorndike says there are plenty of artists, who, like herself, adored you (they have never played with you, you demon) and would do anything for you. Ellen Terry had a benefit and a testimonial that enabled her to retire and die in comfort, leaving her daughter independant.

I am rehearsing *Major Barbara*; and my time for writing is cut down to nothing. What do you think of the Benefit idea?

I wonder could we get you a Civil List Pension. How many Cabinet Ministers have you insulted?

If the telephone and electric lighting people—the people with summary powers of cutting you off—are troublesome, why not send their bills to me? I am always paying such things; one more or less will make no difference.

This letter is only to draw your fire. D.D. thinks you will be indignant if I breathe a word to you.

ever
G.B.S.

64, Pont Street, S.W.1.
20th February 1929

Joey dear,

You don't "draw my fire"—I know how to take punishment like a man. I am not starving—I eat more than you do—my electric light burns brightly—and my telephone is in order—and there's a good fire in my grate—and please, please, please—you who once wrote that you were "my friend world without end"—come and read your play to me, Thursday, Friday, I am free until 4.30, or Saturday.

You cannot dare to make my poverty an excuse!

I don't want a Benefit, I sent a cheque for £25 to Ellen Terry's (which she acknowledged with a letter beginning: 'Dear Sir'—she had not deciphered my signature!)

A Civil List Pension, indeed!

My love to you and your merrymaking.

Stella.

4, Whitehall Court, S.W.1.
20th Feb. 1929

Splendid! all those flags flying; but that is how the Stella Stellarum would go down. I am not easy.

I have just been smitten with a frightful and probably infectious cold—I, who never catch cold!—and I will not risk giving it to you this week, nor next, because I am up to my neck in rehearsals of *Barbara*. We produce on the 4th.

G.B.S.

◇◇◇◇◇◇

Sybil Thorndike was the Major Barbara of the revival.

The new play for Mrs. Campbell was The Matriarch, *her last resounding success. It was an adaptation by* G. B. Stern *of her own novel of that name.*

"Nancy" is Lady Astor, and "Guinness" the Hon. Benjamin Guinness. A later letter—25 August 1937—makes the situation more clear.

26th March 1929

Dearest Joey—

I wonder if you are ever coming to read your play to me?

I went to *Major Barbara*, and marvelled at you all over again—it was hard on her to sit perched up by the wall and by that gun for so long—That's where my Indian hypnotism would have been useful—the long speeches would have seemed less tedious if the expression of her face had followed them, or if she had turned her back and looked over the wall. I think her eyes should have expressed deepest interest.

You must get out of the way of saying I 'throw money into the sea'!

Nancy, D.D. and Guinness so far are secured by my Life

Policy I wanted to sell it out last year and pay them in part, but D.D.'s brother, who is a lawyer, said it was better business to leave things as they were, and now it looks as though he might be right, if this play I have been engaged to open in—the part of an old Jewess of 70 (with an Austrian-French-Yiddish accent) is a success!

Don't be surprised if you hear some day that I have sold one or two of your books.

My love to you.
Stella.

4, Whitehall Court, S.W.1.
31st March 1929

My dear Stella

The honest truth is that I am too shy to read you the only scene in that play that would interest you. Its scandalous climax is a reminiscence of Kensington Square. Perhaps you will never speak to me again when you have read it—or seen it. Ask D.D.

Heavens! I did not want an audit. It is not your personal expenditure that I fear: it is these terrible plays that are no good. I hope the Jewess will be a success. If only I had the writing of her!

Of course, sell the books. Sell everything you can lay hands on whilst the boom lasts.

I cannot get my temperature up after the flu: neither can Charlotte. So we are off to the Adriatic for a month or so on Low Sunday.

G.B.S.

2nd April 1929

My dear Joey,

How glorious to be off to the Adriatic.

I have written to D.D. and asked her what you mean, for

314

I cannot imagine any reminiscence of Kensington Square that should make you too shy to read a particular scene of your play to me.

You and I may be proud of the battle we fought; I think I fought it—odd as it may seem—for Charlotte's sake.

They gave me £100 for *Widower's Houses*, so you see you are helping me financially.

You don't seem to me to be a bit tired—

Charlotte must be very wonderful, and I take off my hat to you both and I would like to give you my remaining years to add on to your own.

My love to you
Stella.

The 'Jewess' will disgrace me if I make a success of her, and I will never get another engagement if I make a failure. Arnold Bennett said I must accept the role—it would be a fine gesture! I suppose he meant publicly to face age—throw vanity to the winds and along with it pre-Raphaelitism, *race*, and the rest of it—

64 Pont Street, S.W.1.
5th April 1929

Dear Joey,

D.D. writes:—

G.B. Shaw has put you into his play as the Egeria of the King—1960. There is first a conversation between this lady supported by the Civil List—with rooms in Buckingham Palace—and the King which is extremely witty and amusing, in which it is conveyed that your relations are innocent—but that you want to be Queen, and he does not want to shock, or desert his wife Jemima. I forget how it ended, but that is the only appearance of Stella. I asked him why he did not get you to play it—and he said 'no one could play themselves'.

I know why you feel shy—the scene isn't true, though it may amuse you to fancy it so.

But please come and read it to me before you go away.

It doesn't look nice of you to refuse, after saying you would, and you have no legal right to put me in a play without my knowledge, or permission—damn you!

My book put you right with the world—

Didn't a strange man come up and shake my hand and thank me for showing the real Shaw—a man with a heart—to the world!

Up to that time the world has realised only your brain, but since, they love you yourself—which is a very different thing—it makes them *listen* to you.

I ran away from you at Sandwich because I wanted to remain Queen of the Kingdom of my heart—but I suppose you mustn't humble the King in your play like that—

I know the loveliness of breeding—not of the flesh—but of the intellect, and you loved like a King—bless you . . .

Please come and read it before you go away—

Stella.

Do look out for the change in the weather.

4, Whitehall Court, S.W.1.
6th April 1929

D D remembers the ending only too jolly well. It is not for nothing that you call me Joey. It is an ending of the red hot poker order: wildly disgraceful.

Of course the scene isn't true; but you will recognize bits and scraps of it. And there are perhaps gleams of truth in it here and there. Which of us knows the whole truth? Not I.

But I can't read it to you now because I do not possess a copy. I had to send the only one in my hands to Barry Jackson this morning to show to the Lord Chamberlain on Monday. I am trying to retrieve another somewhere; but I doubt whether I shall succeed before our departure for Italy on the 14th. It has been put off for a week by the death yesterday of my sister-in-law. The funeral will take us to Shropshire on Monday.

However, when I come back I will read the scene to you. The shyness has in it, perhaps, a fear lest you should set me expanding the scene and upsetting the balance of the play; but I will risk it.

Yes: you were right, Sandwich and all. And wrong, I suppose, to get married.

G.B.S.

64, Pond Street, S.W.1.
8th April 1929

Dear Joey,

That is the kindest letter you have written to me for many a long day.

I am sorry you had to go to the funeral, one easily gets a chill, standing about, and with a sub-normal temperature too—

I am rehearsing this week, but I could get back for you any afternoon by 3 o'clock, before the 14th if you will let me know.

Stella.

Ayot St. Lawrence, Welwyn
10th April 1929

Tell you I aint got the script.

When I go up tomorrow I have to pack and buy things and get passports and tickets and see people (mere people—nobody I want to see) and hurry and scurry and register and devil knows what. I shall be much too distracted to do anything else until I come back.

317

Everything went off beautifully: lovely weather and lovely flowers. I supplied the requisite comic relief.

G.B.S.

64, Pont Street, S.W.1.
11th April /29

Dearest Joey,
You *must* come and read the play to-morrow Friday at 3 o'c or after.

It cannot be done without my permission, I'll have you up for an illegal act—

And listen—I am told that in America your letters to me are worth £200 each—those of 8 and ten pages—more—I have 93— £20,000. Also I am told the only way I can prevent their being published over there (I would like them published they are so lovely—one in particular should be placed between two leaves of gold)—is to have 12 copies published here—

Now please dont be too busy to remember that I love you, and you love me and come any time to-morrow Friday between 3 pm and 2 am.

My love to you,
Stella.

4, Whitehall Court, S.W.1.
11th April 1929

Woman,
Be not faithless but believing. The one copy I had kept for my own use was requisitioned by Barry Jackson last week for the Lord Chamberlain, in whose clutches it now is. You don't suppose I know the thing by heart, do you? I, who never can remember three words at rehearsal unless the actor prompts me.

The letters are worth a good deal; but nobody can publish them without my authority. The copyright belongs to me: the material objects—the pieces of paper on which they are written, belong to you. If I had copies I could publish them without consulting you; but as I have none, you have control of the situation by your power to withold the sheets of paper. Such is the law. This has nothing to do our feelings, but it is important to know the precise legal situation, as there are sharks in the relic trade as in others.

There are two ways of selling: 1, by private contract to Gabriel Wells or some other dealer (he is a really nice patriarch), 2, by sending the letters to Sotheby's to be sold by auction. In the latter the auctioneer is apt to quote appetising passages in the catalogue. They are picked up and broadcast by the press.

I must go to bed. I am dead beat after a very full day.
Goodnight.
G.B.S.

64, Pont Street, S.W.1.
12th April 1929

Well dearest, my point of view may be that of a fool, but if I die—and you may be gone too—these letters will be in the hands of Stella and Pat.

If the letters then get to America, who is going to start lawsuits should they be published there? And the law has an odd way of demanding bonds to be placed in the country before anything can be done. I tried to get $2000 owed to me—so I know.

I sat here for two hours with a man from Dulau—he knows a millionaire who wants the letters for his private collection. This fellow said: "At the death of the millionaire who will prevent his heirs from selling and publishing?"

It was this man who said to me that the only way out of the difficulty was the publication of 12 copies here.

319

In my opinion the letters should be published here at once "with the permission of Mr. and Mrs. Bernard Shaw"—By now I am sure Charlotte knows that to stand by your sweetness is the sweeter way! Or I can return all the letters to you—except two. Please *you* decide.

Your Stella.

P.S.—I haven't seen Gabriel Wells—I thought it better to finish with Dulau's man.

4, Whitehall Court, S.W.1
12th April 1929

The effect of publishing 12 copies here would be to void the American copyright. Mr. D. could take care to buy the 12 copies. Then he could publish a collectors edition in America before anyone else and live happily ever after.

Tell him with my compliments that if he really wants to know what is to prevent people, here or in America, from publishing letters the copyright of which belongs to me, he had better ask the gentleman who last tried it—poor wretch! I was not asked for a bond then; but bonds, which mean only security for costs, present no difficulty to me.

What an unteachable devil you are! Dont you understand that the copyright of my letters belongs to me and the sheets of paper to you, and that the copyright of your letters belongs to you and the sheets of paper to me? I could sell your letters; but the purchaser would not have the right to publish a line of them, or even to make copies to show to his friends.

If you sell, be careful to keep copies.

Gabriel Wells is an honest man as far as that is possible in his business. Mr. D's proposal to publish 12 copies (just let him try it: that's all) needs explanation.

In great haste—packing.
G.B.S.

64, Pont Street, S.W.1.

13th April 1929

Dearest Joey,

The following is what Dulau's man writes:

"The publication question and protection of copyright is more difficult than you have imagined. The copyright in England is automatically protected and is Mr. Shaw's own by the virtue of the very fact that the letters are written by him, but in America the only protection of copyright for an author is if the material is set up and printed in the U.S. Mr. Shaw knows all about this, of course, and even if only 12 copies were printed the copyright would be protected. One copy must be deposited at the National Library of Congress and at least 12 copies must be offered for sale. They need not necessarily be sold, but they must be offered for sale at a definite price. One may ask £1,000 a copy if one wishes, but the formality of offering them for sale must be undertaken.

"I would very strongly emphasise in your interest, the necessity for the greatest possible care in handling this transaction—whoever buys the letters—and without going into details it should be necessary to indicate that the only method of insuring yourself against any embarrassment in the matter, is to entrust the sale to someone in whom you feel the greatest possible personal confidence. Promises are so easily made, as you know, and unless you personally have the confidence that the person who makes the promise will fulfil it to the best of his ability, I feel certain that you would be laying up for yourself infinite trouble in allowing these letters to pass out of your hands.

"I hope that a further opportunity to discuss them and their eventual fate will occur, and that whatever you do about the letters, you will do nothing without taking me into your confidence."

It's no use—you are not helping me a scrap—It's the

responsibility that troubles me—I may fall down dead at
any moment during these Jew rehearsals, and then you'll
be sorry.

A glorious time to you on the Adriatic.

My love,
Stella.

Hotel Brioni, Istria, Italy.
18th April 1929

I apologize to Mr. Dulau. I gathered from your letter that he wanted to publish 12 copies *in England*. Of
course it would be necessary to print and publish some
copies in America if the letters were published in England;
but they won't be. Any further publication of our correspondence during Charlotte's lifetime is absolutely out of
the question. All you can do is to sell the letters. For this
you do not need Mr. Dulau's help, as Gabriel Wells will
probably give you the top price obtainable by private contract, and Sothebys will sell them by auction for you,
though in that case I must bar actual quotations in the
catalogues.

It is clear that Dulau is thinking of publication, which
disposes of his quite correct advice, as publication is barred.

Gabriel Wells will pay you on the nail: he is a good-
hearted old bird. But you must make it clear that there is
no chance of my consenting to publication.

In great haste, and with an icy
wind called the bora blowing every
generous sentiment out of me.

G.B.S.

64, Pont Street, S.W.1.
12th May 1929

I have'nt had a minute and I wanted to write and
tell you I saw Gabriel Wells, but did'nt like him well

enough to show him even one letter. I saw his mouth watering.

What he paid me for the books has lifted a load of debt—But how I *hated* parting with them, he haggled and I tried to—he won—it was a loathsome business.

By the way—just to make your hair stand on end—there is a letter from you giving me permission to publish the letters, saying there is a gentleman's agreement between us! ! and another asking me how I would like to play "St. Joan"!

From what D.D. says you must let me play the Queen in the *Applecart*—if that's the part—unless of course its too unbearably offensive to me!

I gather it would give a gentlemanly balance to the whole business.

I enclose a letter I have had from Mrs. Robert Loraine to show you I am a capable actress—return it to me and dont tell her you have seen it. I worked very hard at this jewess charade—Ethel Irving is a Jew by the way.

Major Vernon the producer concocted the scenario, if only G. B. Stern had done it alone it would have been far better—with me in her mind's eye. . . . Dont go to your grave dearest regretting I did'nt play in your *Applecart*.

My love to you

Stella.

Malvern for a week in August will suit me. I have friends living there who will put me up.

◇◇◇◇◇◇

"Winnie" is Winifred Loraine, who played Roxane to her husband's Cyrano in the 1927 revival. Irene Rooke was a gifted actress who made her reputation at the Manchester Gaiety

Theatre in repertory under Miss Horniman. The new play for Mrs. Campbell, The Matriarch, *had been presented on 8 May at the Royalty.*

Dubrovnik, Yugoslavie.
20th May 1929

Bravo Winnie! First rate of her to let herself go like that. But her letter does not prove that you are a capable actress, but only that you are a witch, which I know better than anyone already. And as your spells are apt to interfere with mine, and to blight my unfortunate company, their potency alarms me. *The Apple Cart* will be safer with Edith Evans; and the King will have a fair chance instead of being upset and unhinged. However, bewitch Barry Jackson if you can. It is not a question of a few performances in Malvern: a short season in Birmingham and then a London production are in the program as well.

For the Queen I want Irene Rooke; but I don't think you mean the queen. I hope the other lady will not prove offensive; she has gone very well at the readings at Lady Astor's; but that the scene is amusingly scandalous and even disgraceful (though Platonic) is undeniable. One or two passages will not be new to you. I believe D.D. remembers it better than she pretends to. I dont believe you could (or would) play it; but you would most certainly play the devil with the whole production, and perhaps make me behave badly and leave me ten years older, which is more than I can afford at 72. I am accustomed to be made much of and spoiled in the theatre now.

You must not try to blackmail me with that gentleman's agreement. It was not carried out. I bargained to be only one little star in a galaxy of adorers; but your worshipper's executors refused to compete, and left Barrie and myself to face the music. I could have managed the situation for you;

but you would not trust me; and I had to make the best of a bad job for you.

Gabriel is all right. You must have opened your mouth very widely indeed; but if he filled it enough to save the situation I rejoice. Did he have the Blake, Virgil, Fred Evans book which I gave you, and which you never opened? That is really unique and ought to fetch something handsome.

I have seen no notices of the play (being cut off from the papers here) and you tell me not a word of it except that you despised the producer. I daresay you told him so. But what happened? Is the play a success? It might so easily be with you in it—if you would let it, whatever it may be.

I have just returned from a stupendous climb (in a car) over the mountains to Cettinje, and am tired and ill humoured. I am treated here like a King: nothing can be more exhausting.

G.B.S.

❖❖❖❖❖❖

"The play by the pseudo-G.B.S." was G. B. Stern's The Matriarch. *It ran for many months.*

Hotel Royal Danieli, Venice
30th May 1929

I wonder where that book has gone to. Possibly you still have it, but think it a dirty old calfbound volume of no value except to stand saucepans on. Its history is this. Frederick H. Evans is a retired bookseller whose hobby was photography, at which he became extraordinarily skilful. One of his diversions was to to make enlarged photographs of the best wood engravings, and make platinotype prints from them to send to his friends as Xmas cards. At last, when he became quite sure of himself, he made a set of enlargements (not big horrors, of course) from William Blake's illustrations to Virgil's eclogues, and tried to sell them to conoisseurs. I don't know how many sets he printed: probably not more than 25. Anyhow, I bought a set. They made a very nice quarto, perhaps an inch thick, the platino-type paper being good. As one always connects Blake with the old golden brown calf bindings, I chose a seal leather and had the book bound by Douglas Cockerell. Then, to find out whether you really knew or cared about books as collectors do, I wrote an appropriate (or perhaps infatuated) inscription, and gave the book to you one evening at Kensington Square when, as it happened, you had some people to tea. You took it with a polite gush of gratitude for the benefit of the company, but without the smallest interest; and it was presently shoved out of the way, an ugly brown book, on the small table in the O.P. upstage corner of the room, near the door, where it lay on some other larger book that served equally as furniture.

I think I saw it once again in the same place. Then either it was moved or I ceased to notice it.

Now you may say what you please, and Miss Morris may say what she likes and may have been with you for 300 years; but that book is *somewhere*. And before the war it was most certainly in 33 Kensington Square with the rest of your belongings. And it is worth three figures if it is worth a halfpenny.

I have read three or four notices of the play by the pseudo-G.B.S.; and they seem conclusive as to your having, like Mrs. Minnie Maddern Fiske in America, staged a sensational Come Back. And they all agreed that you are the goods, and not the play or the company. Which is cheering news for poor authors and for the "support". Mrs. M.M.F., by the way, though she must be at least 130, has actually made a beauty success for the first time in her life. She at-

tributes this, in a private letter which I have seen, to the fact
that she learnt the art of make-up eighteen months ago from
a specialist, having up to that time thought (like yourself)
that nobody could teach her anything.

There is a wicked caricature of you in Punch, clever
enough to be talked about, in a notice of the play which is
good business for you. Let us hope the play will run long
enough to re-establish you as a money magnet.

If Oscar Wilde had been a woman he would have changed
his famous line to "For all blackmail the men they love"
etc. etc.

G.B.S.

64 Pont Street, S.W.1.
7th June 1929

I went to the Selfridge Ball and met Miss Edith
Evans, who gazed eagerly at me saying she was playing *me*
in the *The Apple Cart* at Malvern and in Birmingham and
London—

I spent the whole of Sunday with B——, who talked of
nothing else at lunch, at tea, and at dinner—"the infamy of
it"—and that I must write to you at once—that she would
"walk out of the theatre"—that she "wouldn't go to the
theatre", etc. etc.

Miss Morris raises her eyes to Heaven and says: "It is a
national calamity, an insult"—

About the precious book—Miss Morris and I feel very
foolish—There is just one place we haven't searched—a place
where I keep old papers and 'parts' of plays—and we hope,
by some divine miracle, we will find it there—but I will
swear it hadn't anything in it written by you—and so will
Miss Morris, for we ever kept any written word of yours
apart.

Had you explained the value of the book to me, I can hardly believe I would not have remembered it. My Blakes have always been kept together.

I am truly distressed about *The Apple Cart*. I cannot imagine why D.D. didn't tell me about it when she first heard you read it.

My love to you
Stella.

4, Whitehall Court, S.W.1
20th June 1929

My dear Stella,

The craze for relics has now reached a point at which it is no longer true that private sales are as lucrative as auctioning at Hodgson's or Sotheby's. But they do not involve the publicity of the auction room.

B—— must not talk too much. There is of course nothing that could give any clue to the public—above all to the Press. It can be a secret between us.

As if *I* did not know better than anyone what may or may not be done, and exactly how to do it! The presumption of these infinitesimals. ! . . .

I should read that scene to B—— if I could trust her not to hide you behind the curtains. Though, after all, why shouldn't she?

Goodnight
G.B.S.

64, Pont Street, S.W.1.
25th Jun. 1929

Dear Joey,

How can it be a 'secret' between us—when Edith Evans told me she was playing *me*?

It is unkind of you not to keep your promise to read this play, or to send it to me.

A husband cheats—a friend tricks—and the comic thing is human dignity.

My love to you,
Stella.

I have for the moment forgotten about the letters and the greed in Gabriel Wells' eye.

4, Whitehall Court, S.W.1.
27th Jun. 1929

My dear Stella.

. . . Edith Evans guessed of course. D.D. knows; B—— knows; Nancy knows; perhaps half a dozen others know; (or think they know! for only you and I will ever know); but the Press must never get hold of it. The lady in Warsaw got stage fright and forgot her lines, making a mess of it, as far as I can ascertain, on the first night. It puzzled the audience considerably.

I ought to know whether you will like it or not; but I don't.

Do you go to America with *The Matriarch*? Presumably Shubert included you in his bargain.

First rehearsal of *The Apple Cart* on Monday. I have to read it to them; a killing job, and I so old.

G.B.S.

64, Pont Street, S.W.1.
8th July 1929

Dear Joey,

I haven't felt at all inclined to answer this last letter of yours and I don't know why I do—

You should have sent me your play to read. You are out of tune with friendship and simple courtesy.

Why do you always speak of age. Where no disintegration is setting in—it is more splendid than vain, foolish greedy youth.

Bless you.
Stella.

4, Whitehall Court, S.W.1.
11 July 1929

Stella

Do you mind if it runs this way?

ORINTHIA: I can give you beautiful, wonderful children; have you ever seen a lovelier boy than my Basil?

MAGNUS: Your children are beautiful; but they are fairy children; and I have several very real ones already. A divorce would not sweep them out of the way of the fairies. . . .

And so to make it *our* immortal play I have changed "Orinthia: It is out of the question: your dream of being queen must remain a dream" to "Orinthia: We are only two children at play; and you must be content to be my queen in fairyland."

Does that cure the soreness at your heart? It makes mine feel much better.

G.B.S.

64, Pont Street, S.W.1.
12th July 1929

Joey,

All that nonsense Magnus says in criticism of Orinthia is dreadfully commonplace and vulgar, to my thinking, and why make Orinthia run down your wife? That isn't funny from any point of view—but the kitchen's.

Has Charlotte ever heard that I asked you to show her your letters to me, and that I didn't know until after I had sent them back to Hutchinsons—blackened out in spots by you—that you hadn't done so—a letter I had of yours to me mentions this. . . .

People like to think it is by choice you are not a chivalrous gentleman, they will know better when they see this scene—they will not recognise the joke you find in it—and if it is meant as a palliative to Charlotte's nerves or vanity, it can but mystify the public.

My love for you was the love of a child who feels safe, the woman in me recognises the twist!

As you sat in my room yesterday and read to me—I suddenly knew you—saw you.

Stella.

Ayot St. Lawrence, Welwyn.
12th July 1929

Dearest Stella,

Fret not thyself because of evildoers . . .

There are no personalities in the narrower sense in the scene. Orinthia's husbands are not Patrick or George: they are items in the many millions of men and women, who, seduced by a splendor that dazzles them, bite off more than they can digest. The story is as old as Jupiter and Semele. Do you not know that though you are marvellous, as all the flappers say, you are gey ill to live with: indeed impossible. You cannot have it both ways. I have made a superb picture of you, God forgive me! and you must play the game.

But you must also be as discreet as human nature allows. You talked in a restaurant, and your celebrated voice carried as far as Warsaw, where I had to choke off a story about the name in the English version being Stella, and Orinthia being you, and Heaven knows what.

Do not think of the scene as having been projected into a vacuum. We must not be handed down to history by ig-

331

noble gossip and venomous slander. The world may very well laugh at us; but it had better have splendid fun than dirty fun. Our parts are fine parts; and if you really prefer Lady Patricia to Orinthia you deserve to be whipped at the carts tail from Sloane Square to Drury Lane.

As to your postscript, could I help it? Perhaps I should not have come; but how else could you have heard the scene? I held off long enough, knowing well enough that an old ruffian of 73 cannot shelter himself in a mist of illusion. But my vanity prevailed; for even the wreck of G.B.S. must be more interesting than an average coaling schooner in full sail. I'll send you a copy of the play presently, if I may. In fact I will whether you like it or not. The test will be how you take it.

G.B.S.

◇◇◇◇◇◇

G.B.S.'s answer to this letter was written in red ink on the side of the letter itself and apparently so returned to Mrs. Campbell at a much later date.

64, Pont Street, S.W.1.

22nd July 1929

Dear Joey,

I think it right to tell you that I will never be able to bear in silence the implication of that scene in your play, its mischevious vulgarity, and untruthfulness. D.D. writes: "The scene should never have been written"—and alluding to the reading of it says: "the whole thing was in execrable taste".

What Nancy thought, or thinks, I don't know, and neither I suppose do you. I fancy her chaffing you—and Charlotte too perhaps—set the scene going in your brain.

If I had the script here I would talk it over with my lawyer—I am sure in its suggestiveness it is libellous and ought not to be presented.

Tear it up, and re-write it with every scrap of the mischevious vulgarian omitted, and all suburban backchat against Charlotte and suggested harlotry against me, and the inference of your own superiority wiped out.

People will only say that old age and superhuman vanity have robbed you of your commonsense.

Please do as I say—you will feel strangely relieved.

Stella.

[Notes written on this letter by G.B.S., begun in red ink and finished in pencil:]

I don't feel it to be a bit wrong. It plays magnificently. Orinthia never loses her distinction and beauty even when she rolls on the floor. If she did I would amputate her without a moments hesitation, and be ashamed of her. But I'm not. So stand she shall to all eternity. Besides Orinthia is not a portrait: she is a study for which you sat as a model in bits only—though the magnificence of the picture is due to you. And again I am an artist and as such utterly unscrupulous when I find my model—or rather when she finds me.

4, Whitehall Court, S.W.1.
24th July 1929

Dearest

You are such a fool! Oh, such a, *such* a, SUCH a fool!

Goodnight
G.B.S.

◇◇◇◇◇◇◇

Lysistrata is Magnus's wife in The Apple Cart.

333

64, Pont Street, S.W.1.

26th July/29

Dear Joey,

I feel it the greater honour to be the fool you call me—

I hope your Lysistrata is strong in the wind—and Magnus' breathing sound, and that you have had a happy Birthday.

Stella.

P.S. I recall at rehearsals you prided yourself in not hurting peoples feelings—and chided *me*—you mountebank.

4, Whitehall Court, London, S.W.1.

28th July 1929

Belovedest,

How troublesome you are! . . .

When I suggest that you are an Orinthia you repudiate the likeness as an outrage. When I introduce any detail that differentiates her from you, you want me to alter it and make the portrait complete and recognizable. However, I shall now be able to say that you revised it yourself, and dictated some of the best bits.

Of course we are a pair of mountebanks; but why, oh why do you get nothing out of me, though I get everything out of you? Mrs. Hesione Hushabye in *Heartbreak House*, the Serpent in *Methuselah*, whom I always hear speaking with your voice, and Orinthia: all you, to say nothing of Eliza, who was only a joke. You are the Vamp and I the victim; yet it is I who suck your blood and fatten on it whilst you lose everything!

It is ridiculous! There's something wrong somewhere.

G.B.S.

334

Ayot St. Lawrence, Welwyn.

4th August 1929

But if it distresses you why do you tell me these wildly funny stories . . . You may not be able to laugh at them yourself; but can you expect me to refrain? These adventures have no relation to your real self: marriage, as King Magnus shrewdly remarked, is not Orinthia's job. . . .

On Tuesday I go to the Malvern Hotel, Great Malvern, Worcs.

everest

G.B.S.

◇◇◇◇◇◇

This concerns The Matriarch.
The remainder of the word beginning "jab—" has been accidentally blotted, and it is impossible to guess what it may be if it is not "jabbering."

Ayot St. Lawrence, Welwyn.

20th Sept. 1929

Stella: what a play! What a job for you! Two hours of artless vindictive realism, almost as unbearable as the reality, during which this horribly clever Sheeny woman (nobody but a Jewess dare put in that shocking touch about the ham) revenges herself savagely on her family and her race for the tyranny and boredom of her domesticity in childhood; and YOU have to keep the audience from rushing out of the house and violently down a steep place into the sea. You are too busy doing all that singlehanded to notice how intensely disagreeable the scenes are, or to realize that the audience is held not only by the fact that it is Mrs. Patrick Campbell who is jab—, but by the hope that presently a big bit of drama will come her way. And when the half hour of real stuff at last comes you are left to sleep

335

it out in an invalid's chair, dreaming of ham and plums! I hope they pay you an *enormous* salary.

You snatched just one bit of acting out of it. That scene on the sofa with Cohen, in the very clever red dress (whose idea was that?), was extraordinarily good; but oh! if G.B.S. Junior had only known her business and let the audience know why Cohen was refusing and that Anastasia was offering him an empty safe! Still, even at that disadvantage, you got away with it.

Now tell G.B.S. to go to the Queen's Theatre and see how much duller people than her uncles and aunts can be made deliriously entertaining, and what a gorgeous success you are when *I* write your part. She owes you another play; and as she has tremendous talent she can do it if she will. You have saved her from being stoned.

G.B.S.
(Senior).

64, Pont Street, S.W.1.
12th June 1931

An American private Collector offered me £3,000 for your letters, and is still keeping the offer open—One letter made him jump about the room and clap his hands, another made him weep and one made us both feel we'd said our prayers! You have penned your immortal portrait—an honest, modest man gifted with a divine intelligence in your appreciation and understanding of me—this in spite of your Orinthia foolery—

Unless you want me for your new play, I must hurry back to the States—no work and the rain are more than I can bear.

Stella.

The "Lord Chancellor" was G.B.S's nickname for Patrick Beech.

4 Whitehall Court, S.W.1.
13th June 1931

. . . you DARE give yourself airs with ME. It out Orinthia's Orinthia. . . .

In my new play there are two rowdy flappers and one ridiculous old woman. Therefore nothing of any use to you.

This year my correspondence with Ellen Terry will be published for the benefit of her estate (she did not leave enough); and if it inflames the American imagination a demand may rise among the collector-maniacs for our whole correspondence as distinguished from separate letters. It may therefore be more provident—if you can afford it—to keep the letters together and bequeath them to Stella junior. Or, if you sell, sell in bulk. But whatever you do, do not part with them without keeping copies, even if I have to pay Miss Dickens for typing them.

I believe I have your letters (a pitiable weakness); and the whole budget might help out your grandchild the Lord Chancellor when we are all dead, as Ellen's grandchildren will be helped; but I cannot yet answer for what may happen to them.

G.B.S.

This typewritten letter has the words "Copy," "Dear Joey," and "Perhaps I tore it up myself in indignation. Stella" added in Mrs. Campbell's own handwriting.

337

14th June 1931

Dear Joey,

Couldn't you make the old lady in your new play not quite so old, and rehearse me on approval?

The enclosed is from an American lady of 88—See what she thought of my work last March! You knew her, she was going to see the first night of *Saint Joan* with you and Nancy Astor, but was afraid of missing the boat at Southampton.

I haven't thought of selling the letters except in bulk—and the bulk is worth £100,000 to you and your publishers, and would give the world, including Russia and Japan—hours of joy—125 letters, many postcards, and three poems—all respectable but one—and yet I cannot destroy that one.

Somebody has taken the letter that made me blush so deeply that I didn't feel the hottest summer known in England for years. Among other things it said my vanity was such that I would be dressed in sable from head to foot, and wear your fig leaf in my bonnet.

I hope it won't appear on posters in America, and here upon sandwichmen:—

"G. B. S's fig leaf for Mrs. Pat's bonnet". Perhaps I tore it up myself in indignation.

Stella.

[*The letter enclosed, from Mrs. Cornelia Lunt, of Illinois, is a touching tribute to Mrs. Campbell's power of transporting a playgoer to the heights of imaginative rapture: "To stir one to the depths, to rouse to the heights—what a bestowment!"*]

30 June 1931

Dear Joey,

My letters are worth 2d.—yours 50 quid—so don't bother to answer.

An offer has come from Gilbert Miller for me to play a

horrible Countess with pince-nez looking for a Gigolo—to play it both here and in America—do help me out with the old lady in your play—

Stella.

4, Whitehall Court, S.W.1.
3rd July 1931

My dear Stella

Gabriel Wells says that Benjy Guinness would give £4000 for the Letters. Is this true? Because if it is I might offer to throw in your letters if he would go to £5000 in brewery shares or even in cash, though you would probably either spend that in a week or take a theatre with it and produce some hopelessly bad play. I had much rather they were in B's possession than in anyone elses bar yours. If they ever come into mine they will almost certainly be destroyed.

I cannot save you from Gilbert. The old lady in my play is quite irreconcileable with your personality. You would be condemned to comic landladies for the rest of your life if you touched it; and the play has no prospect of either an early production or a popular success like *The Apple Cart*. So jump at the horrible Countess.

wearily
G.B.S.

64, Pont Street, S.W.1.
14th July/31

Dear Joey,

I have lost a little dog "Swizzles" my companion of eleven years—griffon—such a gay brave, merry-hearted little creature—my flat is dead—I feel lost—it hurts, and hurts, and hurts—

339

I once sent you her photo—if it could be found and returned to me how glad I would be! but that is too much to
hope—

D.D. tells me you go to Russia to-morrow—I hope you
get the right food.

I am glad you saw Conger Goodyear—a nice man—he was
enchanted with you—"a glorious fellow" were his words, So
dont talk or think about age—I am not going to let him have
the letters for £3,000 neither am I going to let Benjie have
them for £4,000.

The other day a publisher valued the letters at £10,000,
and the publishing rights at £20,000—What arrangement
can we make, you and I? You know I am to be trusted—
I have guarded them for 19 years—when you return from
Russia I will send you the few letters that mention Charlotte.

I knew you were playing the "solicitor stunt" it creeps
into all you say, and write and do,—with the exception of
one or two lovely letters to me—the stunt that wearies me
so much—that has worried me for years—that has stood in
the way of your being a Shakespeare—a poet—

I have discovered that if one thinks of Religion and
Relativity as great and good behaviour—both God and Relativity are easy to understand and solicitors unnecessary—

goodbye
Stella.

WESTERN UNION CABLEGRAM

London.
1931 18th Dec. P.M. 11.06

NLT. Mrs. Patrick Campbell, 927 Fifth Avenue,
New York.

Publication impossible. Sell letters keeping copies if

you must but after Terry and Harris neither I nor the market can bear any more.

Joey.

◇◇◇◇◇◇

Copy of card attached to letter of 29 March 1932.

With Bernard Shaw's compliments
    Another discovery among my papers, add it to your collection.

G.B.S.

The Barclay Hotel, New York City.
29 March 1932

Dearest Joey,
    I don't know where you are, in England or Africa; I only seem to get so far in the newspapers as the articles on the kidnapping of Lindbergs' Baby.

I post this to Whitehall Court and hope it will be forwarded to you; and that in your answer you will not sacrifice me to the annoyance others may have caused you.

The publishers here, and many people unceasingly ask me: "why are Shaw's letters to Ellen Terry published and not his to you?" I answer that I believe you think the publication of your letters to me might perhaps in some way offend your wife. Then the conversation gets a little modern, until I convince the company we were most respectably 'in the clouds', as indeed we were! [1]

You know I have behaved like a gentleman for nineteen years over these letters—I could have sold them time and again for $350 and $500 each—one hundred and twenty-five

---

[1] These last four words have been added in handwriting.

of them—I did not, though pressed hard for money; now, times are very much harder, almost unbearable.

I feel the moment has arrived when it is little short of a crime to be ladylike any longer. Please be patient with me dear Joey, and listen:

These letters are still in my possession—

Their financial value is doubled by the public value of *both* our names—

I am in part responsible for their inspiration—

The market value of the letters at the moment, is very high. Are you then fair in withholding the permission for their publication? Why do you, with your just and fair mind, withold what is in part mine?

If I were to sell the paper the letters are written on, I lose control of my rightful share, and should the buyer wish to raise a little ready money he might part with some of the letters to a newspaper. . . .

I think you must have known when you agreed to the publication of your letters to Ellen Terry, and refused your permission for the publication of mine, you put me in a strange and not too comfortable position.

It seems to me there are only two fair ways to deal with the situation: to destroy the most beautiful thing you have done, or for you to keep to that dear "gentleman's agreement between us" that you sent to me years ago, and to trust to my integrity—I would swear to treasure your wife's sensibility.

Of course, there is a third and savage way out of the difficulty—to throw my bonnet over the mill, and let you go for me and the publisher 'hell for leather'—that might cause a little amusement in these miserable dull times.

Dearest Joey, what objection can there be? Letters written so long ago, and all three of us on the verge of the grave! And anyway you said to me that you were willing

that they should be published some day; why not now? If
it is a question of 'dignity' what at our age! And in the age
we live in; to put dignity before intelligence! to say nothing
of taking away the other fellow's half a loaf!—impossible!—

When you wrote these lovely letters, some whisper in me
of my beautiful Italian mother inspired you, awoke the impersonal ideal, set your genius on the plane where angels
and poets pass the time o'day. Please don't think, or let
anyone think, that I am such a foolish creature as to look
upon these letters as bouquets to *me* "No, sir"—as the
Americans say, with the accent on the 'sir'.

Besides their beauty makes a golden besom to brush away
a little of the dust that has gotten strewn around. They im-
mortalize your youth—generations will smile joyfully at the
glorious 'love charade' and will call these letters a feast for
the Gods.

I would like to write the preface in the form of a letter to
you, and link up the letters in some truthful and interesting
fashion, to include my own if you have kept them, and they
are not too silly.

If I felt I was making a hash of it all, (a suburban dish),
I would ask you to suggest someone, or to approve of someone, to help me.

After "Orinthia" I could not let you touch the business;
Orinthia taught me a great deal about you.

The Greeks, as you no doubt know, had a mythical animal that haunted conversation, it was called an "Amphisbaena", a creature with a head at each end, and walking in
different directions.

Joey you are an Amphisbaena, and must on no account,
be trusted with these letters.

For your own sake, and in view of the offers now assum-
ing a gigantic size, please write to me, not an insulting letter, be *fair*, as you, better than anyone else in the world,
know how to be.

343

This thing has to be looked at squarely in the face, or something more than petty injustice is being done to me.

My love to you dear. Joey write to me soon—please.

Stella.

P.S. Naturally you would dictate the contracts. I have read the Ellen Terry book, and the Harris book, and Gordon Craig's—and I can well imagine what the buzzing of bees must have been.

Ayot St. Lawrence, Welwyn.
16th April 1932

My dear Stella,

You should have sold those letters (keeping copies, of course) when the boom in my letters was at its height. It could not last, because it procured such a glut of Shaw letters that even before the financial slump prices had fallen by about ninety per cent. Edy Craig, who sold every scrap of my handwriting, and also sold the copyright in her mother's letters, at once, has come out very handsomely indeed, whilst the purchaser and the publishers are cursing the day they ever heard my name.

[Re] the publication of the Terry letters . . . The circulation has been big and may be bigger still. And, as publishers are as sheeplike as other people, many of them would grab at the chance of repeating the success with another set of letters. Only, so many recent books have been peppered with letters from me (to Frank Harris, for instance) that nothing will serve now but another correspondence of Abelardesque and Heloisian completeness.

And that is not to be had. Ellen and I never saw one another and therefore put everything on paper. Ellen painted a wonderful portrait of herself in her letters, and held her own and a little more against the best that I could do, clever as I am. It was this portrait that broke my resistance to Edy's

iron determination that it should be published to shew the
world how silly the Sweet Nell convention was.

Now we—you and I—dealt with one another *tête à tête*.
Except when we infuriated one another and wrote squab-
bling notes, we had everything out viva voce. I wrote some
things which the public has already sampled in your book.
The rest was not edifying. You would not come out of it
with a halo like Ellen's. I should come out better, because,
though I amused you handsomely, you kept your head and
were never enchanted as I was. Perhaps you have written
love letters, but not to me. Ellen, though she came through
with me *virgo intacta*, gave herself away heart and soul without a thought of reserve to me as she did to everyone else
who invited her confidence. You had no confidence in me;
really small blame to you, Stella: do not think I am re-
proaching you. When it was absolutely necessary for business purposes I had to break in sordidly and indelicately,
and be duly reviled for interfering with your affairs. I ex-
ploited you, made money out of you, got two stage characters out of you (Hesione and Orinthia) and will perhaps
get six more out of your manifold nature; but except for a
little harmless waving of my scalp at first you could get
nothing out of me, could not believe in me, shrank from
letting me touch anything you were doing, made it impossible for us to work together in the theatre, and now finally,
when you want to publish our letters, are mortally afraid
lest I should want to write the preface or see a line of the
story instead of thanking God that you have expert help at
hand to save you from making a dozen *gaffes* in every
chapter.

Now this may be my fault or your fault or the work of
our guardian angels or the Act of God or what not. That
is not the present point, which is, simply, that under such
conditions it was impossible for you to do what Ellen Terry
did: get down on paper a series of letters which brought her

out with flying colors from a correspondence with so artful
a practitioner as myself. The whole thing was on paper; it
was a correspondence with nothing else; it was literature.
But the Stella—G.B.S. (Joey) idyll was acted, not written:
it was not on paper and is not literature. A volume of the
letters incidental to it would give no idea of what it was
like, and would be an anti-climax after the Terry volume.
It is conceivable that if you wrote an elaborate connective
tissue and I overhauled it and completed it, something really
vital and artistically true might be the result: but that is just
exactly what you dread. You would not let me produce
you; and you cannot produce yourself. It cannot be done;
all you can do is to sell the letters.

As to all your threats, dear Stella, you were not born to
be a blackmailer; that is why you do it so badly. No publisher would dare touch my letters without my authorisa-
tion; and no publisher can touch yours because they are not
in his possession nor in yours. If I have really kept them (I
daren't look) I shall keep them until you are dead and I am
preparing for the festival of my hundred and fiftieth birthday, when I shall buy the copyright for ten guineas from
your greyhaired grandson—no, by the way; it will have ex-
pired—and publish it as Mes Souvenirs with my own account of the affair.

I have to disregard the money aspect of the affair ruthlessly. Unless the rumor that B.G. left you £500 a year
(which would last you a week) is true, you must be starving. Very well: starve: everybody is starving. . . . I do
not know how you have managed to live these last ten
years, but conclude that since you have succeeded you can
live on air for another ten years. At all events for me you
are an insoluble problem; and I have callously given it up,
as there is no use making myself unhappy about it.

I feel apologetic for my existence now that all decent
men of my age are committing suicide. I felt very apolo-

getic indeed that day when I read Orinthia to you, and added to all your worries the shock of my senility. But I can still write to some purpose, and so must brazen it out until some assassin saves me the trouble of shooting myself.

And now your letter has mysteriously disappeared, and I shall have to wait perhaps until I find it, as I have no other note of your address. Maddening!

G.B.S.

20.4.32

I will chance your Fifth Avenue address rather than keep you waiting.

Ayot St. Lawrence, Welwyn.
2nd May 1932

My dear Stella

What a damned thing? Your cable, unsigned, and naturally not in your handwriting, completely mystified me. I never connected it with you, as there was no hint in your big letter of any intention of returning; and the Riviera is full of wild people with fixations on me. To complicate matters I mislaid your letter, which I have just found in the pocket of the old overcoat which hangs in my garden shelter. I answered it at considerable length, but, being unable to lay my hands on it, asked Miss Patch for your address. She gave me the one in Fifth Avenue to which we used to cable; and thither dear Stella, that long answer of mine has gone. Perhaps it will come back to me; but the American postal ways are not our ways.

The gist of it was that the bottom has fallen out of the Shaw market—and indeed out of all the markets—and that even with the Terry correspondence the publishers have burnt their fingers badly . . . And as the Terry affair was all on paper and ours was lived and not written, the publication that did Ellen justice would belittle you. There is noth-

347

ing for it but to sell the letters (keeping copies); and even that could not occur at a worse moment than the present.

Winifred Loraine reduced me to stupefaction by telling me that you were wonderful and beautiful as O'Neill's Electra, which, as it happened, I had just read. Next day she wrote to say that she had made a slight error: that it was Clytemnestra, *not* O'Neill's.

Heartbreak House flopped badly on Hesione, the poor lady being very ill, and underplaying hopelessly. It is picking up a little, and may possibly survive. Edith Evans repeated her Orinthia success. So there!

G.B.S.

Villa L'Enchantement, Mougins. A.M.

12th May 1932

Dearest Joey,

How stupid of me I thought I had signed 'Stella', and as the cable was sent from the boat, you would know I was on my way home. However I left my address behind me, so I will be sure to get your letter eventually.

I am glad Winifred Loraine was pleased with "Clytaemnestra". I read Haigh's Attic Theatre, and tried to evolve something that would give pleasure to someone.

I found O'Neill's *Mourning Becomes Electra* horrible. Nazimova had one fine emotional moment, worth something to see, but not all I suffered that afternoon and evening.

You are right, the publication of Ellen Terry's letters to you, did her justice. It is impossible you are in earnest when you say the publication of yours to me will 'belittle' me, that is very absurd, and impossible, and when did you begin to be concerned about my belittlement? Joey I am ashamed of your unsubtle fibbing.

The offer for Magazine rights—$25,000 holds good. And

348

the publishers are willing to advance me one thousand pounds to work at peace on the book, and cancel my American tour. This really means the saving of my life, for my last lecture tour nearly killed me—I am not paid enough to travel a maid, picture me at my age packing and unpacking, ironing out crumpled gowns, catching trains alone at unearthly hours, (I never sleep on trains)—standing on the lecture platform for an hour and a half on end, in the cursed steam heat (no friend nearby should I fall in a fit) shaking hands with hundreds of people—it always seemed to me like thousands.

In Detroit at the Statler Hotel in an enormous Ball Room at eleven o'clock in the morning before an audience of a thousand persons, I gave a programme that included—*Pelleas and Melisande*, "Lady Macbeth", Hecuba's speech from *The Trojan Woman*, scraps of your dear 'Eliza Doolittle', scenes from *The Second Mrs. Tanqueray*, *Magda*, *The Matriarch*, *Romeo and Juliet*, the 23rd Psalm, a modern poem, verses from the Bible, Imitations, Anecdotes, remarks on stage management, and stage managers and producers, and a little of my own special wisdom on the art of acting. All this three and four times a week with travelling in between. Paying out of my salary 10% to my agent, 10% English Income Tax, and 7½% State and Federal Tax. —At the end of that tour I had to hide in an Hotel in New York where nobody knew me, and lie in bed for days staring at the ceiling until I *willed* myself back to life and energy.

The thought of facing it all again is a nightmare.

I have had a lovely little house at Cap D'Antibes lent to me by Mrs. Gerald Murphy from the 7th June, a real "dream-come-true" place, with an orange grove where the nightingales sing all night long. A paved courtyard with electric light, open fires, milk, cream and vegetables within a stone's throw. To this "Ferme des Orangers" I go to write, write and write, it is all mine rent free for so long as I like. Perhaps you will come and see what is happening.

You say you found my letter in the pocket of the old overcoat that hangs in the garden shed. Put on the overcoat with the letter in the pocket, and find again the man who taught me to walk, and jump on the bench in Richmond Park—who promised to be my friend "world without end".

Send me a telegram: "go ahead and be damned to you", tell Miss Patch to send me what letters you have of mine. I will not fail you in any way, there will be no belittling. I forgive you all your disloyalties, as the world will forgive you—these letters of yours soar above personal obligation.

My love to you.
Stella.

Villa L'Enchantement, Mougins A.M.
21st May /32

Dearest Joey,

At last your letter has been forwarded to me from America. I pass by those remarks that make me ashamed of you, without comment.

Years ago our lovely friendship was disturbed by jealousy, and interference—this caused a disloyalty in you that pushed me to one side. Don't try to explain it in any other way.

You know why we "couldn't work together in the theatre"—that actors that are original artists cannot be cluttered up with other people's opinions and ideas. You never could resist the temptation of using my wits as your 'marceline spring-off' board—intolerable at rehearsal—, but I did well for you in *Pygmalion* and deserved another chance.

At their request I had long talks with Putnams, Hearsts, and Harpers. A mutual friend arranged a meeting at her house with Mr. Adams and myself; he spoke quite frankly, so I know pretty accurately about the business.

I am quite convinced—and I am not alone in this—that no man should touch up, or tone down his own love letters for publication, or write the 'connective tissue', he would be smothered in contemptuous accusations of vulgarity and vanity. . . . A great and humble Dante, perhaps—but not you, my dearest Joey. Who is going to believe that your desire was to "save me from making a dozen *gaffes* in every chapter"?

My aim will be as you say to write "Something vital and artistically true", but not too elaborate. Of course it is understood that I submit my effort to you—and with gratitude for your help—but if your criticisms are too devastating, I must burn the whole thing on a funeral pyre at "Ferme des Orangers". Now should that happen, I will not be able to return the publishers their advanced thousand pounds, and you would have to help me out! Perhaps it would be better for you to make the advance, and hold a lien on the letters?

If in spite of all you have said and written and allowed to be published of your private life and feelings, you still persist in refusing me your permission, do give a reason that I and the world may regard as fair and sincere, and that doesn't conflict with the permission given to other publications.

Joey can it be that you are just modest about your own true heart—yes, I believe it is that—afraid of the best that is in you well, well for 76 years you have said you are God, and here you are afraid of yourself! or is it my stupidity that fills you with alarm? You will control that with your criticisms; and if I am three parts a Zany, there is that fourth part that is alight!

Do put fear on one side, and send me that telegram to enable me to cancel my cruel American lecture tour, and settle down here to write. The moment is a very grave one for me, much graver than appears in this letter. It would be wonderful, to feel sure of your help *and* sympathy.

What is all this nonsense you write about senility? Does the embrace of the Botticelli [1] angels mean nothing to you? Then you have my tears as well as my love—

Stella.

4, Whitehall Court, S.W.1.
12th June 1932

My dear Stella,

I should have written before; but I am overdriven just now, and am trying not to do anything.

All that about the letters is nonsense. You had the first whack; Ellen Terry's memory had the second; Mrs. Frank Harris has gleaned what was left. There are certain successes that cannot be repeated and certain sacrifices that cannot be made twice.

I have nothing else to say that would interest you in the least. I know how exhausting the lecturing road is in America; in fact I know everything better than you do. And I havent a scrap of unkind feeling about you. But as to the letters: N O. The Fates, not I, decree it.

G.B.S.

◇◇◇◇◇◇

Another gap of nearly three years.

605, North Elm Drive, Beverly Hills.
14th Feb. /35

Dear Joey,

It was nice of you to answer so promptly. I dont mind confessing to you that had I been able to face the

---

[1] The name is altered from "Mantegna" in Mrs. Campbell's writing.

352

financial risk I would have gone to New York and had a look at the part. The papers said there was a blizzard raging, fourteen inches of snow so perhaps it is as well things turned out as they did.

I don't grieve to have left England to spare my little dog the Horror of Quarantine. When David is King I pray he will abolish that most vile law.

I wish you would write an article that would drown man's spite—that's what it is—spite. I wish you would visit one of those Quarantine homes and see the little well-bred dogs sobbing softly to themselves—their tears jellied around their eyes—in small barred cages—so that the rats cannot get at them at night. In the daytime when a bell rings or a door opens they hear all the larger dogs 300 or 400 of them howling and scratching the bars of their cages hoping their masters have come for them, and this happens 30 or 40 times a day. These small little pet creatures have to suffer this torture for six months through November fogs, and dark cold winter days—no play—no grass—no voice they love to call their name—think what that means to a dog—never to hear its name! . . . For four hours on a stretch I watched so that the cruelty of it would sink into my bones—then I found it quite easy to put my dog before my country and my Career! A porter told me a sad story of an Irish woman who landed with her dog not knowing the law—The officials took the dog from her and put it in a basket she slipped her shoe off and put that in the basket too. The porter said "it was 'ard on us watching 'er limping along the platform to catch 'er train".

If you ever have time send me a letter.

Keep well,
Stella.

◇◇◇◇◇◇◇

The new play was The Simpleton of the Unexpected Isles, *which was to all intents a repetition, on an inferior dramatic level, of* Heartbreak House—*as perhaps the best of Shaw's dramatic critics, Sir Desmond MacCarthy, has pointed out. The play by Margaret Kennedy was* Escape Me Never.

17th March 1935

Stella, Stella,

How often must I tell you to take on as many enemies in front as you please, but never to leave one behind!

As it turns out you are lucky to have missed the part of Prola—not, O most Just God, Pralo—for the critics have fallen on it with such fury that it has flopped completely and is now playing to the Guild subscribers only, which means $8000 a week for a few weeks and then, extinction. The politest notice describes me as a dignified monkey shying cocoanuts at the public. However, that does not account for the failure; for the critics went just as savagely for Margaret Kennedy's play with Elisabeth Bergner, and it has had an overwhelming success. I have just had the flashlights of the production, which was lavish and earnest, but all wrong. Nazimova, in *your* part, appears as a slinking sinuous odalisque. She should have been straight as a ramrod: an Egyptian goddess. My four wonderful young Indian deities, clothed to the wrists and ankles in silks and bangles, and full of mystery and enchantment, came out simply as a naked cabaret troup in the latest Parisian undress. And so on and so forth. When I am not on the spot the harder they try and wronger they go.

However, that is not what I have to scold you for. You should not have snubbed The Guild even if they were in the wrong. You are not their governess; and it is very important for you that they should be very sorry they missed you, and very eager to get you another time. You should have touched your hat and trusted for a renewal of their esteemed orders. But they were not in the wrong. If you want New York engagements it is your business to live within half an hour of Broadway exactly as it is the business of a London stockbroker to live within half an hour of Capel Court. And it is because you want engagements as a film actress that you live within half an hour of Hollywood. This almost forces you to choose between the two branches of the profession unless you are prepared to pay travelling expenses; for you cannot expect New York to pay travelling expenses from California just as you could not expect London to pay travelling expenses from the Hebrides. You must either live on the spot or get to it at your own expense. That is hard lines; but it is business; and you must not insult The Guild for being businesslike.

To offer you a part without sending you the book would, I grant you, have been a little disrespectful if the play had been by some nobody; but damn it, Stella, a play by me—by ME—by M E ! ! ! ! ! What were you dreaming of?

All this is to guide you in your ways in future; for it always makes me uneasy when I think how very likely you are to *mourir sur la paille* if you persist in governessing people and quarrelling with them. Quarrelling *dates*, it drags one back to Whistler. Governessing is pure Croydon.

In short you shouldnt have left that poor young lady at The Guild offices with a sore derrière by dealing a quite useless parting kick instead of sending her a bouquet and saying how flattered you were by being honored by an invitation to act for the leading highbrow theatre in the U.S. if not in the world.

Now do you like being tutored? Well, that's how other people feel when you lecture them.

As you apparently do not keep a press agent one never

knows what you are doing or where you are. As for me I am repulsively old, as I fancy you realized suddenly when last we met. In November last I dropped down dead, but was officiously revived. I slept for three days and remained in bed for seven. That cured me (I was completely over-tired); but I was no sooner on my feet again than Charlotte got bloodpoisoning and very nearly died. Now at last we are both able to travel. We start next Thursday (21st March) for a voyage round Africa, and shall not be back in England until the middle of June.

And that's all my news, except that I shall spend the voyage finishing a play I began a year ago called *The Millionairess*.

G.B.S.

◇◇◇◇◇◇

Moonbeam was the white Pekinese dog for whose sake Mrs. Campbell said she would never return to England (because he would have to endure quarantine). In her unpublished papers we find homage of this sort: "I made Moonbeam a leash two yards long, but it was no use—he sat down in the road with tears in his eyes—shamed before the other dogs who were free. And now I have taught him to obey—though it is really the other dogs that have helped me by obeying me and leaving him alone. It is so hard for a Peke to obey—a sacred Royal dog—it is for him to give orders—and I do my best to obey him."

Address from 11 April 1935:
Sunset Tower, 8358 Sunset Boulevard, Hollywood.

8/4/35

Dear Joey. It was very cheering, and very happy [*sic*] to get your letter.

You both seem to have been quite ill, I hope the African tour will make you quite well again. I daresay you know how to travel without fatigue—it just kills me.

356

The Guild with their 'subscription list' are a little intolerable; they treat Artists like bales of cotton, but what management could keep its head with such a certain support! More than once in my life have I noticed the queer effect a 'subscribers list' has on a management.

I enclose my photograph taken 6 months ago—you will see I still hold together should you want me for your Millionairess—wouldn't that be wonderful? I wonder what she is like? What sort of things she says and does. Hollywood and the Camera have taught me humility—deep humility: nobody need be afraid of me anymore. Thirteen weeks work *in 16 months*—think of that misery—it has almost broken me up.

The studios say I am too celebrated for small parts, and too English to 'Star'—that Kalamazoo, Bute Montana, and Seattle, would not understand my English style and speech . . . Can it be that I still have some pre-Raphaelite atmosphere? No: surely not. Whenever I ring up my agents they answer: "M.G.M. is thinking of you but nothing suitable has come along"—

B.G.—dear B. did attempt to keep me from *mourir sur la paille* but her money isn't enough for Hollywood. In retirement in Florence it would be ample—but the urge wont be silenced . . . yet!

Its odd too that I don't mind brazenly cadging from you . . . I am in a very nasty jam—I can go on for 6 weeks perhaps, but it will be six weeks more before my allowance comes again, and then it won't be enough to put me straight.

Will you help me? . . .

What do you mean by saying I found you "old" when we last met—you seemed to me a little unkind, and cold, and had I thought a guilty air—I wondered why—we, you and I, could never be 'repulsively old'—

Your veto on the publication of your letters—your lovely letters—lost me a fortune. I have behaved like a gentleman over it haven't I? One particular letter I sometimes read when I want to set my heart aglow—I showed it to a brilliant lady the other day—her words were: "It is more beautiful than anything he has ever written, what a crime the world doesn't know this man"—

I know you will realize I am up against it—that I dont like whining. I don't mind being in the battle to the finish, but in this place one gets left in mid-air. . . .

Give a glance at "Moonbeams" Picture—could you have shut him up for 6 months? To him I am a goddess; he trusts me implicitly, how could I betray him?

Do dear Joey take care of yourself and laze a little—my letter is too long.

As always,
Stella.

◇◇◇◇◇◇

The "quondam chancellor" of this letter is Mrs. Campbell's grandson, Patrick Beech.

4, Whitehall Court, S.W.1.
11th August 1937

My dear Stella,

My antiquity, now extreme at eighty-one, has obliged me to make a clearance among my papers and take measures generally for my probably imminent decease. I find that I have done a very wicked thing: I have kept all your letters in spite of my rule never to keep anything but necessary business memoranda. I kept Ellen Terry's because her handwriting made pictures of them which I could not burn: it would have been like burning a mediaeval psalter or a XV Century French Book of Hours, I have no such excuse in your case. They *would* not be burnt, I suppose.

Now, if I keep them, the next thing that may happen after I die is their sale by my trustee to Gabriel Wells for the benefit of my estate, with incalculable subsequent adventures. Your only control over them will be your copyright in them, which will make it impossible for anyone to publish them for fifty years after your death without your authorization.

There is only thing to be done—to send the letters back to you so that you may have the complete correspondence in your hands. This will add to its value if you have to sell it. Gabriel who has a mania for buying letters of mine (he has bought thousands) tells me that he would buy without hesitation but that you make impracticable conditions. But what conditions can you make except those that the law secures for you? Legally I have not the right to make copies of your letters; and I have not done so and shall not do so, as I should certainly die of angina pectoris during the operation. But you ought to make and keep copies of them before you part with them (if you do) as otherwise you will have a valuable copyright which you will not be able to use because you will not be able to supply the text; and the owners of the letters as material objects will be able to blackmail you for access to them.

As the last address that I had is a Hollywood one, and the interview that was lately published by James Agate placed you in New York, I asked Stella where you were. She gave me the last address she had; but as it was three months old I cabled you for confirmation. Your reply has arrived.

I learn incidentally that the quondam chancellor has made you a great-grandmother. Fancy that! As Tesman says.

I shall wait long enough to give you time to reply by post. If you dont, I shall send the letters on.

I rejoice to learn from the things you said to Agate that you ought not to have said that you are still Stella. I wish I were still Joey; but I have to be content now to play Pantaloon.

Always yours
G. Bernard Shaw.

Mrs. Patrick Campbell,
Hotel Sevilla,
17, West 58th Str.,
New York City.

P.S. I intended to buy from one of the fashionable locksmiths and safe manufacturers a beautiful jewel box big enough to hold the correspondence. But this would involve difficulties at the custom house and affidavits and deuce knows what. The only safe and easy plan is just to stuff the letters into a vulgar set of registered envelopes and post them to you. So you must just buy the box yourself and send me the bill. And if you decide to have the whole correspondence typed as a simple precaution against fire you must let me pay for that too, as it will cost as much as a new hat.

Ayot St. Lawrence.
14th August 1937

My dear Stella,

I have now, with infinite labor and a little heartbreak packed all the letters, from the polite one to dear Mr. Shaw in 1901 when you wouldn't be Cleopatra, to your last cablegram, into six compact envelopes: five of them the official registration ones and the sixth an ordinary one such as typed playscripts fit into without folding. When you have received the six you have received the whole collection and *nothing else*. I underline nothing else because you need not open the envelopes until you want to deal with the letters, which will be meanwhile conveniently packed for you. The official envelopes are fairly stout.

I cannot remember anything in these letters that could hurt anyone. But all letters need editing. I have given Ellen Terry's letters to the British Museum; but they were not all printed nor unedited. For instance, her description of Mrs. Kendal as "my idea of hell" could hardly be published during Dame Madge's lifetime. And Gordon Craig had to be considered.

There can be no question of publication in our case until Charlotte's ashes and mine are scattered in the gardens of one of the crematoria in which I hold shares. After that, the correspondence will be a valuable literary property which may be helpful to Stella junior if not to yourself. . . .

And so, blessed be your days, dear Stella.

G.B.S.

◇◇◇◇◇◇◇

Sir James Barrie died on 19 June, aged seventy-seven.

117, West 58th Street, New York.
25th August 1937

Dearest Joey,

Both your letters have come and I expect the registered envelopes will soon be here. Oh dear me! There's a clutch at my heart . . . the desire to feel a child again will tempt me to read them—to feel sure goodness and fearlessness bring us nearer heaven's gate than any wisdom can. I always felt a child with you—that was your magic and that is my hunger now. . . .

Stop this about 81 and Pantaloon! I agree there is something funny in age—feeling one's heart more tired than one's head—this finding the joker in the pack of cards!

I don't understand why your ashes and Charlotte's ashes

361

have to be scattered over the ground before your letters to
me may be published. It must be something to do with that
Policeman's garb you used to don to try and frighten me
into good behaviour. But then you *must*—you should *know*
best. I don't *know* Charlotte—you wouldn't let me.

In 50 years time life will be lived in the AIR—Nobody
will read books—only those on gas and engines and screws
and light-signals and such things. Books of wit and wisdom
and beauty and drama and history and poetry will only be
read aloud by cripples on the radio, and nobody will listen
—But your letters to me will be carried in the airman's lug-
gage because of the thrush in your throat! How it sings in
your letters to me and in everything you write. That song
will cease if those letters wait 50 years to be published. 81
indeed! Remember the age of the song of the thrush—81
thousand years or more!

Barrie's going makes one pause and so many others—
speeding on. The mood of tidying up comes upon us, I
wonder if anyone does tidies up in time!

You write you have "with infinite labour and a little
heartbreak" packed the letters—those words make me mur-
mur: 'darling, darling Joey . . . the typewriter is so blood-
less and to decipher my writing is too much fatigue for
anyone.'

Gabriel Wells will be here soon now—I expect he told
you your letters were in this country, but he doesn't know
I have had two photostated copies made of them, and I
have put them into a steel drawer, for which I pay $15 a
year, in the safety vaults of the Chase National Bank,
Grand Central Branch, Lexington Avenue at 43rd Street,
and there my letters to you will go when they too are
photostated.

Our correspondence is all I have to leave my great gran-
daughter—"Jennifer Stella Sigrid". . . .

When Gabriel Wells returns in September he will be

asking me out to tea—He lives nearby—We go to a little Hungarian tea shop.

I am afraid if I sell the correspondence to him he may sell some of the letters *singly* (I was offered $700 for one—I resisted)—and that single letter might get published—then what happens?—An alien cannot take legal action, I am told, without first putting up a $10,000 bond—

Another torment is Harrods, of Brompton Road, they will soon be meddling with my possessions furniture, pictures, books and things to sell part of them to pay my bill for storage. I just will not let that thought interfere in my interviews with Wells. The plain fact *is* that *I don't want to part with your letters before they are edited and published.*

I cannot help feeling responsible—I wish I could hear your voice on the telephone—Of course that would be expensive for you—but what a joy for me. And you wouldn't have time to put on your policeman's garb. . . .

B's £500 a year provides for me. . . . I live simply in the cheapest hotel in New York—furnished bedroom, sitting-room, bathroom and kitchenette, service and electric light—$83 a month—and a refrigerator!! . . . Believe me a new hat is an event.

Stella loves her daughter-in-law—who is, from all I can gather, an affectionate, clever, very capable, pretty girl—Pat is happy—he writes to me that his little daughter "grows more beautiful and adorable each day". Their Registry Office marriage wasn't legal in Sweden. I had the luck to be able to send them the money (Radio work and some pupils) to fly to Sweden and to be married again there. Gunnel's mother sent me a joyful message saying I had given her a further ten years of life.

I send you a profile of Moonbeam to melt your bosom and to convince you that country and career must be sacrificed before such a being can be put in Quarantine, shut up for 6 months in a cage with criss-cross bars—

I send you also a chapter of my book—40,000 words are
written and 40,000 more should be written—it won't do, it
doesn't hold up! I have nothing more to say—it sickens me.
If you read this chapter you will understand my running
away from Hollywood up into the mountains 7,000 feet
above the sea and living there for seven months in a log
cabin—wonderful months—indescribable beauty—no roads
—no lights—no noise—no paths but those made by the little
feet of wild deer—A Virgin forest at the top of San Ber-
nardino Mountain called "Skyforest"—Carpets of pine
needles—the scent—and the birds!! Two rooms and a little
kitchen, cracks where the logs joined—The antennae of
small beasties feeling through curiously—a wood stove with
the flue going up into the wall. A road-mender's wife had
the cabin next to mine—she used to come in and 'do' for
me an hour a day, and when the time could be spared we
used to go into the woods together for half an hour and
pick up sticks and 'pine knots' for the stove. . . . I wrote
at my book all day and half the night. Then alas! blood
pressure and fainting fits started—The Doctor's diagnosis
was "working too hard in too high an altitude" Down he
sent me to Lagune beach—there I felt suicideal and I came to
New York and crept into a little room in a nice hotel—expensive but I was too tired to search for another. My room
looked out upon a well and I stayed in bed for nearly nine
weeks—John Gielgud found me there and brought me
flowers with tears in his eyes—the Terrys weep easily—He
took me for a drive in the Park—gave me his arm and I
walked slowly—and Moonbeam ran about. He asked me to
come and see his Hamlet and criticise. I did.

I only saw the one doctor before I left "Skyforest"—they
charge so much—He gave me the name of a heart specialist
but I knew better than that! The dear Irish housemaid used
to come in on tip-toe every morning and say in a cheerful
voice as I opened my eyes: "Sure and I thought it was dead

you were, and there you are smiling and Moonbeam wagging his tail". Once she whispered: "I have some of my wages saved—if it is hard up you are—and not too proud to be taking from me"—I told her to stop her talk—that emotion set my heart and head pounding and pumping, and pins and needles all down the left side of me—a dear generous, warm-hearted creature if ever there was one—

Now I am quite, *quite* well. I have just returned from playing in two summer theatres—Cohasset and Connecticut —An ovation, calls, and a cry for a speech each night were comforting so far as these things go. I could still make a fortune for you if you hadn't preferred actresses who are "easy to work with" and if you could have forgiven me that I could not "be a cog in the collective machine—only the dust, but in it there is also fire, lighted now and then from, the winds of the sky" . . .

I mustn't go on scribbling—You'll never read it! . . .

That man Agate! acceptable only to heaven because of his great love of horses! . . . I was his guest—it was a mean trick to turn my nonsense into "copy"—*he* started luncheon with two cocktails I don't drink, as you know—Then a bottle of champagne followed, and he finished up with a double brandy. I had to amuse *him*! But if his article brought me happily to your mind I am content.

I agree with Ellen Terry, and the words shouldn't have been 'cut'. I know the daughter—the deaf one. I knew in spite of Madge's dignity and her bonnet—she was a devil!

After *Macbeth* she came on the stage taking no notice of me, and when I thought she had flattered Hackett enough I said to her "And how did you like my *street walking* scene, Mrs. Kendal"—you remember Hackett wouldn't let me play in an antechamber but insisted that I walk on the ramparts—her mouth twitched—she had a sense of humour —she asked me to luncheon next day—I knew better than to go.

I must not write any more. I could go on for weeks—I would like to tell you about the friends I have here, and the books I have been reading, and that I went to Radio City today and did a dialogue with Peggy Wood. They gave me a copy of your *Back to Methuselah*—absorbing—I would have liked to have read "Eve" but they had engaged all their people.

I don't expect you to answer this letter—I wanted you to know what I had been doing with life these last few years.

God bless us all, and you most especially, dearest Joey, for all the wit and wisdom and truth and justice, and love of fair dealing; the genius of your work—that you have showered upon the world so bountifully.

It is your affection for me that will raise me a little out of the rut and place me somewhere near your side. I am proud and happy that it is so.

Stella.

Hotel Sevilla, New York.
27th Sept/37

Dear Joey—

They have arrived after taking nearly three weeks to make the journey. Five registered envelopes, and one manuscript registered envelope. The five were opened by the Customs—looking for dope I suppose. I understand if permission to open had been written on the envelope, this would not have happened.

As I gaze at this heap I realize the trouble you have taken, and other things—and I am deeply touched. . I think it must be fear of ghosts, or of grammar—I cannot look into a single envelope: later on I must of course.

I know that before publication your dear dust has to be scattered, and Charlotte's too, but there is my dust to be considered,—my dust will not lie in peace, neither will it scatter, if anything that might displease you happens to our correspondence.

Picture the nightmare of Gabriel Wells selling the letters here by auction, and the auctioneers remark as he misreads and misquotes, and his jokes on "Joey and Mrs. Pat"!

If a Publisher would buy an option and wait until the years pass! Anything to ward off Wells. Please advise and guide me.

I have thought that Jack Mackail might edit and bridge the letters, and write a preface; the preciousness of his style would keep at bay all cheapness or vulgarity that might otherwise creep in.

Perhaps there is someone you might prefer, and Mackail might be unwilling, or his dust too be scattered!

I am so anxious no blunder is made.

Dearest Joey do cease your comic allusions to age or you'll be missing the glory of the sunset, and the divine humour of readiness.

My love to you
Stella.

I would like to thank Charlotte—will you for me?

[CABLE]   28 February 1938
George Bernard Shaw
    Whitehall Court
    London (England)

Have heard from an old friend here that it is necessary in this country to have a legal document embodying your generous gift to me and permission allowing me the right to publish the correspondence at the time stated in your letter of August 14th. Otherwise trouble might befall my heirs and publishers through some unforseen complica-

tions hope not tiresome of me Dear Joey to ask you to send
such a document without delay Love

Stella.

———————

1938 Mar 1st

London
Mrs. Patrick Campbell, Hotel Sevilla
   117 West 58. New York.
        I forget everything I wrote last August you must
send me a copy and explain the present transaction.

Joey.

Hotel Sevilla, New York.
9th March /38

Dearest Joey,
        Thank you for your cable. I enclose as you ask, a
copy of your letter of August 14th, 1937, not having heard
from you again I sadly accepted it as—Hail, and farewell!
   So far there has been no transaction. I saw Gabriel Wells
—the auctioneer in his eye decided me definitely not to part
with the letters.
   You know that my desire has always been that under no
circumstances the letters be thrown upon the public in
some cheap fashion. I have been trying to arrange a Trust
to render that impossible.
   Dear Joey I do indeed apologise for troubling you.

Stella.

4, Whitehall Court, S.W.1.
18th March 1938

My dear Stella,
        Now that you put me to it, I find this business of
the letters much more complicated than I thought. I can do

no more than confirm to you the gift of the pieces of paper on which your letters to me are written. The pieces of paper on which my letters to you are written are your property without question.

I can also declare, and do hereby declare, that my executors will be acting according to my wishes if, after my wife's death and mine, they consent to the publication of the letters for your benefit, or, if you also are no more, for the benefit of your daughter Stella. Failing her, the interest in the letters becomes an unencumbered part of my estate.

This is all I can do at present. If I become a widower I may be able to make the situation clearer by a codicil to my will; but if she becomes a widow this will not be possible. She will inherit the copyright in my letters with all my other copyrights; and you may regard it as certain that she will not consent to publication, and had better not be reminded of the existence of the correspondence. On her death the copyrights will go to the Public Trustee; and then publication will be possible.

The position will then be that nobody can publish without your consent, because only you will possess the letters; and in any case you have the copyright in the letters written by yourself. This makes you mistress of the situation to the utmost extent now possible. But you must hold on to the letters.

I strongly advise you to have two copies of the correspondence typed in sections of three or four letters at different offices so as to prevent the possibility of surreptitious copies. Send one copy to Stella and tell her to take special care of it. This will act as a fire insurance. You keep the originals yourself. The third copy will do for the printer; and if it also is kept in a separate place it will be an additional insurance against loss by theft, fire, accident, carelessness or the like. I have no copies myself, nor have I ever shewn your letters to anyone.

I think this is all I have to say, except that as you are nine years younger than we are your chances of surviving both of us are fairly good.

always
G.B.S.

Hotel Sevilla, New York.
5th April /38

Dearest Joey,

I have your letter of March 18th. Your letter makes it quite clear that I possess nothing that enables me to continue my attitude towards the publication of the letters.

You have often urged me to sell the letters this I will now do. I will not sell them collectively but singly.

Circumstances may make it necessary for me to publish my letters to you, with notes to make them comprehensive [*sic*].

Sometime ago I wrote telling you that two photostated copies of all your letters to me were in the Chase National Bank. You had so often begged me to have copies made, and photostated copies seemed the safest.

Should the time come when the ban is lifted from your letters there will be these photostated copies in the possession of my family.

My love to you
Stella.

Hotel Sirmione, Lago di Garda.
3rd Sept /38

Dear Joey. It is miserable to read of your illness in the newspapers I wouldn't dare bother you with a letter were I not sure you would not read it if you are bidden not to tire yourself unnecessarily.

My beloved Italy has done wonders for me—I was

370

carried on to the boat when I left the States, and off the boat when I arrived at Boulogne—a rheumatic knee—four months of agony, and the American Doctor had said "18 months and crutches". When the Italian Doctor saw it, he smiled and said: "I will have you dancing in a fortnight"— And sure enough 12 radium-mud-packs for 12 days—the wonderful mud they get from under the beautiful Lago di Garda—has completely cured me.

Your last letter of March 18th with its: "*if the executors consent*" and: "*When you and Stella are no more the letters to become an unencumbered part of my estate*" appears to me rather like somebody's grandmother used to describe as 'foolish with roguery' compared with your previous letter—however it had the effect you wanted.

I read the scrawls and scribbles of mine you returned— there are several letters missing—my secretary always kept copies referring to *the* letters: these are the missing ones— I have the copies.

But the only thing that matters now is that you should get better—and feel less tired—and the illness be arrested—it troubles me very much.

My love and my prayers.

Stella.

The Impney Hotel, Droitwich.

20th September 1938

My dear Stella,

The doctors seemed to have cured me by stabbing me in the seat once a fortnight or so with a monstrous hypodermic syringe, and injecting one of the newest hormones into me. The Chinese have known all about it for the last two thousand years. So for the moment I am not dead, though keeping me alive is pure officiousness, as I am 82, and look it.

Your cure is much better news.

I forget all about the letters. I forget everything now ten minutes after it has happened. All I can say is that when I worked out the legal situation and combined it with the susceptibilities that have to be considered I found it full of impossibilities. Your quotation from my last letter is true only of *the copyright* in my letters. You have all the letters I have been able to find of mine as well as those you wrote to me; and you can sell them as if they were a pound of cheese to any collector; but he mustnt publish them. He wont want to, probably, as it would destroy their uniqueness. If there are any missing I probably tore them up or burnt them because they contained something that might have made mischief. Ellen Terry, in a letter to me, described Madge Kendal as "her idea of hell". You may very well have indulged in some criticism; and in that case I would have thought it better not to keep it.

You really are a fool in some things, Stella, concerning which I am full of vulgar cunning.

Will you stay in Italy or return to New York or to London?

We shall be here until the end of the month.

I haven't seen the *Pygmalion* film yet; but it has won *la coppa Volpi* in Venice.

I stuck in a very expensive scene of Eliza's success at the ambassador's party. The whole thing cost about £75,000 reported in the papers as £150,000. All the élite of the profession over forty rushed down to Pinewood to super in it. Apparently they are so hard up that they will do *anything* for ten guineas.

I return your letter to add to the collection. Ridiculous.

Sempre a te—Giuseffino.

Hotel Brighton, Rue de Rivoli, Paris.

9th Dec. /38

In your last letter you said my letters to you were ridiculous—this put me off writing for the moment—

And of course it is ridiculous of me to imagine that you have time to be interested in me.

I was overjoyed to hear of your miraculous cure—The Gods were good to have ordained the jabbings would do the trick—I know a poor lady who had to eat a quarter of a pound of par-boiled bleeding liver twice daily—and she never touched meat!

It was nice too, to hear of you and Charlotte at the Book Fair "shown around like Royalty" and why not—and "both looking so well." Also from a friend I heard of the huge success of *Pygmalion* at the Odeon Theatre Chesterfield with a population of 23,000—there were 21,000 seats sold in the week. And I hear that the miners came in their rough clothes straight from the mine and enjoyed every word of your wit.

And you on a percentage! You must be making more money than you know what to do with. I wonder if you remember all the trouble I took—how I took the play to Tree and begged him to ask you to come and read it to him—and said I would play Eliza—How I stood your insults at rehearsals! How I worked day and night over the accent —how loyal I was to you when Tree came to me just before the curtain went up and begged me to "cut" the bloody (I would have liked to have heard the miners laughter) how I spilt my heart trying to make Eliza common and beautiful—something about her—to fit into dreams —of course you have forgotten everything or you would send a Christmas box!

You ask me if I am going back to America. No: it isn't in me somehow. You say I haven't your "vulgar cunning" I am not at all sure I cannot be cunning—if driven to it—

vulgar No: Do be very careful and cunning this time in America—however giddy and out for a good time they *expect great men to be serious*. I fought bravely explaining "Boob" was short for "Booby" a term of endearment used by lovers.

Sometime ago I sent you a chapter from my book I don't suppose you read it—and I wrote you a private and rather long letter about my life at the moment in New York you sent neither back to me—Do you think Miss Patch could find them and return them to me?

I am in one little room here, but I have an open wood fire —and a lovely view over the Tuileries Gardens—and the sun all day. The covered colonades go all down the street so I can go out wet or fine. The Duke and Duchess of Windsor live three doors down on my right. He looks tranquil—she looks calm.

Take care of yourself and dont let them tire you out over there.

Christmas blessings upon you dear Joey and I hope you keep well and fit.

Stella.

◇◇◇◇◇◇◇

[*Note attached to letter:*]

With Bernard Shaw's compliments.

I have just come across this, which I suppose I should have sent back to you, but what a ridiculous practice! If only I had time to write your reminiscences for you I'd make you the most famous woman in Europe and America.

G.B.S.

Ayot St. Lawrence, Welwyn, Herts.
    9th January 1939.

374

9th December 1938

My dear Stella,

I could swear I sent you back those letters. Probably they are in some Italian Post Office, marked 'Gone Away'. However, Miss Patch shall search.

Pygmalion, they say, is making millions, but I have not seen the color of them yet. Wendy Hiller, the new Eliza, is to get £5000 for her next film, and £10,000 for her fifth.

The Jews, including my ruined Austrian translator, will get all the money people have to spare this Christmas; and you will get nothing.

I will tell you how to earn some. Write the true story of *Pygmalion* and you will make all Britain and North America laugh uproariously, mostly at me. Hutchinsons will advance a thousand pounds without winking. But mind! it must be the utter grotesque truth. The dismal string of lies in your last letter is not worth twopence.

I don't think I can have got the letter you mention with a chapter from your book. What book? At 82 one forgets everything; but surely I should have remembered that. And I don't.

Joseph.

Hotel Brighton, Rue de Rivoli, Paris.

15th Dec. /38

Dear Joey,

What do you mean "a string of lies"—even if your memory is failing you, you cannot have forgotten that I speak the truth. In the House of Life there are many windows, and from each a different view—And so in the home of the spirit—where imagination dwells. Only villains and weak women tell lies.

So far as I am concerned the story of *Pygmalion* is rather

a dismal one for me, and not worth two pence to anyone else.

Do you remember coming on the stage at the St. James' at a performance of *Belladonna*, and accusing me of speaking too carefully?—(probably you were thinking at the time that I spoke better English than anyone else in the world—a Frenchman told me I had succeeded in making an ugly language beautiful)—I said to you: "If you will write me a cockney part I will show you what I can do." (its possible that you had already written *Pygmalion*—you didn't tell me so therefore I couldn't know).—I thought it was from this conversation that you got the merry idea of making me a cockney, and Alexander—who was so painfully gentlemanly on the stage—a Dustman—.

You told me Alexander refused the play—perhaps he thought you were pulling his leg—and he hadn't the wit to see the fun of Higgins—probably you didn't read the play to him.

Quite some time after this—I had a copy of the play— *I took it to Tree, and I begged him to ask you to read it to him.* I told him I was free to play "Eliza". You came and read it to him—(this is where my Christmas box comes in) —Tree was enchanted—somebody else was there, I forget whom—and we were all your slaves. Tree also refused the part of the Dustman—such a pity, he would have been immense.

I have a delightful letter from Lucy telling me that as Eliza's accent improved she must copy Tree's German accent—but I knew only *you* must make fun of the artist!

At long last came the rehearsals—Oh my God! . . . I was 25 years too old for the part—something about my figure, my movements, my voice, my natural Italian grace annoyed you, you wanted to break it up—the girl wasn't common enough to amuse you—(or it may be you wanted to take me up in your arms and kiss me, and as you couldn't you bullied me unmercifully—) I was having infinite trouble with the accent, I wanted to get rhythm into it, and no comic adenoid effects—nothing to worry the audience—I have one letter of yours, written just before the first night, that would have made a weaker woman commit suicide.[1]

You must remember you nearly killed Tree—and when you make that sickly suburban pun that convulsed the staff, the artists, and the electrician fell off his ladder, and Tree turned purple, and nearly had an apoplectic fit—I took him to the stage door for air and tried hard to comfort him—what I said about you! in spite of everlasting affection for you.

There was a Manager risking a fortune to produce your play—who had agreed to pay you handsome royalties—and paid artists call out: "I say Tree must you be so Tree-acly" —And you have dared to go about the world saying that *I* am "impossible in the Theatre"—

The outcome of it all was that your want of respect and appreciation of my hearts-blood efforts suddenly made me explode—I stamped my feet and said in the voice of a Peacock: "If Mr. Shaw doesn't leave the Theatre I will"—With supreme dignity you gathered up your papers and left— without a raising of your hat to my valour—(If only I could have burst into a flood of tears how different my career would have been).

To this day you haven't forgiven me—you have written to me—spoken to me—branded me as an "impossible woman in the Theatre"—

I have remained calm and watched role after role being covered in green baize that I could have made sing down the ages. The Portuguese Jew [Pinero] knew there would have been no "Mrs. Tanqueray" if he had interfered with

---

[1] See page 179.

the amateur. Some people recognize and can manage a "blood 'orse" some cannot—(and I would then as now have eaten out of your hand).

I am going to tell you a tragedy that came upon the world of Art through that cocksure critical attitude of yours—Its no use for you to be indignant and deny it—for it is pathetically true.

Ambrose McEvoy was painting my portrait—so far as he had gone it was *most rarely beautiful*—I made the mistake of taking you to see it—I say "Mistake" because you didn't know the man and had no idea of his sensitiveness. You showed no reverence or recognition of what was *on* the canvas, but called in critical tones for what was *not* there—

The next day I went for my sitting—he had blackened the portrait completely out. After his death his Wife and I searched through more than a hundred canvases but could find no trace of it—she said he must have painted another picture over it. There's a dismal story if you like, dismal as hell. . . .

Yes: I suppose if you haven't the long letter and the chapter and another long letter I wrote to you before I went to Italy, they have gone astray. *Town and Country* gave me £100 for two chapters—One appeared in the November issue, and one in this month. That is how I managed to settle up in Italy and start again here.

By the way among my letters you returned there was one to you from Constance Collier—I must say that made me laugh!

The Letters of T. E. Lawrence have just arrived—there is something terrific in the way we are all thinking of to-morrow—yesterday has lost so much of its importance—

I cannot think of you as anything but Joey. Suppose I was to ask you to call me Beatrice or Rose they are both

my names . . . and Joey has a strange significance for me
—the tragedy of baffled sincerity—
My love to you and my prayers that you continue well.

Stella.

❖❖❖❖❖❖

*"Morgan" is Charles Morgan, distinguished novelist and es-
sayist. Since the death of A. B. Walkley he had been chief dramatic critic of* The Times. *His handsome wife writes under the
name of Hilda Vaughan.*

4, Whitehall Court, S.W.1.
19th December 1938

My dear Stella

Your consciousness is so entirely imaginary that I
give you up as hopeless. There is not one item in those reminiscences of yours that has the remotest derivation from
the truth, much less foundation in it. It is a pity; for the
true story has some comedy in it, and some interest as a
record of your queer psychology.

If only you could write a true book entitled WHY,
THOUGH I WAS A WONDERFUL ACTRESS, NO
MANAGER OR AUTHOR WOULD EVER EN-
GAGE ME TWICE IF HE COULD POSSIBLY HELP
IT, it would be a best seller. But you couldnt. Besides, you
dont know. I do.

I return Morgan's letter and yours. It is polite of him to
call you a flame; but flames are now six a penny: their mass
production in California has overdone that game. And then
you say you were 25 years too old for Liza. Well, Liza is
at least 18; so you claim to have been 43 (I was the more
deceived) in 1913. That was 25 years ago, which makes

you 68. Morgan says he cannot be ready for two years or so. You will be 70. Morgan, who married the prettiest woman in Wales, will not want a flame of 70. You will have to take the theatre seriously and study and act for the first time in your life. And Morgan, who imagines you just a "difficult" genius instead of an impossible fiend who would start trying to disconcert and humiliate him at the first rehearsal, and pay no attention to his play, would quarrel with you straight away. All authors are not angels, like me.

I havent any money (too much invested) and I have huge sums to pay next month; for *Pygmalion*, which is said to be making millions, has not sent a penny my way as yet. As to bringing you over, I had as soon bring the devil over. You would upset me and everybody else. You dont know how I have blessed that wretched little dog. And, anyhow, France is the cheapest place to live.

Geneva is a horrible play: I went to see it the other day and it made me quite ill. Splendid for the actors though. The performances are like election meetings.

But I must stop making myself unpleasant, though I believe you can taste nothing but Cayenne pepper. I have to write letters like this, just as I have to write plays like *Geneva*. It is not that I want to. Joey was the cleverest thing you ever invented,

by far, by far, by far
G.B.S.

◇◇◇◇◇◇

W. B. Yeats, the great Irish poet and playwright, had died four days earlier, aged seventy-three.

Mrs. Campbell encloses two quotations from Shaw's letter of 3 April 1913:

(1) "I drove into Dublin today" to "the young lions of the St. James's stalls."

*(2) "So if you are still idly curious to know whether I am
still in love with you" to the end of the letter.*

Hotel Brighton, Rue de Rivoli, Paris.

1st Feb./39

Dear Joey,

A letter and a card from you lying on my table for
3 weeks, and I without a smile to answer with. . . .

A friend has died—my great grandchild caught cold and
was very ill—A Director came here from Ealing to beg me
to play a part in a picture—I read the script—Over, and
over, and over turned my stomach—a wooden Duchess—
with just enough lines to give the other parts a chance to
continue—to Seymour Hicks dancing, singing, tipsy Duke
——I've lived too long—I have no business in this world at
all—there's another great-grand child baby expected in
June—I must pick up crumbs. . . .

The Director—Robert Stevenson—quite nice—he thought
I was Stella—that I looked so many years younger than
when I played in *The Matriarch—BORN 9th FEB 1865—
Who's Who* has it correctly—he laughed merrily, and was
very curious to know why people called me "difficult". I
told him he must ask *you* since Henry Arthur Jones—
Boucicault and Alexander were dead and all the rest had
loved me. Pinero—Tree—Robertson—Bancroft, Hare, Gerald du Maurier . . .

This last letter of yours is full of craziness, and unbe-
lievable unkindness:

"No Manager would engage you a second time if he
could help it"

Six engagements with Alexander—counting two revivals—
and please remember I gave in my notice. . . .

Nine engagements with Robertson—until Hamlet and his
pretty wife left no place for me.

Four plays with Gerald du Maurier. . . . *Two* with Hare

381

Four with Tree . . . but what's the use of bothering about your wilful nonsense, and by now I daresay you have forgotten all you wrote in this last letter!

And you dare to accuse me of humiliating people! Since you first dipped your pen in the ink-pot what else have you ever done?

You say I "invented" Joey—for some reason that makes my eyes smart, and you add: "and it is the cleverest thing you have ever done by far, by far, by far". Your written words inspired me, if they were false, then Joey is an imposter—

Without inventions there would be no life. God—Architecture—Beethoven's Pastoral Symphony—that passage when all the birds in the universe burst into song . . . Toscanini conducting "La Mer"—400 men following him with rapturous obedience and he—without a score—humming every bar—his left hand uplifted blessing them over the dangerous places—(I only a few feet away weeping—I had been sent an invitation to the Radio Concert in New York)

Yes: I am glad I invented you, and that it is the cleverest thing I ever did—

And women's inventions!—the silly creatures—that friends are true—husbands faithful—that their babes will be kings and queens—But there I am not going to waste your time with any more of my 'ridiculous' letters—if ever you want another you must ask for it. We will meet in heaven, you will bow, I will curtsy, and the angels will say to each other: ". . they did not snatch at joy and spoil the winged world"—

Take every care of yourself for all our sakes.

Stella.

P.S. I heard again what a tremendous success *Pygmalion* is and that it comes back to London in June—that Pascal has to account to you for 10% of the total receipts—you cant have *invested* that money yet! Christmas-box time has passed—and the New Year—but my birthday is on the 9th of this month.

I believe you have eaten your own heart . . . read this bit of an old letter of yours I send you—letters that make me laugh, and letters that make me cry, and letters that are just foolish noddings of the feathers in your cap—What *am* I to do with them? *Think* . . . it would take me a year's work to knit them together and heavens what a Preface you could write! If you have an order to give me about them— *give it*—such a fountain of joy they are.

I hope you will be spared to treat me abominably many years longer . . .

Its grim and sorrowful that Yeats has gone—that imagination that blue-blood of Irish kings—that strangeness ah! what a quality.

"Goodbye" unless you ask me to write again.

Stella.

◇◇◇◇◇◇

G.B.S. had sent a note saying that Constance Collier desired a part in the Major Barbara *film. It concluded: "Are you seriously in the field?" This is Mrs. Campbell's last letter to G.B.S.*

Hotel Calais, Rue des Capucines, Paris.
28th June/39

Yes: I am still "seriously in the field", but you know not as cannon fodder.

Constance Collier deserves anything worthwhile that is given to her—Heavens how they treated her in Hollywood!

A week or two ago I thought I would be heroic—I offered myself to the English Theatre here at £25 a week, or less. In answer they sent me a play to read; my part a Jewish Mother with an idiot son whose weakness is to kill little girls and hide them in his Mothers rag box, after first covering them with the oil cloth from the kitchen table. The Mothers dialogue consisting of: "Oi; Oi; tch: tch: we shouldn't have left him alone". I asked Stirling what made him wish to produce such a play? he said: "We must give them a novelty, something they cannot see in London"; at my astonished query "they? who?" he replied: "The English tourist".

The Brighton Hotel raised its price for the Season, so I came here to one room en pension—saving time and money. I sincerely hope to get away to the South of France to a little hotel at the same price but set in beauty—The lovely "Ferme des Orangers" with its nightingales, and the scent of the orange groves has been sold or my friends would have let me have it again.

I am getting used to poverty and discomfort, and even to the very real unhappiness of having no maid to take a few of the little daily cares for me, and give me an arm when I cross the road carrying "Moonbeam" through the terrifying tearing traffic.

Stella.

◇◇◇◇◇◇

And this is Shaw's last letter to Mrs. Campbell.

4, Whitehall Court, S.W.1.
21st August 1939

My dear Stella

The giant is decrepit and his wife crippled with lumbago.

Constance Collier tried for the part Pascal wanted you

384

for; but he had engaged Marie Löhr for the season and could not afford to have her eating her head off. He gave you up because you would not be separated for six months from your dog. For Heaven's sake, when that wretched animal perishes in the course of nature or is slain by an automobile, buy a giant panda or a giraffe or a water buffalo or a sea lion, any of which you can take with you anywhere. They make affectionate pets, though the water buffalo has a dangerous preference for black children. They are also splendid advertisements.

Cheetahs are real dears: I have petted one.

I am keeping away from Malvern this year; but my new play has enlivened the Festival. It is all about Charles II, his wife, two of his whores, an actress, Isaac Newton, his housekeeper and housemaid, Kneller the painter, George Fox the first Quaker, and James II (Duke of York in the play). I have given up producing; I am too old, too old, too old.

G.B.S.

INDEX

A NOTE ON THE TYPE

This book was set on the Linotype in JANSON, *a recutting made direct from the type cast from matrices* (*now in possession of the Stempel foundry, Frankfurt am Main*) *made by Anton Janson some time between 1660 and 1687.*

Of Janson's origin nothing is known. He may have been a relative of Justus Janson, a printer of Danish birth who practiced in Leipzig from 1614 to 1635. Some time between 1657 and 1668 Anton Janson, a punch-cutter and type-founder, bought from the Leipzig printer Johann Eric Hahn the type-foundry that had formerly been a part of the printing house of M. Friedrich Lankisch. Janson's types were first shown in a specimen sheet issued at Leipzig about 1675. Janson's successor, and perhaps his son-in-law, Johann Karl Edling, issued a specimen sheet of Janson types in 1689. His heirs sold the Janson matrices in Holland to Wolffgang Dietrich Erhardt.

The book was composed, printed, and bound by THE PLIMPTON PRESS, *Norwood, Massachusetts. Typography and binding designs are by* W. A. DWIGGINS.